Class Voice
Fundamental Skills for Lifelong Singing

Class Voice
Fundamental Skills for Lifelong Singing

Brenda Smith, DMA
Ronald Burrichter, MM

5521 Ruffin Road
San Diego, CA 92123

e-mail: information@pluralpublishing.com
Website: https://www.pluralpublishing.com

Copyright © 2023 by Plural Publishing, Inc.

Typeset in 10.5/13 Garamond by Flanagan's Publishing Services, Inc.
Printed in the United States of America by Integrated Books International

All rights, including that of translation, reserved. No part of this publication may be reproduced, stored in a retrieval system, or transmitted in any form or by any means, electronic, mechanical, recording, or otherwise, including photocopying, recording, taping, Web distribution, or information storage and retrieval systems without the prior written consent of the publisher.

For permission to use material from this text, contact us by
Telephone: (866) 758-7251
Fax: (888) 758-7255
e-mail: permissions@pluralpublishing.com

Every attempt has been made to contact the copyright holders for material originally printed in another source. If any have been inadvertently overlooked, the publisher will gladly make the necessary arrangements at the first opportunity.

Library of Congress Cataloging-in-Publication Data:
Names: Smith, Brenda (Brenda Jo) author. | Burrichter, Ronald, author. | Sataloff, Robert Thayer, contributor.
Title: Class voice : fundamental skills for lifelong singing / Brenda Smith, Ronald Burrichter.
Description: San Diego, CA : Plural Publishing, 2022. | Includes bibliographical references and index.
Identifiers: LCCN 2021054262 (print) | LCCN 2021054263 (ebook) | ISBN 9781635503265 (paperback) | ISBN 9781635503272 (ebook)
Subjects: LCSH: Singing--Instruction and study.
Classification: LCC MT820 .S696 2022 (print) | LCC MT820 (ebook) | DDC 783/.043--dc23
LC record available at https://lccn.loc.gov/2021054262
LC ebook record available at https://lccn.loc.gov/2021054263

Contents

Foreword by Robert T. Sataloff, MD, DMA, FACS — xi
How To Use This Book — xiii
   A Message to Students — xiii
   A Message to Teachers — xv
Getting Started: Studying Singing Together — xix
Acknowledgments — xxvii
Contributors — xxix
Reviewers — xxxi

Introduction: Class Voice and Strategies for Lifelong Singing — 1
   Songs: With and Without Words — 1
   Instruments Versus Voice — 2
   Human Growth: Musical, Physical, and Aesthetic — 2
   Speaking Voice and Singing Voice Use — 2
   Musical Skill Training and Singing — 3
   Issues of *Fach* and Longevity — 3
   Conclusion — 4
   Discussion Questions — 4
   References — 4

1 Skills for Learning to Sing — 5
   Brenda Smith
   The Basics of Singing — 6
      Relaxation — 6
      Posture — 8
      Breathing — 14
      Resonance — 18
   The Why and How of Warm-Ups and Cool-Downs — 20
   Discussion Questions — 20
   References — 20

2 Anatomy and Physiology of the Voice — 23
Robert T. Sataloff

Anatomy — 23
Physiology — 29
Conclusion — 34
References — 35

3 Skills for Learning to Sing Music — 37
Ronald Burrichter

Introduction — 37
Musicianship Skills — 37
   Singing and Rhythm — 38
   Basics of the Printed Page — 38
   Other Rhythmic Tricks — 40
   Singing and Note Learning — 41
   Understanding Aural Skill Levels — 42
   Strategies for Lifelong Music Learning — 43
Conclusion — 44
Discussion Questions — 44
Resources for Further Reading — 45
   Music Learning — 45
   Online Resources for Music Learning — 45
   Choral Singing — 45

4 Skills for Learning to Sing Text — 47
Brenda Smith

The Italian Language and Singing Skill — 47
International Phonetic Alphabet — 48
   Tricks for Learning IPA — 48
   The Value of the International Phonetic Alphabet — 48
   Learning the IPA in English — 49
   Consonants — 51
   Singing Versus Speaking Vowels and Consonants — 52
   Using the International Phonetic Alphabet as a Tool — 52
   Phonetic Transcriptions and "Rhyming Vowels" — 53
Sounds in Italian, German, and French — 54
Diction in Context — 55
Conclusion — 55
Discussion Questions — 55
Resources for Further Reading — 55
References — 55

5 Singing Solo — 57
Brenda Smith

The Singing Art in the Western World — 57

Bel Canto, Legato, and the Even Scale	58
Range, Registration, and Tessitura	59
Messa di Voce or "Measuring" the Voice	60
Tone Quality and Vibrato	61
Conclusion	61
Discussion Questions	61
Resources for Further Reading	62
Reference	62

6 Singing With Others — 63
Brenda Smith and Ronald Burrichter

Singing Together in Choirs	63
A Brief History of Early Choral Singing	63
Unison Singing	64
Choral Breathing	65
Canons	66
Suggested Canons for Class Voice Use	67
Two-Part Singing	67
The Singing Life of Choral Singers	67
Singing Soprano in a Choir	67
Singing Alto in a Choir	68
Singing Tenor in a Choir	69
Singing Baritone or Bass in a Choir	69
Choral Singing and Tuning	70
Challenges of Choral Singing	70
Score Marking	71
Conclusion	72
Discussion Questions	72
Resources for Further Reading	72
Reference	73

7 Skills for Mastering Repertoire — 75
Brenda Smith and Ronald Burrichter

Warm-Ups and Voice Building	75
Relaxation and Posture	75
Breathing and Resonance	75
Cool-Downs	78
Solving Vocal Problems in Repertoire	84
Repertoire Learning Skills	84
Learning a Song: Step 1 Is the Text	84
Word Mastery	85
Understanding Vowels	86
Materials for Score Preparation	87
Establishing the Context for a New Song	87
Sample Fact Sheet for Vocal Repertoire	89
Musical Preparation	90

Practice Strategies	90
Sample Practice Logs	91
Sample One	91
Sample Two	94
Sample Three	95
Practice Styles	98
The Role of Mindfulness and Joy in Practice	99
Performance Anxiety and Musical Preparation	99
Tips for Mindful Preparation	100
Performing and Mental Toughness	101
Physical Factors and Performance	101
Singing and Sharing the Stage	101
Conclusion	102
Discussion Questions	102
Resources for Further Reading	102
Practice Skills	102
Performance Anxiety	102
References	103

8 Vocal Skills and Repertoire — 105
Brenda Smith and Ronald Burrichter

What Singers Sing	105
Folk Songs	105
Early Italian Songs and Arias	106
British and American Song	106
German Lieder	106
French *Mélodie*	107
Learning Vocal Skills Through Repertoire	108
Suggested Vocal Repertoire and Lesson Plans for Class Voice Study	108
Breath Coordination and Gentle Onset	108
Legato and Phrasing	113
Vocal Agility and Flexibility	115
Vocal Color and Text Painting	116
Range and Registration	118
Messa di voce	120
Opera, Singspiel, and Operetta	123
Musical Theater	123
Suggested Musical Theater Repertoire for Class Voice	123
Spirituals and African American Art Songs	126
Putting It All Together	127
Interpreting Text and Music	127
Performance Strategies for Class Presentations	128
Midterm and Final Projects and Performances	128
Midterm Presentation	128
Final Presentation	129

Program Notes and Research	129
Performance Etiquette	129
Criteria for Evaluation	131
"An die Musik" ("To Music")—An International Calling Card for Singers	133
Conclusion	134
Discussion Questions	134
Recommended Online Resources	134
Resources for Lesson Planning	134
Resources for Repertoire Acquisition	134
Resources for Music Purchase	134
Resources for Further Reading	135
References	135

9 The Singing Life — 137

Considerations for the Adolescent Singing Voice	137
Vincent Oakes	
Singing Fundamentals for the Adolescent Voice	138
Phonation Onset and Duration	141
Nonpitched Exercises for the Adolescent Voice	142
Limited Range Exercises for the Adolescent Voice	144
Aural Development of the Adolescent Singer	144
Balance and Physicality for the Developing Singer	145
Additional Considerations	146
Conclusion	148
Discussion Questions	148
Resources for Further Reading	148
References	149
Singing and Women	150
Brenda Smith	
Finding Your Voice	150
Women and Choral Singing	151
Healthy Voice Use	151
Maintaining Your Voice	151
Vocal Aging: To Sing or Not to Sing	152
Vocal Limitations and Strategies	152
Conclusion	153
Discussion Questions	153
References	153
Singing Life of Men	154
Ronald Burrichter	
The Singing Life of Tenors	155
Men's Falsetto Voices	155
The Singing of Life of Baritones and Basses	156
Conclusion	158
Discussion Questions	158

Resources for Further Reading ... 158
Gender Spectrum Voice ... 159
Erin Nicole Donahue
    Working With the Gender Diverse Population ... 160
    Transition and Hormones ... 161
    Aspects of Voice and Verbal Communication ... 162
    The Transgender or Gender Diverse Singer ... 167
    Considerations for the Music Educator ... 167
    Conclusion ... 169
    Discussion Questions ... 169
    Resources for Further Reading ... 169

10 The Science of Healthy Singing ... 171
Erin Nicole Donahue
Vocal Health and Wellness ... 171
A Brief Overview of Anatomy and Physiology ... 172
    Respiration ... 172
    Maximizing Vocal Health ... 174
    Voice Disorders and Laryngeal Pathology ... 182
    The Voice Care Team ... 183
Conclusion ... 184
Discussion Questions ... 184
Resources for Further Reading ... 184

Conclusion: The Benefits of Skillful Lifelong Singing ... 187
Brenda Smith and Ronald Burrichter
Singing Alone and With Others ... 187
The Intrinsic Value of Singing ... 187
Singing in the 21st Century ... 188
21st Century Vocal Pedagogy ... 188
Maintaining Fundamental Skills for Singing ... 189
Cautions and Strategies ... 189
Conclusion ... 190
Discussion Questions ... 190
Resources for Further Reading ... 190
References ... 190

Glossary ... *191*
Bibliography: Resources for Research and Learning ... *201*
Index ... *209*

Foreword

In its 2019 Impact Study, Chorus America reported that more than 54 million people in America sing in amateur choral organizations (Grunwald Associates LLC & Chorus America, 2019). Singing activities include people of all ages, races, genders, and creeds. Amateur singers, who sing for the love of singing, rarely have an opportunity to develop vocal skills in a systematic way. *Class Voice: Fundamental Skills for Lifelong Singing* is an accessible resource to help beginners master basic singing skills and train them in the presence of others. This book is different from other Class Voice books because it is intended for flexible use so that the teacher can design the curriculum to fit the student population as opposed to the usual format of brief didactic information and a huge anthology of songs. This open format also makes the book more useful as a reference in the future. For the student who continues training and becomes a voice teacher or choral conductor, its content can function as a ready reference for lesson building, warm-up and cool-down exercise design, rehearsal planning, and more. Because each class member presents with a unique vocal instrument, students of singing quickly develop a sense of personal identity as well as perspective.

All students in a voice class are potential professional voice users. A convincing speaking voice is required for nearly every profession. The attention given to effective posture and breathing for singing is foundational to all healthy voice use. The "speaking voice" and the "singing voice" are one instrument that is used in slightly different ways. In Class Voice, students prepare spoken and sung presentations that enlighten classmates and foster habits for lifelong healthy voice use.

Relying upon evidence-based voice pedagogy, the authors dispel many of the myths that confuse and confound untrained singers; and they are well qualified to do so. For example, Dr. Brenda Smith has not only taught, lectured, and performed extensively, she also has coauthored texts on choral pedagogy and other topics. Her expertise is internationally recognized. Vincent Oakes wrote "The Young Singer" chapter in *Choral Pedagogy, Third Edition* and has expanded upon it in this text (Oakes, 2013). Erin Donahue is a singing voice specialist who was a double major in voice performance and speech-language pathology at the University of Florida. She has been at the Blaine Block Voice Center in Cincinnati since she received her master's degree from Miami University and became a certified speech-language pathologist. Ron Burrichter just retired after 37 years of studio voice teaching and choral work. The course includes comparative listening and class discussion—exercises that serve to enhance the ear, the mind, and the heart, fostering understanding of a wide range of voice types, performance styles, and best practices. Such training sophisticates the student's capacity to listen, observe, and compare tastes, ideas, and opinions with others.

As the singing voice ages, changes are inevitable. The chapter in this textbook on the singing life contains a set of short essays that describe the developmental growth of the human voice from birth to old age. When setting goals and expectations, it is important for students of singing to identify where they are in the growth process and what lies ahead. The textbook prepares students to find their place and to thrive in a singer's world as amateurs or as professionals.

For students seeking to become music educators, the class approach is directly applicable. The book contains information regarding terms, gestures, and exercises used commonly by singers, music educators, and choral conductors. It also provides a user-friendly chapter (Chapter 2) entitled "Anatomy and Physiology of the Voice" adapted from other publications that I have written. The chapter provides references to other print and online resources for further study. With this information, instrumentalists, conductors, teachers, and aspiring singers will acquire a fundamental understanding of the human voice as a musical instrument.

The resources in the book can be adapted to any population. The assigned repertoire can be chosen to suit the abilities and goals of each student. The instructor is free to design the syllabus and weekly work around personal preferences and expertise. The book seeks to train instrumental music education majors, non-music majors, and adult learners in fundamental skills for singing. Its contents, which are very useful in the classroom, also can serve as an invaluable reference for future use.

Class Voice is a community of singers. The late Thomas Lux, in his poem "Regarding (Most) Songs," said that "The human voice can sing a vowel to break your heart" (Lux, 2001, p. 25). A singing voice has the capacity to ignite emotions, inspire reminiscences, and invite human relationships. Singing produces a camaraderie uncommon to other forms of communal music making. The Class Voice experience prepares each student for participation in choral settings of many kinds.

The development of basic singing skills and good vocal health habits is vital to lifelong singing. It is indeed possible to grow old gracefully as a singer if fundamental skills are mastered. After completing the course, students should be motivated to join or start one. Singing with others brings joy to life at every age, and healthy singing can sustain that joy through even the final decade of life.

—Robert T. Sataloff, MD, DMA, FACS

References

Grunwald Associates LLC, & Chorus America. (2019). *The Chorus Impact Study: Singing for a lifetime.*

Lux, T. (2001). *The street of clocks: Poems* (p. 25). Houghton Mifflin.

Oakes, V. (2013). The young singer. In B. Smith & R. T. Sataloff (Eds.), *Choral pedagogy* (3rd ed., pp. 189–204). Plural Publishing.

How To Use This Book

A Message to Students

Welcome to Class Voice! This textbook seeks to train you in the fundamental skills required to sing for a lifetime. Whether you are a music education major, a non-music major with an interest in singing, or an adult learner, you will find this book of special value. Unlike other class voice textbooks that contain an anthology of vocal repertoire and advice for performing it, this book provides you with foundational information and training in singing skills that can be applied to any vocal selection or style. In current times, there is no reason to limit what you learn. Using various digital means, you can acquire most songs or arias that interest you in a key or arrangement that suits your needs. Through consultation with your instructor, you can plan a course of study that answers your questions, teaches you skills, and trains you in the songs you care to sing.

Why is Class Voice the appropriate forum for your work? By its very nature, singing involves a community made up of those who sing and those who listen. Because the voice is the only instrument that the "player" cannot see, touch, or accurately hear, the community provides essential feedback, inspiration, and encouragement. You have chosen wisely to begin your study of singing in the presence of others.

Why should anyone want to sing better? The voice is an instrument used for speaking and singing that is central to daily life. Your voice grows and changes as you age. Your expectations for your voice as a singer and speaker advance from year to year, too. There is hardly a profession or pastime that does not require an effective, convincing voice. No matter what career you select, you will be what is known as a "professional voice user"—someone for whom professional success relies heavily upon vocal consistency and power. Basic singing skills support your vocal instrument the way personal training contributes to your physical strength, balance, and well-being. Singers are classified as "vocal athletes"—humans who use every aspect of their being to produce beautiful tone and deliver meaningful text. As you learn to sing, you will become more aware of your body, your mind, and your spirit as well as your voice. They coordinate to help you express yourself in song and speech. Class Voice is the training ground where you will equip yourself with the tools needed to appreciate, use, and preserve your voice.

Why learn singing skills with others? We learn to sing by observing and hearing others sing and by having others report to us what they see and hear when we sing. As singers and speakers, we do not perceive the sound of our own voices as others do. In the book *This Is the Voice*, John Colapinto writes:

> This is because it reaches us, not solely through the air, but in vibrations that pass through the hard and soft tissues of our head and neck, and which create, in our auditory cortex, a sound completely different to what everyone else hears when we talk. (Colapinto, 2021, p. 22)

If you doubt this information, consider your response after hearing your recorded voice played back on a message machine. Most people ask, "Is that really how I sound?" Your teacher and classmates will act as your "outside eyes and ears," assuring you that the sounds you make display your talents at their best. You will hone your critical observation and listening skills by observing the posture, gestures, and vocal sounds of your classmates.

The basics of singing are relaxation, posture, breathing, and resonance. Each singer strives for a body attitude that is sustainable and advantageous for creating the best tone. In a classroom of singers, an instructor must offer several approaches for the achievement of each skill to meet the needs of each student. You will have the opportunity to try more than one method and to observe how others respond to each. In a private voice lesson, you would receive individual attention all the time but might wish for a means of comparing alternative ways of working. Here you will learn various "roads to Rome." If your chosen field is teaching, you can stockpile your Class Voice teacher's methodology for future use with students of varying learning styles. When your classmates report their singular strategies for practice and preparation, you can analyze and incorporate their "tricks of the trade" into your procedures. If you are a non-music major who wishes to learn as much about singing as possible, you will receive in this class a broad perspective as well as individual assistance. If you are an adult learner, your life experience will be of great value to you and your classmates.

How can you keep your voice healthy? The Class Voice course covers a broad range of topics involving solo, choral, and speaking voice issues. The course acquaints you with the singing life at every age and gives useful advice for preserving your voice through vocal hygiene. The authors hope that your participation in the course will result in a framework for a lifetime of healthy singing and speaking.

What songs will you sing? Because the syllabus will be based upon your abilities and interests and those of your classmates, there is flexibility about the exact content and flow of the class. Everyone will have a chance to learn about how singing evolved in Western culture. A portion of class time will be spent singing together songs that build specific vocal skills. With your teacher's guidance, you will learn and perform alone songs that fit your unique voice and temperament. Because you are developing fundamental skills for singing, the repertoire designed for "acoustic" singing or nonamplified performance is featured. Once you master the fundamental skills, you can easily expand your field of interest and expertise to include skills specific to music created for amplified circumstances.

How is Class Voice different from private lessons? In Class Voice, you will learn with others how to improve musicianship skills, how to practice voice, and how to minimize performance anxiety. Because most chapters conclude with discussion questions, you can explore a wide variety of issues and share a diversity of opinions with your classmates. The suggestions for further reading will expand your understanding of voice science, vocal literature, and performance practices. In a private lesson, you would not receive this broad exposure as readily.

What skills does singing teach? Unlike any other musical genre, singing involves the expression of poetic texts in English and other languages. There is a chapter on the basics of "singer's diction" to help you sing with confidence and clarity. Diction skills are easily transferred to the articulation of spoken text. No matter what your career plans, you will rely upon your voice to communicate your ideas. In the chapter on vocal health, you learn how to preserve your talent. Class Voice will train you to use your voice for singing and speaking effectively and healthfully.

What performance skills will you learn? Learning to sing with others will afford you the chance to observe peer performances as well as to perform. Your instructor and classmates will share best practices for studying music, memorizing text, and preparing public performances. As you compare other methods with your own, you can design a personal plan for success. Many students have found it valuable to record practice sessions and rehearsals. Since singers do not hear themselves as others do, a recording can satisfy a singer's curiosity, affirming growth and alleviating fears. If you upload your recordings of your practices to your instructor, you can receive constructive feedback and confirmation of your progress. Your class experiences combine with the resources provided in each chapter to prepare you for your midterm and final presentations. Your performances in class will produce responses from your peers and instructor. The presentations are capstone experiences that verify your growth as a singer and help you set meaningful goals for the future.

Can you sing for a lifetime? Lifelong singing is an achievable goal. The human voice is fragile and finite. Class Voice gives you tools for maintaining a healthy voice for speaking and singing. Through comparative listening and class discussion, you will develop a context for life as a voice user, expand your horizons, and set goals for lifelong singing. The authors are aware that this course might be your only opportunity to learn about singing. The content of the course includes materials of interest to the beginning singer, potential music educator, and adult learner. We hope *Class Voice: Fundamental Skills for Lifelong Singing* will be a valuable resource to you for years to come. May your Class Voice experience allow you abundant opportunities to exercise your voice, enrich your knowledge, and share the joy of singing in a supportive community!

Reference

Colapinto, J. (2021). *This is the voice* (p. 22). Simon & Schuster.

A Message to Teachers

Most singing around the world is done by amateur singers in choirs, whether they are affiliated with schools, religious organizations, communities, barbershop quartet clubs, or other organizations (Smith & Sataloff, 2013, p. 3). Singing with others can be a hobby or a profession. It is an activity that can nurture friendship, artistic goals, and well-being for a lifetime. It is, therefore, fitting that the basics of singing be learned in a group setting such as Class Voice.

Who will take this course? The short answer is simple: potential professional voice users. Whether the course is a music education requirement, a nonmajor voice class, or a course for adult learners, it will be useful to students interested in dramatic arts, speech-language pathology, and all subject areas that require knowledge of the human voice. Expect the class to attract students with a wide range of abilities, interests, and ambitions. There will be students with extensive singing experience and musical expertise as well as novice singers who present with a deficit of skills. Class Voice teachers frequently "discover" fine talent—a student whose voice and personality soar after years of hesitation or shyness.

How is this textbook different from others? This textbook is designed to meet the needs of all the students in the course. *Class Voice: Fundamental Skills for Lifelong Singing* does not contain an anthology that could limit what is sung or taught in class. In the 21st century, almost any musical score is available through a digital means in a range of reasonable keys and arrangements. Using the principles and resources of this book, you can design an action plan for each student in your class. You need not compromise your repertoire preferences or force a student to sing something that does not suit their interests, abilities, or temperament. The course plan can be topical or general, chronologic, or strictly contemporary. Music education majors, preparing for student teaching internships, might request to learn repertoire used in high school assessment festivals along with musical theater repertoire. Non-music majors might prefer a wide range of styles as well as appropriate audition materials. Students may share an interest in the music of women composers or a desire to sing spirituals, gospel, jazz, or folk songs. Selections from the American Songbook might be especially attractive to adult learners. Imagine the satisfaction of finding songs that fit the voice and personality of each student. Also consider the intrinsic value in showing students how a single song can unlock and fortify the vocal gifts of an individual singer.

There may be chapters in the book that are not necessary for those currently enrolled in your class. If everyone is an able music reader, you can skip the chapter on musicianship skills. For students aspiring to careers in private or classroom music teaching, the material may be a useful resource for developing their future lesson plans. Non-music major voice students may not be aware of the importance of foundational musicianship skills. Some adult learners might not have a desire to study the nuts and bolts of music, preferring instead to spend class time learning and singing songs with others. Others may be curious to know more about negotiating the musical score. Though learning music by rote or imitation works, it is known that solid musicianship skills instill confidence in singers and help preserve their vocal health. It is assumed that Class Voice may be the only course of its type that your students experience. The content of the book is intended to inform students of singing about matters of interest today and in the future.

In the online companion website associated with the textbook, you will find resources to spark your imagination and secure your success with each student. The online companion website contains suggested syllabuses and weekly plans designed for three different Class Voice populations. They are entitled "Class Voice for the Instrumental Music Education Major," "Class Voice for the Non-Music Major," and "Class Voice for the Adult Learner." Use the materials to design the syllabus that meets your expectations and those of your students. May this approach enliven your teaching of Class Voice and allow you to meet the needs and gifts of any population.

Why is Class Voice essential for success in certain careers? Many human beings are surprised to discover their chosen career depends upon the success of their voice. Almost everyone in training is preparing to be a professional voice user. Most careers require effective voice use for speaking while others consider singing skill an asset though not a necessity. In lessons and rehearsals, instrumentalists communicate musical ideas to other players by singing how specific passages of the music should be played. From time to time, band and orchestra instructors cover for an absent choral colleague. In the amateur and professional theater, many acting roles include a singing assignment. Commonly, speech-language pathologists use singing voice exercises to achieve proper speaking voice use habits.

How does singing training facilitate speaking voice skills? The basics of singing are relaxation, posture, breathing, and resonance. A convincing speaker must also relax, stand tall, breathe deeply, and project an appealing vocal tone. Singing instruction increases the range of vocal timbres and prosody or vocal flow. Both are assets useful to any speaking voice.

What can students expect to learn from Class Voice? While becoming thoroughly familiar with their own voices, students in your class will identify and appreciate the gifts of others. This awareness gives a perspective and depth to the learning experience. Frequent in-class performance opportunities engender confidence and minimize anxiety. As you discuss age- and size-appropriate repertoire, challenges inherent in performance situations, and issues of vocal health, your students glean vital information about the preservation of their vocal instruments. The course prepares each student to travel the pathway of lifelong singing.

Why is a sense of community essential? Learning to sing is a process of trial and error. In her book *The Inner Voice: The Making of a Singer*, Renée Fleming described singing as "an exercise in vulnerability" (Fleming, 2004, p. 20). A sense of community is advantageous for the training of essential skills such as relaxation and deep breathing. You, the teacher, coax your students to experiment with vocal sounds that are applicable to the music you assign. Having the freedom to select repertoire appropriate and desirable to each student is a true advantage in a Class Voice setting. Each voice is valuable because of its unique qualities and every question will advance the training of each singer.

How is the material sequenced for learning? The course is designed for a 16-week semester plan, punctuated by a midterm presentation in Week 8 and a final presentation in Week 16. The book contains the rationale for warm-up exercises and cool-down routines as well as sample procedures, discussion of repertoire by language and genre, and suggestions for using repertoire to develop specific vocal skills. This textbook addresses the fundamental skills for singing and treats repertoire designed for "acoustic" singing or nonamplified performance. After building a strong technical foundation, students can easily expand their field of interest and expertise to include skills specific to music created for amplified circumstances.

The resources are adaptable and should appeal to students interested in classical and CCM (Contemporary Commercial Music) as well as choral music, musical theater, popular music, and folk song. At the end of each chapter, you will find suggestions for comparative listening, questions for discussion, and opportunities for further reading. Suggested assignments and evaluation criteria for the midterm and final presentations are given in Chapter 8 along with assessment forms.

What technology might facilitate student learning in this course? Students with minimal keyboard skills benefit from any one of several applications available on the internet. There are apps that teach music note by note and others that make accompaniments available in multiple keys and tempi. Video and aural recordings of practice sessions and rehearsals can be uploaded for review and feedback by the instructor or the class. It is desirable, though not essential, to employ a collaborative pianist to accompany students in the assessment events.

In his poem entitled "Elevator Music," Henry Taylor wrote: "We are all in this together, the song says, and later we'll descend. The melody is like a name we don't recall just now that still keeps on insisting it is there" (Taylor, 1996, p. 15). We hope you will enjoy your exploration of singing in a class setting as you teach the fundamental skills for lifelong singing.

References

Fleming, R. (2004). *The inner voice: The making of a singer* (p. 20). Viking Press.

Smith, B., & Sataloff, R. (2013). *Choral pedagogy* (3rd ed., p. 3). Plural Publishing.

Taylor, H. (1996). *Understanding fiction: Poems 1986–1996* (p. 15). Louisiana State Press.

Getting Started: Studying Singing Together

A song or aria, like many other works of art, has the capacity to change a life for both singer and listener. Vocal music melds poetic thought with music that represents a collaboration of artistic minds in pursuit of a common expression of ideas, feelings, and beauty. Singing is an art form designed to be shared. In Class Voice, you and your instructor develop vocal knowledge and skills in the presence of others. Class Voice consists of human beings who will support your growth through their example and encouragement. Everyone in the class will improve body awareness, sharpen listening abilities, and train speaking and singing voice skills. By listening together, students and instructors alike deepen their appreciation of various singing styles and trends by listening.

Learning to sing with and for others brings satisfaction as well as singing success. You will become familiar with the vocal gifts of others and identify aspects of your own. Each student of singing brings experiences and observations that broaden the musical horizons of everyone present. Together class participants learn the foundational skills for a healthy singing life, skills that are applicable to every genre of vocal expression.

Creating a Safe Space for Singing

In Class Voice, the unique talents of each singer in the class will be celebrated. Learning new knowledge and skills involves experimentation and exploration. Voice teachers of all kinds *coax* students to try new ways of standing, sitting, breathing, and singing. Because singers neither see nor hear themselves as others do, they need encouragement and reassurance. In private lessons and Class Voice, students experience exciting "breakthrough" moments that occur after hours, or even weeks, of frustration and doubt. On stressful days, beautiful singing may not be as easy to achieve as on leisurely ones. In Class Voice, the spirit of the room, where students sing as a group and as soloists, must always be one of acceptance and expectancy.

Constructive feedback is essential for the solo singer and for the group. The famous composition teacher Nadia Boulanger (1887–1979) once said:

> You can squash people. One remark made in a certain way, on the other hand, can encourage and give confidence. One must tell the truth, but with a view to inspiring confidence and liberating the inner self; it is very difficult,

and collective education doesn't allow for it. (Monsaignon, 1985, p. 59)

Actually, it is possible to be truthful and inspire confidence in a group setting. After a singer or group of singers performs in class, look for what has been positive about the experience. What did the instructor and class members "like" or even "love" about a student's performance? If there are corrections to be made, the instructor should be the one who determines the most constructive means of communicating them.

Corrections addressed to one singer can enhance the learning of everyone in the room. The authors suggest that the instructor preface any corrections with a positive comment and then use the word "and" (rather than "but") to describe another method to achieve the goal. For example, "Your singing was very expressive and attuned to poetic nuance *and* your eyes could reflect even more clearly the intense sorrow of the last poetic phrase." This is preferable to, "Your singing was expressive, *but* we did not 'get' the sadness implied in the poetry." Whether you are the instructor or a student, strive in Class Voice to acknowledge positive attributes and suggest additional ways to work. The growth of each individual student should be of equal importance to everyone in the class. Diminish any spirit of competition between classmates by investing in the success of everyone. Performance anxiety is a "fight or flight" syndrome born in the fear of reprisal. Every performance should be an act of exploration and discovery.

Assessing Interests, Experience, and Expectations

Welcome one another to the class by comparing interests, experiences, expectations, and goals. The following are two tools for gathering basic contact data and essential information regarding individual preparation for Class Voice. The forms can be completed in class, as homework, or online. The first form is more detailed and applicable to a small class. The second one is more general and appropriate for a larger enrollment. You may want to use one of the following forms or adapt one that suits the needs of the class. It could be that everyone prefers to make their introductions in class. If so, you may want to designate one person to transcribe the pertinent data. Compile the responses and use them as criteria for setting the pace and content of classwork.

Sample Information Forms

Class Voice: Fundamental Skills for Lifelong Singing
INFORMATION FORM

FULL NAME _____

    I prefer to be called _____

    My pronouns are _____

CONTACT INFORMATION

    Mailing Address (Optional) _____

    E-mail Address _____

    Phone (Cell/Home) _____

MAJOR _____ MINOR (If applicable) _____

MUSICAL INSTRUMENTS (If any) _____

Circle appropriate response: Lessons? Yes No (If yes, how long? _____) Self-Taught

Circle appropriate response: Lessons? Yes No (If yes, how long? _____) Self-Taught

SINGING EXPERIENCES (If any)

Solo Voice Training: Lessons? Yes No (If yes, how long? _____)

    Soprano   Mezzo   Alto   Tenor   Baritone   Bass

Solo Voice Performance Experiences (If any):

Selection: _____ Date: _____

Performance Venue: _____

Selection: _____ Date: _____

Performance Venue: _____

Choral Experiences (If any):

Group _____ Length of Participation _____

Soprano I   Soprano II   Alto I   Alto II

Tenor I   Tenor II   Baritone   Bass

Group _____ Length of Participation _____

Soprano I   Soprano II   Alto I   Alto II

Tenor I   Tenor II   Baritone   Bass

Group _____ Length of Participation _____

Soprano I   Soprano II   Alto I   Alto II
Tenor I   Tenor II   Baritone Bass

What is your favorite song? _____

What is your favorite musical or opera? _____

Why have you enrolled in *Class Voice: Fundamental Skills for Lifelong Singing?*
Circle all appropriate responses:

   Academic Requirement   Professional Development   Personal Development

Name one goal you hope to achieve in this course. _____

List your hobbies, sports, and special interests. _____

In the following space, please feel free to share any information you believe the instructor should know about you, your voice, or your health. If there is a particular song you would like to learn, please mention it.

Class Voice: Fundamental Skills for Lifelong Singing
SURVEY OF VOCAL EXPERIENCE AND COURSE EXPECTATIONS

Name _____ Preferred First Name _____

Pronouns _____

Contact Information (e-mail) _____ (phone) _____

Years of Voice Study _____

Years of Instrumental Study _____

Years of Choral Experience _____

Years of Band/Orchestra Participation _____

What do you consider to be your voice part? (Circle all that apply.)

    Soprano   Alto   Tenor   Countertenor   Baritone   Bass

At what age did your voice change occur? _____

Which, if any, of the following musicianship skills have you studied?
(Circle all that apply.)

    Treble Clef   Bass Clef   Key Signatures   Meter Signatures

What other languages than English, if any, have you studied?

What musical skills do you hope to learn in our class?

What style of music do you listen to most often?

Do you have a favorite song/aria you wish to learn this semester?

Creating an Action Plan for Learning

Class Voice attracts students with a wide range of interests, experiences, expectations, and goals. Some members of the class may have professional ambitions while others hope to enjoy singing as a hobby. Class Voice may be a required course for an instrumental music education major. One student may have been a singing star as a child with professional credits while another may never have sung before. Adult learners may lack confidence due to lapsed practice. They may also have many questions and misgivings about current vocal technical methods. Some students may have "perfect" or "absolute" pitch and others may not yet match pitch at all. All class participants harbor personal expectations, private hopes, and myriad questions. How shall the class work together to meet the needs of everyone?

After the initial gathering of the class, consider the following steps toward designing a learning plan. (Note: Should several students express an interest in a topic beyond the scope of this textbook, such as "belting" or "riffing," the instructor can identify online and published resources that address the topics or include outside materials to supplement the textbook.)

- Collate the information gleaned from the forms and/or opening discussions
- Identify the "burning issues"
  - Topics of immediate interest to everyone
  - Topics of urgent interest of individuals
- Determine priorities
  - Vocal skills
  - Musicianship skills
  - Performance-related skills
  - Other
- Collect individual repertoire requests
  - Group singing
  - Solo singing
- Assign repertoire
  - Group selections
  - Solo selections

(Students will use online and library resources to acquire repertoire.)

- Shape the lesson plan (two 8-week segments)
  - Daily schedule within each segment
  - Deadlines for assessment events
    - Quizzes
    - Reports/response papers
    - Midterm and final presentations

Every Class Voice syllabus is structured around the theory and practices of special interest to the students and their instructor. The theoretic part of the course entails basic knowledge acquisition (anatomy and physiology, music history and theory, vocal health, and hygiene). Practice comes in the form of music making (vocal, musicianship, and repertoire learning skills). The instructor reserves the right to organize the syllabus/learning plan and adjust it as necessary.

Before active singing begins each day, the class will engage in a warm-up appropriate to the skills and repertoire to be studied. A regular reminder of the "basics of singing" (relaxation, posture, breathing, and resonance) helps everyone "assemble" their vocal instrument properly. Each class should conclude with a brief cool-down routine. Class discussion and comparative listening are useful exercises that fortify student learning outcomes.

Implementing the Learning Plan

In any learning community, structure brings freedom. Open the class period with a review of the material covered in your previous meeting that will keep everyone accountable and correct any misunderstanding. As a group, discuss reading or listening assignments. This will help everyone read and listen more critically.

Developing a Context for Singing

For most human beings, singing is a natural ability that is identified in childhood and enjoyed throughout life with little instruction. Students of singing discover there is a great deal to know about the art form, the anatomy and physiology of the voice, and vocal acoustics. Because no two voices sound alike, every voice deserves its own serious study. In Class Voice, students have the chance to gather intriguing information that deepens their understanding of their own instrument and enhances their enjoyment of listening to other voices. Consider attending "live" recital performances as a group or as individuals during the semester. Discuss your observations in class or in written response papers. Save the program, program notes, texts, and translations for future reference.

Impacted by political, religious, and artistic circumstances, singing styles change with each historical period. Every culture has its own preference for literary and dramatic subjects. As you learn the context in which vocal repertoire was composed and performed, you expand your worldview and shape your performing perspective.

Conclusion

Class Voice is an occasion for singing students and instructors to explore together the topics and vocal repertoire of interest to them. A course plan designed by the entire learning community brings satisfaction and yields excellent results. Enjoy your time together, learning and performing the music that interests you.

Reference

Monsaignon, B. (1985). *Mademoiselle: Conversations with Nadia Boulanger* (p. 59) (R. Marsack, Trans.). Carcanet Press.

Acknowledgments

The authors wish to express sincerest appreciation to Dr. Robert T. Sataloff and Nicole Hodges for suggesting the creation of this publication. We are grateful to Valerie Johns, Christina Gunning, Jessica Bristow, Megan Carter, Lori Asbury, Kristin Banach, and Emily Pooley for their kind and competent production assistance. We express our thanks to Dr. Deborah Caputo Rosen for her grace and generosity in the completion of this volume. Our sincere gratitude goes to Leslie Weisstein Antman and Dominique Baeta for their experience and insights. Our colleagues Dr. Paul Basler, Dr. Rich Pellegrin, and Dr. James Sain kindly shared with us the latest music theory resources for our readers. We thank University of Florida undergraduate music students Simon Lynch and Isabella Stolarczyk for demonstrating skills captured in photos by Dr. Thaddaeus Bourne. The author headshots were created by Mike Shea Photography. We are grateful to the reviewers of this manuscript for their useful comments and suggestions that improved the final result.

As college professors, we are very pleased and proud to feature the writings of our former students Erin Donahue and Vincent Oakes. Since completing undergraduate degrees at the University of Florida, they both have distinguished themselves in their chosen fields. Finally, we extend our love and unending thanks to Dr. Elizabeth Graham, internationally recognized operatic star and longtime head of the Voice Area at the University of Florida. Dr. Graham's vision, leadership, and concern for students have been a beacon of light through all the voice studios at UF. We appreciate her support of our work and her devotion to lifelong singing.

Contributors

Erin Nicole Donahue, BM, MA, CCC-SLP
Voice Pathologist and Singing Voice Specialist
The Blaine Block Institute for Voice Analysis and Rehabilitation
The Professional Voice Center of Greater Cincinnati (ProVoice Center)
Cincinnati, Ohio
Chapters 9 and 10

Vincent Oakes, BM, MM
Artistic Director and Director of Choral Music
Chattanooga Boys Choir
The Baylor School
Chattanooga, Tennessee
Chapter 9

Robert T. Sataloff, MD, DMA, FACS
Professor and Chairman
Department of Otolaryngology-Head and Neck Surgery
Senior Associate Dean for Clinical Academic Specialities
Drexel University College of Medicine
Director, Otolaryngology and Communication Sciences Research
Lankenau Institute for Medical Research
Chairman, The Voice Foundation
Chairman, American Institute for Voice and Ear Research
Faculty, Academy of Vocal Arts
Conductor, Thomas Jefferson University Choir
Philadelphia, Pennsylvania
Chapter 2

Reviewers

Plural Publishing and the authors thank the following reviewers for taking the time to provide their valuable feedback during the manuscript development process. Additional anonymous feedback was provided by other expert reviewers.

Patricia Boehm, PhD, MM, BM
Professor of Music
University of Mount Union
Alliance, Ohio

Cynthia Clayton, MM
Professor
Moores School of Music
University of Houston
Houston, Texas

Michael Hix, DM
Associate Professor of Voice, Coordinator of Vocal Students
University of New Mexico
Albuquerque, New Mexico

Natalie C. Lerch, DMA
Professor of Music
Cornish College of the Arts
Seattle, Washington

Brent Rogers, DMA, MM, BM
Associate Professor of Music and Dean
College of Arts and Sciences
Dickinson State University
Dickinson, North Dakota

Meg Stohlmann, DMA
Assistant Professor, Choral Music Education
Appalachian State University
Boone, North Carolina

Susan Wallin, MM, BM
Professor of Voice
Baldwin Wallace Conservatory of Music
Berea, Ohio

Nathan Windt, DMA
Associate Professor of Music (Voice)
St. Ambrose University
Davenport, Iowa

Dedicated to Meagan Burrichter Fratiello
Benjamin Harmon Sataloff
Johnathan Brandon Sataloff
Isla James Deacy Donahue
Emilia Josephine Donahue
Brandon Thomas Oakes
Luke Vincent Oakes

Introduction

Class Voice and Strategies for Lifelong Singing

Songs: With and Without Words

Singing sounds surround our lives with and without words. Singing is a quintessential element of life on earth. Fragments of melody encircle us in swaying tree branches, squeaking hinges, and humming bees. Wordless singing is rare among human beings, but it is common in nature. Each creature has a characteristic sound, an exclamation that announces its presence. Calls and responses ring out to invite community or warn of danger. In the words of the theologian Dr. Tom Troeger: "The song and prayer of birds is melody alone. Their hymns employ no words. Their praise is purely tone" (Troeger, 1994, p. 55).

From its earliest occurrence, singing spontaneously penetrated the silence and described the emotions of the moment. "Early musical instruments were melodic imitators of the human voice; and it took centuries to establish music as a series of sound unrelated to the voice and detached from any verbal association" (Storr, 1992, p. 66). Using stems and strings, bamboo and boxes, people devised sound-making instruments to imitate or accompany the singing. As singing technique and instrument building became more sophisticated, the horizons of vocal and instrumental music expanded, making room for new avenues of musical expression. According to Charles Rosen, vocal music dominated the secular and sacred musical scene well into the 18th century.

> For centuries, of course, there had been pure instrumental music played in public, but it consisted either of arrangements of vocal music, introductions to vocal music (preludes or overtures to church services or operas), interludes between the acts of operas and oratorios, or dance music, which had no prestige whatever (naturally, this did not prevent the creation of masterpieces in that genre). (Rosen, 1980, p. 8)

A knowledge of singing is an essential building block for understanding music making in Western music.

Singing was the first form of music making and may have begun as an involuntary act of human expression. All sounds made by the human voice are powered by the breath. Humans group these sounds into melodies that are organized around a rhythmic pulse that comes from the heartbeat and responds to thought. It is a natural mode of communication known to enchant, comfort, and excite.

Instruments Versus Voice

The human voice is a perfectly designed aerodynamic system with the oscillator positioned directly above the power source and under the resonators. To produce tone, your vocal instrument needs no valves, pedals, or expensive accessories. Your voice is a physical attribute, a unique and personal feature. Do not be deceived by the fact that your voice is conveniently located and easily accessed. You must carefully tend to it and painstakingly train it if it is to function effectively as your main communication tool. The fact that the voice exists within your body is significant. Whatever happens to your body, mind, and heart happens also to your voice. Because your vocal instrument lives within you, it is concealed from your view. Singing vocal repertoire is considered the voice's most "Olympic" activity, requiring complex neuromuscular coordination. Learning to sing means learning to "play" an invisible instrument. The learning process for singers is one of trial and error. It demands an abundance of patience and, therefore, should occur in a safe environment.

Human Growth: Musical, Physical, and Aesthetic

You have chosen wisely to develop your singing skill in the presence of others. Each person in your class presents with an irreplaceable, distinctive voice for you to investigate. When you attend a voice class, you are surrounded by colleagues with differing types of vocal talent, performing style, and experience. Each voice is unique and incomparable. Since human beings age daily, every day is its own idiosyncratic point along one's vocal journey. Singers are more than the sum of their vocal parts. The singing voice expresses the musical, physical, and aesthetic gifts of a human being. Remember the motto of the late children's choir specialist Helen Kemp: "Body, mind, spirit, voice—it takes the whole person to sing and rejoice!"

During this course, you will sing by yourself and receive constructive feedback from the instructor and your peers. You will hear and observe the singing of others, giving you ample opportunities to study vocal timbres and skills. When learning new material, you and your class will join forces to explore ways to address vocal issues. A voice class is a total immersion teaching experience that trains you in the proper use of your body, mind, and voice for singing and speaking.

Speaking Voice and Singing Voice Use

The vocal instrument does many expressive tasks such as singing, speaking, humming, and sighing. The avoidance of vocal injury is essential to lifelong singing. To preserve your voice, you must use it wisely. A voice class addresses more than just singing. Its scope includes healthy speaking and all other voice use. If a jogger trips and sprains an ankle, walking will be an arduous task until the ankle heals. In the same manner, the well-being of your singing voice depends upon the careful maintenance of your speaking voice.

Healthy voice use is based on four principles: relaxation, posture, breathing, and resonance. You will learn to keep a sense of "melody" in your speech and to sing with a core sound that relates to the timbre of your speaking voice. Your body is your instrument whether you are singing or speaking. How you nourish and care for your body really matters. Your physical well-being influences the way your voice works. Class Voice will equip you with foundational information and best practices for maintaining your vocal health and wellness throughout life.

Musical Skill Training and Singing

The voice is governed by the brain and fueled by breath. For speaking or singing, you must "audiate" or "pre-hear" what you wish to speak or sing. The vocal instrument responds to the mental signals you audiate. Verbal thought processes direct your speech. For healthy singing, you must summon the pitch and vowel from an outside source, be it the piano, a vocal model, or a musical score. "Why can't I just sing along with a recording or learn songs by rote?" you ask. Though such methods of note learning may help you pick up a tune, both are acts of vocal imitation. To sing in a healthy way, you must "teach" your voice the exquisite details of the rhythm, melody, and poetry. Class Voice provides you with strategies for developing and teaching strong musicianship skills for singing. Rhythm, the backbone of music and poetry, will be the starting point and note learning will follow. Ever wonder about "absolute" or "perfect" pitch? Or if tone "deafness" exists? Class Voice will help you answer these questions and many others.

Issues of *Fach* and Longevity

You may be wondering about what repertoire you should sing or what voice part you should choose when you join a choir. You may have heard of the German word "Fach" commonly used to classify or assign a voice to a particular part. The term is a technical way to classify vocal range, timbre, and repertoire. For a young singer or a singer in transition, classification is not necessary or even recommended. There will be many seasons in your vocal life. To sing for a lifetime, you must accept the changes inherent in human growth and development. Class Voice will help you know what to expect. There will be times in your life when it is desirable to set high solo performance goals and strive to meet them. There will be other times when choral singing is the best option for staying in the singing game without the exposure and stress of solo responsibilities. Class Voice will introduce you to all kinds of vocal repertoire. You will learn what is appropriate for your specific talent. You will also develop an understanding of the singing skills certain repertoire engenders.

As a singer, teacher, or colleague, you will confront many vocal challenges. Because you cannot see or hear yourself clearly, you will always need an extra set of "eyes and ears" to provide useful feedback. To navigate the singing road, voice users solicit the guidance of qualified voice teachers, vocal coaches, or choral conductors. Class Voice helps you understand the stages of a singer's life from "cradle to grave." You will learn what to expect of yourself and others. Class Voice gives you abundant resources for further inquiry. With the materials found in this textbook, you will be able to set goals and assess your learning objectives and outcomes. Should you become a teacher, the information will help you train others. Class Voice supplies you with the tools and strategies for lifelong singing.

Conclusion

Singing occurs daily in every culture around the world. The singing voice and speaking voice are partners in human communication. To preserve the singing voice, singers must learn to speak healthfully. It has been proven that singing skills are effective in developing a convincing, reliable speaking voice. Teaching music of all kinds requires a dependable vocal technique for speech and song. When explanations fail, instrumentalists demonstrate musical concepts to one another by singing. Studio teachers, vocal coaches, and choral conductors speak text and sing melodic examples as their "way to work." Class Voice brings you the opportunity to learn fundamental skills needed for a lifetime of singing.

Discussion Questions

1. Why is singing central to an understanding of instrumental music making?
2. What elements make the human voice different from human-made musical instruments?
3. Describe the musical, physical, and aesthetic growth of the human voice.
4. How does musicianship training secure the longevity of a professional voice user?
5. What roles do the speaking voice and the singing voice play in the success of a professional voice user? What is "Fach" and why is it important?

References

Rosen, C. (1980). *Sonata forms* (p. 8). W. W. Norton.

Storr, A. (1992). *Music and the mind* (p. 66). Ballantine Books.

Troeger, T. (1994). *Borrowed light: Hymn texts, prayers and poems* (p. 55). Oxford University Press.

1
Skills for Learning to Sing

Brenda Smith

If you play a human-made instrument, you keep it in a protective case until you are ready to use it. Before playing, you open the case to assess and remove each part. You might swipe a soft cleaning cloth over the surface or blow through its tubing to rid the instrument of excess dust or spit. As you assemble the instrument, you align its parts to accommodate your arms and hands. You assume the stance that facilitates your manner of playing. If you are a keyboard player, you lift the lid of the instrument, dust the keys, and adjust the bench to a comfortable height and distance. When you finish your music making, you return the instrument to its storage space.

As a singer, you "live" in your instrument. It surrounds you all the time. In the words of Dr. Jean Abitbol in his book entitled *The Power of the Voice*:

> The voice is the most intimate and the most naked manifestation of our essential self. It is in us; it reveals our highest spiritual conscience. It allows us to dialogue with our inner self and to express our every emotion, our every feeling. The mystery of the voice is part of the mystery of life, a sort of emotional hologram. (Abitbol, 2016, p. 99)

The state of your whole being is the state of your vocal instrument. Your speaking and singing voice will reflect the physical and emotional environment that surrounds you. It will be important for you to prepare your body, mind, and spirit for healthy voice use.

We live in an era of "evidence-based vocal pedagogy," a time when voice users can rely on scientific research to determine best practices. It is commonly believed that a regimen that ensures physical and mental relaxation, fosters a tall posture, and allows for deep breathing are the steps that prepare the voice for efficient resonance or sound production. The individual elements are relaxation, posture, breathing, and resonance, known as the "basics of singing." Moving from one element to the next, you "build" your vocal instrument from simple to complex. The order matters. Each step facilitates the success of the next. By identifying and eliminating unnecessary tension, it will be easier to align your body. A tall, balanced posture helps free muscles needed to achieve a relaxed and buoyant breath. Once the muscles for breathing are awakened and active, your voice will respond with a resonant and appealing tone (Smith, 2018, p. 56).

The voice, guided by neurological signals, is a complex system involving all parts of the body. If you are to sing freely, your mind and body must act as one. In daily life, we use our voices for a wide variety of tasks without thinking much about it. For singing, all the elements must be brought under control. Singers relax, center their thoughts, and seek balance through proper alignment. A singer's posture is a proud one with shoulders wide and rib cage expanded. A singer standing in a "performance ready" position exudes an attitude of hopeful expectation.

Breathing for singing involves mental coordination and muscle antagonism (Appelman, 1967, p. 30), a combination that moves air into and out of your body. The cycle of breath begins with exhalation, the expulsion of air currently in your body, and is followed by a deep, relaxed inhalation. The muscles of expiration stand at the ready during the inhalation process. When the inhaled air is placed under pressure, it reverses course and travels back through the vocal tract. To facilitate the moving airstream while you sing, you must maintain an expectant, stable body position. The vibration of the vocal folds turns air waves to sound waves. The resonators of the vocal tract (the oral pharynx, nasal pharynx, and mouth) act as filters that cause your voice to be audible. The result is sound production occurs, which is called "phonation." "The vocal tract cavities resonate most strongly within specific frequency ranges known as *formants*" (Davids & LaTour, 2021, p. 68). We will examine each individual element or "building block" of the vocal instrument.

The Basics of Singing

Relaxation

Whether you are playing a human-made instrument or your own "natural" voice, you are sure to benefit from a systematic relaxation routine before practicing or performing. Singing is a dynamic act of concentration unlike any other. Being tension free and alert will help you coordinate your mind and body. The singing voice is a fragile instrument, vulnerable to fatigue and injury. Long thought to be the "seat of the soul," the human voice is a control center for communicating wordless utterances as well as speech and song. Singing teachers and choral conductors open every lesson or rehearsal with activities especially designed to release bodily tensions, soothe the spirit, and center the mind. You may have already discovered ways to calm and center yourself through meditation, yoga, or other popular methods. Such techniques will come in handy as you develop your singing voice and help others to sing.

Physical Relaxation

In daily life, you are likely to accumulate muscular tensions. In preparation for singing, search for unwanted tension so that you can gently release it. Muscle tension generally responds favorably to an increase in blood flow. Stretching or massaging areas of tightness will improve circulation and achieve temporary relaxation. Be intentional and systematic about releasing physical tightness. In the following text boxes you will find examples of ways to find and eliminate tension. The examples are designed to move intentionally from larger to smaller muscle groups, addressing each of the regions that will be used for singing.

> **Relaxing the Extremities**
>
> Gently roll your shoulders backward, eliminating any strain.
>
> Stretch your arms across your body and give yourself a warm embrace.
>
> Extend your arms in front of you at shoulder height and squeeze your palms into fists.
>
> Flex and release your fingers.
>
> Wiggle your toes.
>
> Bend and straighten your knees.
>
> Rotate your weight from one leg to another.

> **Relaxing the Thorax**
>
> Twist your upper body slowly to the right and hold. Reverse.
>
> Pull your shoulders up to ear level. Squeeze and release. Repeat.
>
> Bring your shoulder blades together and release.
>
> Release and repeat until all tension in the shoulders, chest, and rib cage is eliminated.

> **Relaxing the Neck and Throat**
>
> Rotate your head to the right and then the left. Hold and release.
>
> Lower your right ear toward your right shoulder and enjoy the stretch.
>
> Repeat on the left side.
>
> Drop your chin toward your chest. Release any tension in the back of your neck.
>
> Stroke your throat with long, comforting, downward motions.
>
> Note: Be careful about rotating the head backward. "Some people with certain cervical spine problems should not roll their heads to the back" (Lyle, 2014, p. 14).

> **Relaxing the Face and Tongue**
>
> Place your palms on your cheeks and massage.
>
> Stroke your forehead and jaw line.
>
> Close your eyes tightly and open them wide.
>
> Make a funny face and then an angry one.
>
> Explore your upper and lower lips with the tip of your tongue.
>
> Flex your tongue side to side, up and down, in and out.

Take note of the areas where you personally found strain or stress. Identify what brought you relief from tension and explore additional ways to achieve relaxation in each of these areas.

Mental Relaxation

Though you may have eliminated physical tensions, your voice is not quite ready to sing freely. Because the vocal instrument resides in the body, it reflects every spiritual and mental stress that occurs in daily life. Anxiety limits your ability to concentrate and coordinate your mind and body. As you build your vocal instrument, your inner life is a factor that must be considered. This principle is one major difference between playing an instrument and singing. If you are distracted, fearful, or sorrowful, you are probably still able to play an instrument. A human-made instrument will perform at your command. It may not be a particularly fulfilling experience for you as a musician, but the audience is unlikely to notice your sadness. Singers, however, find it very difficult to keep the circumstances of the soul from being heard in the sound and fluency of the voice. In his book entitled *Looking for Spinoza: Joy, Sorrow, and the Feeling Brain,* Antonio Damasio, a world-renowned neuroscientist, tells us that our feelings, emotions, and mental images are the "bedrock" of our thinking. Damasio writes:

> But there they are, feelings of myriad emotions and related states, the continuous musical line of our minds, the unstoppable humming of the most universal of melodies that only dies down when we go to sleep, a humming that turns into all-out singing when we are occupied by joy, or a mournful requiem when sorrow takes over. (Damasio, 2003, p. 3)

Singing is a very conscious act in which body systems work together to express feelings and emotions through words and music. Experiences that cause grief or anxiety jolt your physical being. Suddenly, your body tightens, restricting your ability to breathe and sing. Remember: What happens to you, happens to your voice. The following text box provides sample exercises that relax the mind, assure the spirit, and bring the singing instrument into a state of readiness.

Exercises for Mental Relaxation

Close your eyes and center yourself within on a single point. Exhale and inhale slowly.

With your eyes closed, imagine the moon gently spreading its light across the ocean.

With your eyes closed, envision a scene that would calm you. Relax and breathe.

Cover your left nostril and inhale through your right one. Exhale in reverse order. Repeat.

Sense the presence of a bouquet of your favorite flowers or the scent of a favorite food.

Release all negative thoughts and imbibe positive ones.

Squeeze your eyelids tightly and release them with an inner smile.

Posture

Body alignment is the next step in building the vocal instrument. For the vocal instrument to work efficiently, the power source (air) must be aligned with the oscillator (the vocal folds) and the resonators (the vocal tract). Singers generally perform in a standing posture and rehearse in a seated one.

Standing Posture

A standing posture for singing begins with a firm foundation achieved by centering your body weight on the metatarsal heads or "balls" of the feet. Release your knees and keep them loose and flexible. Rotate your body from side to side to free your spine and elongate it. To expand the rib cage, extend both your arms horizontally at shoulder height (Figures 1–1A and 1–1B). With your arms at a 90° angle to the floor, turn your open palms to the ceiling (Figures 1–1C and 1–1D). Notice the openness of your chest and the proud stance you have achieved. Keep your shoulders expanded as you relax and release your arms and hands to your sides. Allow your head to balance easily on your spine, chin parallel to the floor.

Notice the position of your body. Your weight is balanced. Your knees are "soft" or unlocked. Your spine is elongated. Your rib cage and shoulders are elevated and wide.

A

B

Figure 1–1. A. Female student demonstrating step one of standing pose. **B.** Male student demonstrating step one of standing pose. *continues*

C

D

Figure 1–1. *continued* **C.** Female student demonstrating step two of standing pose. **D.** Male student demonstrating step two of standing pose.

Your head is relaxed and balanced. This is a "singer's posture." You have "built" your instrument on a firm foundation. Notice the "order of things" from the bottom of your feet to the top of your head. Study it from a *kinesthetic* point of view, meaning "how it feels." In their book entitled *Singing with Your Whole Self: A Singer's Guide to Feldenkrais Awareness through Movement*, the authors explain how valuable an accurate kinesthetic sense can be for a singer. "Any tension beyond the minimum necessary is both wasteful and harmful" (Nelson & Blades, 2018, p. 15). Become aware of what your body is doing and strive for a sense of buoyance and readiness.

Cautionary notes:

1. As you sing or speak, monitor your knees periodically. It is easy to tighten them unconsciously due to fatigue or fear. Tightness in the knees causes muscles of the thighs and the abdominal muscles to lock.
2. A "singer's posture" is based upon an even distribution of your body weight on the balls of the feet (metatarsal heads).

Be aware that the shoes you wear for singing must be supportive and comfortable. Singers are encouraged to wear shoes with heels of modest height for practice and performance settings. Let gravity work to your advantage by selecting appropriate footwear that helps keep you aligned and grounded. (See *The Effects of Heel Height on Head Position, Long-Term Average Spectra, Perceptions of Female Singers* by Dr. Amelia Rollings.)

Seated Posture

From time to time, voice users must speak and sing from a seated position. An effective seated posture for voice use is based on the balance achieved in a standing one. Start with your standing "singer's posture" with weight centered on both feet. As you lower yourself into a chair, keep your hips forward on the chair's edge so that you achieve a 90° angle between your feet and your knees as well as your knees and your hips. Elongate your spine, open your chest, and expand your rib cage. Bring your head to a neutral position, keeping your chin parallel to the floor (Figure 1–2).

Maintain this tall posture from your "sitting bones" to the crown of your head. Be careful not to cross your knees or ankles while seated for singing or speaking. Monitor your posture, assuring yourself that your alignment facilitates voice use. Should a chair or bench be uncomfortable, do not be reluctant to find a remedy. A pillow might help you support your back. If your feet do not rest easily on the floor in front of you, use a footrest. Feel the same buoyant readiness you enjoyed in your standing "singer's posture."

Good posture is essential if you are to achieve your full potential as a singer and it prevents fatigue. According to Marina Gilman:

> When we begin to think of posture not in terms of how the connections of bones, muscles, and tendons directly interact, but in terms of the flow of movement, of the constant interrelationship between stability and instability in relation to gravitational forces, our ability to problem solve will be very different. (Gilman, 2014, p. 21)

Because voice use is an activity in which you engage all day, try to make your "singer's posture" the way you position your body for life.

A

B

Figure 1–2. A. Female student demonstrating step one of sitting pose. **B.** Male student demonstrating step one of sitting pose. *continues*

C

D

Figure 1–2. *continued* **C.** Female student demonstrating step two of sitting pose. **D.** Male student demonstrating step two of sitting pose.

Breathing

Breath energy inspires us and organizes our thoughts. How we breathe matters. A deep breath slows a racing heart rate and quiets a grieving or frightened spirit. Hectic, constricted breathing upsets the functioning of the mind and body. In stressful situations, we often forget to breathe, ignoring a readily available means for restoring physical and spiritual equilibrium. Breathing, an essential life activity, defines the way we live and think. It is the source of vital energy for living.

Music must also "breathe." No matter what the genre, musical phrases are punctuated with pauses that are intended to conclude thoughts and allow for breathing. If you play a human-made instrument, be it wind, string, keyboard, or percussion, you know that silences play a significant role in communicating the architecture of the composition. Both the performer and the listening audience "breathe" with the music, imbibing and interpreting the audible shapes we call musical "phrases." When you sing, acknowledge every punctuation mark in the text and every rest in the music. A punctuation mark in the text may be an excellent place to breathe, or it may be simply a place to "sing a silence." To comprehend the text's meaning, a listener must "hear" the pause. Without punctuation, spoken or sung text becomes meaningless droning.

Breathing for Singing

Breathing for singing is arguably the most crucial basic technique in a singer's toolbox. The air you breathe serves as the power source for your voice. Though breathing is a vital, natural function, not everyone breathes in the most efficient way. For singing, it is best to inhale with a receptive attitude much as you do during sleep. Singing happens as you exhale. It is an organized process that you shape to meet the vocal demands of the music. The steps described previously—namely, relaxation and posture—create the framework for a thorough exhalation and a calming inhalation of air.

For centuries, singing teachers have used the motto "to breathe is to sing and to sing is to breathe" to make the point that the way you breathe determines much about how you are able to use the air. When you open your body and invite air into your lungs, you mobilize and energize the muscles of exhalation. If you breathe with haste or rigidity, your body is ill-prepared to move the inhaled air with flexibility or intention. A forced or tense inhalation tightens muscles and immobilizes the body's exhalation system. For speaking or singing, relax and enjoy the inhalation process. Perceive it as an enriching, refreshing experience for your body and mind. The "quality" of your inhalation facilitates your capacity to create beautiful tone.

Breathing and Air

The voice is powered by air acquired through the natural act of breathing. According to Evangelista Torricelli, a Renaissance scientist, we are "submerged in an ocean of air" (Walker, 2007, p. 11). Air is an invisible, intangible substance we sense and smell. Take a moment to consider the fact that you have powered your voice daily without seeing or touching either the instrument or its power source. Your body savors air, routinely cycling air through your lungs about 25,000 times a day. Your "vital capacity"—that is, the air in your lungs—is made up of *tidal* and *residual* air or air that refreshes and air that stabilizes. Together they replenish and sustain oxygen levels in your body.

Exhalation: An Essential First Step

The cycle of breathing for singing begins with a thorough exhalation of air. By emptying your lungs, you create the "need" for new air. In his pioneering book, *Respiratory Function in Speech and Song,* Thomas J. Hixon stated: "the stored energy is released and the lungs recoil toward a smaller volume—like a stretched spring recoils when released" (Hixon, 1991, p. 12). This is a passive form of expiration, one in which you relax and release your abdominal muscles. As you expel the air, maintain your "singer's posture." Remain balanced on both feet with "softened" knees, expanded chest, and relaxed arms. Allow the air to escape gladly and easily. This is the "at ease" position for which you will strive at the end of every phrase you sing.

Inhalation

Inhalation can occur exclusively through the nose or mouth or by some combination of the two. Because the nose is equipped naturally to purify, humidify, and warm the air, most medical professionals advocate for nasal inhalation. "Just as important as how much air we can take in is how freely we do so" (Nelson & Blades, 2018, p. 87). Singers train to be skillful at all three ways, each of which proves advantageous in a specific musical circumstance.

In general, solo singing affords more opportunities for a singer to breathe through the nose than does ensemble singing. One voice teacher may espouse an exclusive method of inhalation for all students while another may be open to many variations. Commonly, choral conductors prefer choristers to breathe through the mouth. According to James Nestor, mouth breathing has some disadvantages. "Inhaling air through the mouth decreases pressure, which causes the soft tissues in the back of the mouth to become loose and flex inward, creating less overall space and making breathing more difficult" (Nestor, 2020, p. 27).

Nasal Breathing

Nasal breathing is effective and efficient. When comparing mouth breathing to nose breathing, Nestor writes that nose breathing "forces air against those flabby tissues at the back of the throat, making the airways wider and breathing easier" (Nestor, 2020, p. 27). It can also be a very calming way to receive air. To experience the benefits of nasal breathing, be sure to exhale and maintain your singer's posture. Relax and sense the expansion in your body as air flows easily through your nostrils and vocal tract to your lungs. As you welcome the air into your body, your body temporarily widens. The diaphragm contracts and lungs fill. Without your awareness, the muscles of exhalation have already positioned themselves. Enjoy this moment of calm expectancy.

Mouth Breathing

Mouth breathing is the quickest way to access air. If you suffer from restricted airways due to chronic illness, allergies, or sinus problems, it may be the most effective way to breathe. To breathe efficiently through the mouth, maintain your singer's posture and exhale completely. Relax and release your abdominal muscles as you allow the air to flow gently over your tongue. Your tongue and jaw should be passive, not tightened, retracted, or jutted. The tip of your tongue should be at rest and your jaw relaxed. Allow the same expansion that occurred during nasal breathing. Welcome and receive the air silently. Since you have created the need for the air, the process ensues almost effortlessly.

Combined Nasal and Mouth Breathing

Breathing through the nose and mouth simultaneously is also an option. The principles described previously apply. Part your lips slightly. Allow the air to flow through your nostrils and over your tongue as you maintain a singer's posture. Be careful not to retract your tongue. Singers with nasal congestion or chronic allergies often find this method to be effective.

Comparison of the Three Methods of Inhalation

Strive to master all three methods of inhalation. It could be that one method serves you better than another. If you play a wind instrument, you may find that breathing exclusively through the nose for singing and through the mouth for playing helps you differentiate the muscle groups and techniques required for each activity. The music itself may dictate the use of one method over another. *Where* you inhale air (in other words, through the nose, mouth, or combination of both) is not as significant as *how* you inhale and *how much* air you inhale. Remember: Efficient inhalation for singing depends upon a full expulsion of previously inhaled air and the maintenance of a singer's posture.

Develop a positive relationship with the breathing process. The secret to an effective inhalation for singing lies in an expectant physical and mental attitude. Air is costless and readily available. Remember that you live "in an ocean of air" that will never starve you of its resources. Receive the air gratefully and use it generously. The more air you use as you sing, the faster your body will replenish its supply. The air you breathe inspires you, calms you, and gives you energy for singing.

Reverse Breathing

Effective, efficient breathing for voice use is not the development of a new skill. It involves reverting to a familiar, fundamental one. As a child, you may have been less fearful and more trusting. You may have fallen asleep effortlessly at the end of a tired day. In later years, life presented you with challenges and uncertainty. Unconsciously, you sought internal ways of defending yourself against a real or imagined adversity. You may have stiffened your jaw, tightened your abdominal muscles, and/or locked your knees without noticing. This defensive stance may have given you a sense of strength and well-being. It is unlikely that you considered the impact of such a posture on your breathing patterns. In a clenched body, inhalation occurs by gasping or sucking the air. The chest rises, pressing against the larynx. The lungs cannot fully descend to receive air. Though unproductive, it is common for humans to breathe with tense abdominal muscles. Singing teachers and choral conductors often call this behavior "reverse" breathing. It represents the "opposite" of what is healthy for singing and speaking.

Learning to sing requires that you return to a body position that favors gravity. If locked core muscles seem "habitual" or "normal" to you, a grounded posture (flexible knees, balanced weight, and lengthened spine) may feel awkward to you at first. To reverse the habit, try allowing your abdominal muscles to expand when you inhale. Initially, the experience may seem counterintuitive. It will, however, soon prove its worth. Think of inhaling for sleep. Your body expands and air flows in. Inhalation for singing requires the same gentle expansion. When you inhale in this manner, you can rely upon the muscles of exhalation to govern the movement of your air. This method of breathing ensures that your voice will be governed by a reliable source. The voice, like all wind instruments, requires a steady stream of air for its power. Any physical position that inhibits the neck or torso impairs the flow of air to the voice. A tall, buoyant posture and low breath are essential skills for healthy, lifelong singing.

Breath Management

The term "breath management" (preferable to "breath support" or "breath control") refers to how you engage the muscles of your abdomen, back, and ribs to guide the air steadily back to your vocal folds. Some vocal pedagogues describe the process using the Italian word "appoggio" (meaning "to lean"), implying that the abdominal muscles "lean" on the air column. Through the flow of energized breath, the vocal folds are set in motion. The vibration of the vocal folds turns air waves to sound waves. The sound waves continue through the vocal tract to the resonators where they become audible tone.

> In singing, exhalation becomes synonymous with phonation and phonation must be controlled by the careful management of the breath in such a manner as to produce the optimum tone quality and flexibility.... Hence *appoggio*, in its fullest sense, refers to a complex equilibrium between several sets of muscles at both the respiratory and laryngeal level, in which an image of leaning on the voice is an effective metaphor in breath control. (Stark, 1999, p. 92)

The equilibrium described previously derives from the natural recoil of the lungs that occurs during the process of expiration. Using "muscle antagonism," a singer resists the natural recoil by stabilizing the expanded rib cage and the pressure of ascending air.

Singers of all musical styles manage the flow of exhaling air through muscle antagonism proportionate to the singer's age, voice size, and body type. Voice teachers address breath management and its associated muscle antagonism based upon personal preference. Though there is no single best practice for breath management, teachers agree that a thorough exhalation as well as a gentle inhalation of air and a balanced, energetic use of it are foundational steps to beautiful tone production.

Want to experience the muscle antagonism that helps you manage breath? Try the following procedure (Figure 1–3).

Stand in a relaxed, tall posture.

Expel all remaining air.

Place your thumbs directly below your rib cage, palms open against your body.

Extend your fingertips across your abdomen.

As you inhale, allow your abdomen, sides, and back to expand.

As you exhale, guide your fingertips back to your thumbs.

Sense the natural appoggio or "leaning" of your muscles on the air column.

Relax and repeat.

Figure 1–3. Female and male student demonstrating breathing pose.

Resonance

The fourth basic singing skill is called "resonance." It results from your success with the other three. Now that you can release tension, align your physical instrument and inhale deeply, the next step is to engage the breath to produce sound. Resonance means literally "to sound against." Resonance occurs when the structures of the resonating cavities (oral pharynx, mouth, and nasal pharynx) act as filters to reinforce the sound waves generated in the larynx. Both singers and speakers use resonance intentionally to produce a wide variety of vocal sounds.

Flow Phonation

The sound-making process or "phonation" is based upon the flow and vibration of air in coordination with mental and muscular impulses. You, the singer, *audiate* ("hear internally") the sound you wish to make. The signals of audiation cause your vocal folds and vocal tract to position themselves. With the help of the abdominal muscles, the air you inhaled engages with the vocal folds, setting in motion a vibratory pattern that changes air waves to sound waves. The sound waves "resound" or "sound against" your resonators and make your tone audible. The entire process is called "flow phonation."

According to the late Meribeth Bunch Dayme, "ideal singing comes from being at one with the self, the surroundings, the music and the spirit, coupled with a dynamic balance of the components of the vocal mechanism" (Bunch Dayme, 2009, p. 15). The transformation of air into vocal tone is a "dynamic" event in which a beckoning of the mind invites exquisite physical responses.

"The ability to use the voice to express music through singing is a characteristic of all known musical cultures" (Welsh & Sundberg, 2002, p. 253). Each human voice is a unique vocal instrument. No two singers have the same physical design or complement of musical gifts. The sound of your resonating voice is a one-of-a-kind identifying feature of you, your personality, and spirit.

Onset of Sound

You have learned that vocal sound begins in speech and song when mental and muscular activities coordinate. In other words, you send the impulses for the pitch and vowel and you engage the air. The result of your effort is a vocal sound you "receive." The goal for every speaker and singer should be a balanced, gentle onset of sound. The initiation of a vocal sound, better known as "onset," is crucial to vocal health and success. Through practice and constructive feedback, you will learn to achieve a well-coordinated onset of sound. Many vocal pedagogues refer to this goal as speaking or singing "on the breath."

Until you are completely comfortable with the basics of singing, you may experience an abrupt beginning of tone known as a "glottal onset" or "glottal stop." The *glottis* is the space between the vocal folds that occurs when the vocal folds separate to allow air to flow into the windpipe. Phonation for speaking or singing involves the closure of the space or *glottis*. If this process is ill-timed, the vocal folds are forced together in an uncoordinated manner. The result is a somewhat harsh, effortful sound.

As you work toward developing the skill required for a balanced, gentle onset of sound, you may underestimate the amount of effort required to begin a resonant spoken or sung sound. Such a tone presents with a veil of air. The tone quality is referred to as "breathy." A breathy tone lacks acoustical energy and clarity.

For certain kinds of speech and song, a more forceful approach to vocal onset is popular, known as "vocal fry." It is a vocal quality appropriate to the delivery of emphatic speeches as well as gospel singing, certain kinds of jazz styles, and rock music. The tone has a bit of "grinding" element that emphasizes specific meanings or emotions. The use of vocal fry should be monitored to ensure vocal health and longevity.

Memorizing Sensations

It is essential to understand that you hear your own voice differently than your listener does. The listener hears the results of your resonating voice and the acoustical circumstances in which it rings. You, the voice user, hear some aspects of your vocal sound but not all of them. In principle, you—the speaker or singer—perceive your voice more as an "echo" while your listener hears all its properties. During training, singers develop an acute sensitivity to resonant vibrations felt in the head and face. Your teacher or vocal coach will help you identify and replicate the sounds that represent your voice at its best. If you are a choral conductor, you will assist the choristers in your care.

Both solo and choral singing requires intense teamwork and concentration. It is important to remember that neither the singer nor the choir ever grasps fully what the teacher, conductor, or listener hears. Unlike other instrumentalists, singers require an outside set of trained eyes and ears to discern desired accuracy and beauty in pitch, vowel, and tone quality. With regular practice, singers recognize and "memorize" the positive sensations advocated by a teacher, vocal coach, or choral conductor. If you use the basics of singing (relaxation, posture, breathing, and resonance) as a checklist, you can recreate the circumstances that caused positive sensations day after day.

The Why and How of Warm-Ups and Cool-Downs

The vocal instrument produces many sounds. Besides speech and song, your voice makes sound when you sneeze, cough, grunt, or snore, for example. For each function, the vocal folds position themselves to achieve a specific task. For singing, you want your vocal folds to assume their singing posture. A warm-up procedure prepares you and your vocal folds for singing. Conversely, a cool-down procedure returns your vocal folds to a speaking posture.

To "warm up" your voice, relax your body and mind, establish a "singer's posture," and exhale and secure a deep breath source before connecting air to sound through a sigh or other descending pattern. Create for yourself a checklist.

- ✓ Is my mind relaxed?
- ✓ Are my muscles free?
- ✓ Are my feet balanced?
- ✓ Are my knees loose?
- ✓ Is my spine elongated?
- ✓ Is my chest expanded?
- ✓ Is my head balanced?
- ✓ Is my chin parallel to the floor?
- ✓ Do I feel buoyant, steady, and expectant?

Once the body and voice are ready for singing, consider the vocal demands of the repertoire to be sung. Your instructor will help you develop vocal exercise patterns some of which you will use every day. Others may be created from the repertoire you will be singing. Use warm-ups to help you divide and conquer the vocal problems you face in songs, arias, and choral music.

During the act of singing, the vocal folds are set into motion to vibrate, stretch, and contract. Just as athletes require a cool-down after strenuous activity, vocal folds need to be aided back into a speaking range and posture. Though cool-downs for singing can be brief, they should be considered an essential element and designed with intention. (Sample warm-ups and cool-downs appear in Chapter 7 of this textbook and in the online companion website.)

Discussion Questions

1. How is the human voice a unique musical instrument? How is it different from any instrument you have played?
2. Name the four basics of singing in the order recommended for their use. Explain how the basics of singing "build" the vocal instrument.
3. What does the Italian word "*appoggio*" mean? What role does relaxation and posture play in achieving it?
4. Define resonance. How is it different from "loudness"?
5. Describe how a warm-up or cool-down preserves vocal health and stamina.

References

Abitbol, J. (2016). *The power of the voice* (p. 99). Plural Publishing.

Appelman, R. (1967). *The science of vocal pedagogy* (p. 30). Indiana University Press.

Bunch Dayme, M. (2009). *The dynamics of the singing voice* (5th ed., p. 15). Springer Verlag.

Damasio, A. (2003). *Looking for Spinoza: Joy, sorrow, and the feeling brain* (p. 3). Houghton Mifflin.

Davids, J., & LaTour, S. (2021). *Vocal technique* (2nd ed., p. 68). Waveland Press.

Gilman, M. (2014). *Body and voice: Somatic re-education* (p. 21). Plural Publishing.

Hixon, T. (1991). *Respiratory function in speech and song* (p. 12). Singular Publishing Group.

Lyle, H. (2014). *Vocal yoga: The joy of breathing, singing and sounding* (p. 14). Bluecat Music & Publishing.

Nelson, S., & Blades, E. (2018). *Singing with your whole self: A singer's guide to Feldenkrais awareness through movement* (2nd ed., pp. 15, 87). Rowman & Littlefield.

Nestor, J. (2020). *Breath: The new science of a lost art* (p. 27). Riverhead Books.

Rollings, A. The effects of heel height on head position, long-term average spectra, and perceptions of female singers. *Journal of Voice, 32*(1), 127.e15–127.e23. https://doi.org/10.1016/j.jvoice.2017.03.005

Smith, B. (2018). *So you want to sing for a lifetime* (p. 56). Rowman & Littlefield.

Stark, J. (1999). *Bel canto: A history of vocal pedagogy* (p. 92). University of Toronto Press.

Walker, G. (2007). *An ocean of air: Why the wind blows and other mysteries of the atmosphere* (p. 11). Harcourt.

Welsh, G., & Sundberg, J. (2002). Solo voice. In R. Parncutt & G. E. McPherson (Eds.), *The science and psychology of music performance: Creative strategies for teaching and learning* (pp. 253–268). Oxford University Press.

2
Anatomy and Physiology of the Voice

Robert T. Sataloff

Singing teachers and students should be as familiar with the structure and function of the voice as instrumentalists are with the components of their instruments. The human voice consists of much more than simply the vocal folds, popularly known as the vocal cords. State-of-the-art voice diagnosis, nonsurgical therapy, and voice surgery depend on understanding the complex workings of the vocal tract. The physiology of phonation is much more complex than this brief chapter might suggest, and readers interested in acquiring more than a clinically essential introduction are encouraged to consult other literature (Sataloff, 2017b).

Anatomy

The larynx is essential to normal voice production, but the anatomy of the voice is not limited to the larynx. The vocal mechanism includes the abdominal and back musculature, rib cage, lungs, pharynx, oral cavity, and nose, among other structures. Each component performs an important function in voice production, although it is possible to produce voice even without a larynx—for example, in patients who have undergone laryngectomy. In addition, virtually all parts of the body play some role in voice production and may be responsible for voice dysfunction. Even something as remote as a sprained ankle may alter posture, thereby impairing abdominal, back, and thoracic muscle function and resulting in vocal inefficiency, weakness, and hoarseness.

The larynx is composed of four basic anatomic units: skeleton, intrinsic muscles, extrinsic muscles, and mucosa. The most important components of the laryngeal skeleton are the thyroid cartilage, cricoid cartilage, and two arytenoid cartilages (Figure 2–1).

Intrinsic muscles of the larynx are connected to these cartilages (Figure 2–2). One of the intrinsic muscles, the *thyroarytenoid muscle* (its medial belly also is known as the vocalis muscle), extends on each side

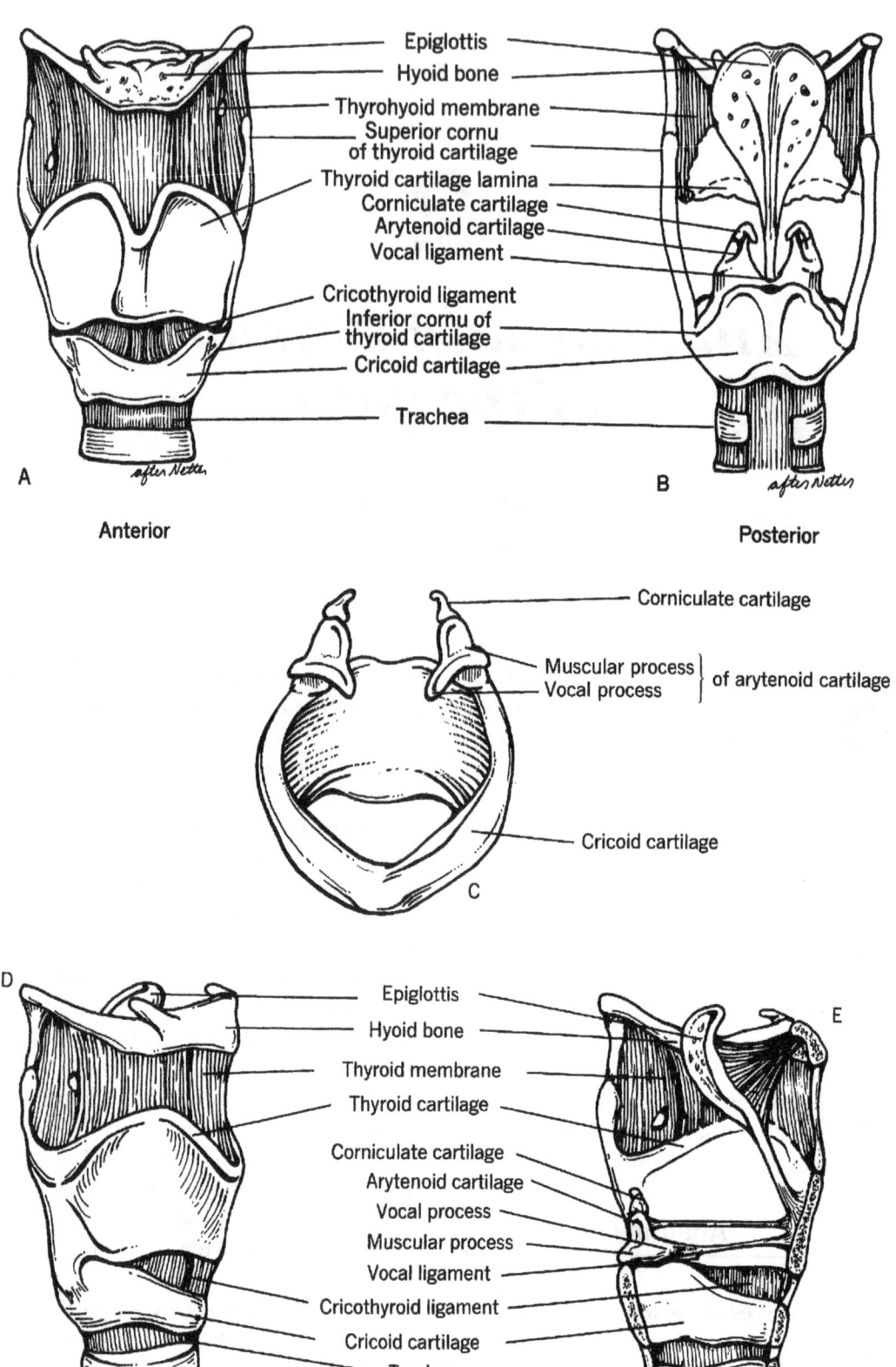

Figure 2–1. Cartilages of the larynx.

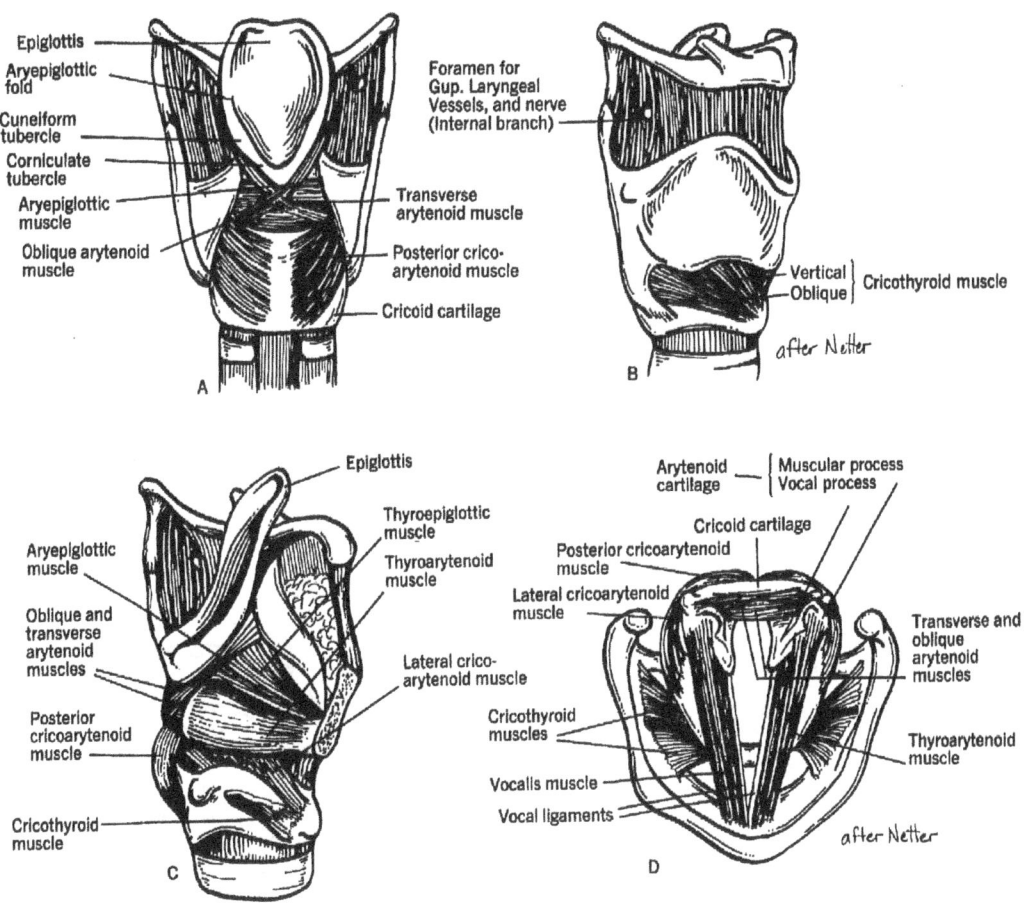

Intrinsic muscles of the larynx.

Figure 2–2. Intrinsic muscles of the larynx.

from the vocal process of the arytenoid cartilage to the inside of the thyroid cartilage just below and behind the thyroid prominence ("Adam's apple"), forming the body of the vocal folds. The vocal folds act as the *oscillator* or *voice source* of the vocal tract. The space between the vocal folds is called the *glottis* and is used as an anatomic reference point. The intrinsic muscles alter the position, shape, and tension of the vocal folds, bringing them together (adduction), moving them apart (abduction), or stretching them by increasing longitudinal tension (Figure 2–3). They are able to do so because the laryngeal cartilages are connected by soft attachments that allow changes in their relative angles and distances, thereby permitting alteration in the shape and tension of the tissues suspended between them. The arytenoid cartilages on their eliptoid cricoarytenoid joints are capable of motion in multiple planes, permitting complex vocal fold motion and alteration in the

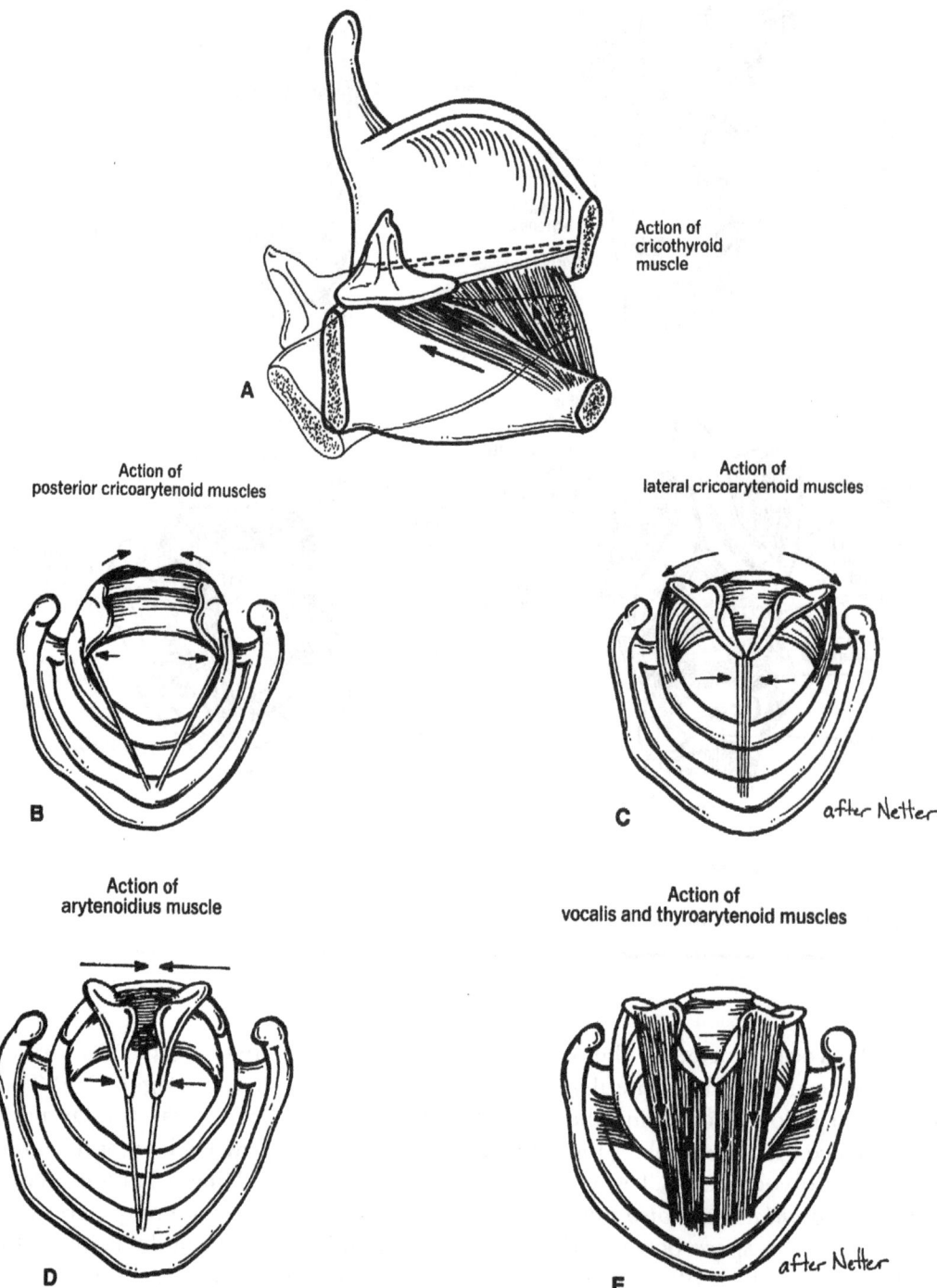

Figure 2–3. Action of the intrinsic muscles.

shape of the vocal fold edge associated with intrinsic muscle action (Figure 2–4). All but one of the muscles on each side of the larynx are innervated by one of the two *recurrent laryngeal nerves*. Because this nerve runs in a long course (especially on the left) from the neck down into the chest and then back up to the larynx (hence, the name "recurrent"), it is injured easily by trauma, neck surgery, and chest surgery. Injury may result in vocal fold paresis or paralysis. The remaining muscle (*cricothyroid muscle*) is innervated by the superior laryngeal nerve on each side, which is especially susceptible to viral and traumatic injury. It causes changes in longitudinal tension that are important in voice projection and pitch control. The "false vocal folds" are located above the vocal folds, and unlike the true vocal folds, usually do not make contact during normal speaking or singing (Sataloff, 2017b).

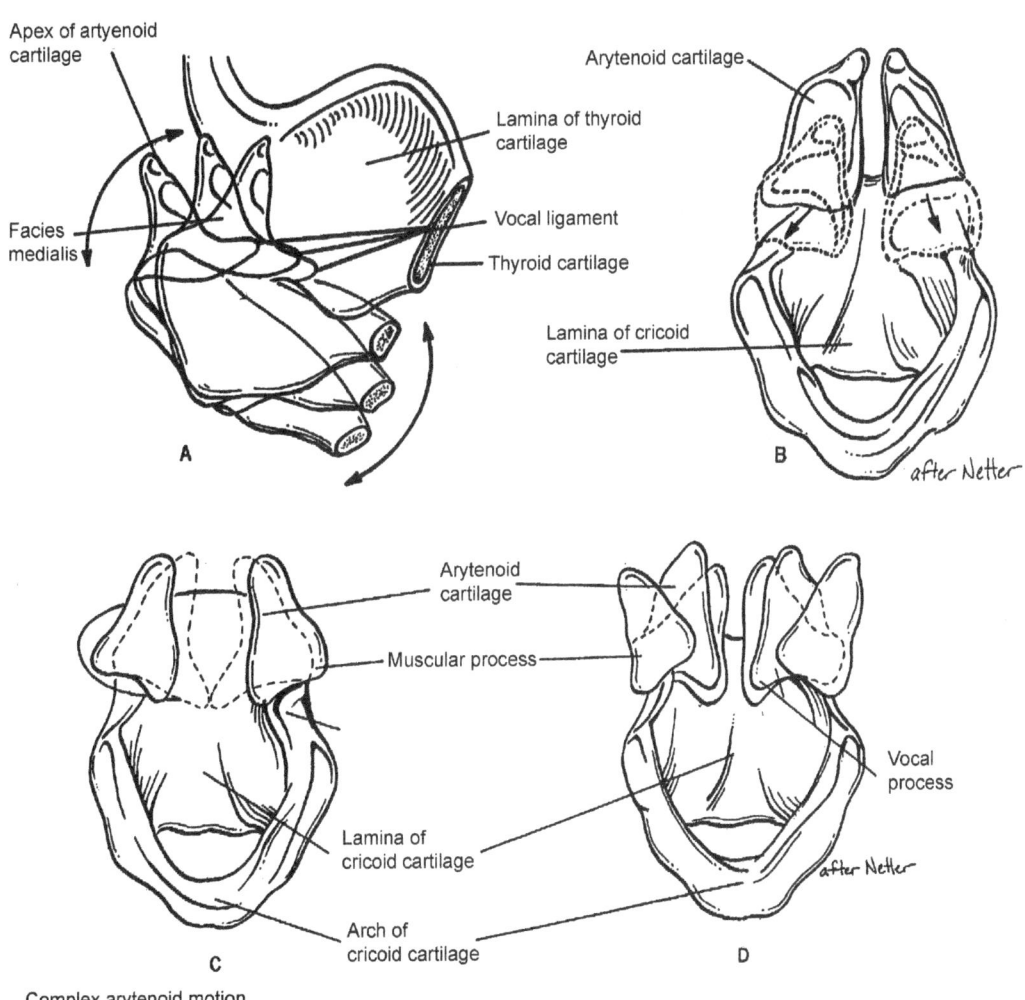

Figure 2–4. Complex arytenoid motion.

The neuroanatomy and neurophysiology of phonation are extremely complicated and only partially understood. As the new field of neurolaryngology advances, a more thorough understanding of the subject is becoming increasingly important to medical clinicians. Readers interested in acquiring a deeper scientific understanding of neurolaryngology are encouraged to consult other literature (Sataloff, 2017a) and the publications cited therein.

Because the attachments of the laryngeal cartilages are flexible, the positions of the cartilages with respect to each other change when the laryngeal skeleton is elevated or lowered. Such changes in vertical height are controlled by the extrinsic laryngeal muscles, the strap muscles of the neck. When the angles and distances between cartilages change because of this accordionlike effect, the resting length of the intrinsic muscles changes. Such large adjustments in intrinsic muscle condition interfere with fine control of smooth vocal quality. Classically trained singers generally are taught to use the extrinsic muscles to maintain the laryngeal skeleton at a relatively constant height regardless of pitch. That is, they learn to avoid the natural tendency of the larynx to rise with ascending pitch and fall with descending pitch, thereby enhancing unity of sound quality throughout the vocal range through effects on both resting muscle condition and supraglottic vocal tract posture.

The soft tissues lining the larynx are much more complex than originally thought. The mucosa forms the thin, lubricated surface of the vocal folds, which makes contact when the two vocal folds are approximated. Laryngeal mucosa might look superficially like the mucosa that lines the inside of the mouth, but it is not. Throughout most of the larynx, there are goblet cells and pseudostratified ciliated columnar epithelial cells designed for producing and handling mucous secretions, similar to mucosal surfaces found throughout the respiratory tract. However, the mucosa overlying the vocal folds is different. First, it is stratified squamous epithelium, which is better suited to withstand the trauma of vocal fold contact. Second, the vocal fold is not simply muscle covered with mucosa. Rather, it consists of five layers as described by Hirano (1975). Mechanically, the vocal fold structures act more like three layers consisting of the *cover* (epithelium and superficial layer of the lamina propria), *transition* (intermediate and deep layers of the lamina propria), and *body* (the vocalis muscle).

The *supraglottic vocal tract* includes the pharynx, tongue, palate, oral cavity, nose, and other structures. Together they act as a *resonator* and are largely responsible for vocal quality or timbre and the perceived character of all phonated sounds. The vocal folds themselves produce only a "buzzing" sound. During the course of vocal training for singing, acting, or healthy speaking, changes occur not only in the larynx but also in the muscle motion, control, and shape of the supraglottic vocal tract and in aerobic, pulmonary, and bodily muscle function.

The *infraglottic vocal tract* (all anatomical structures below the glottis) serves as the *power source* for the voice. Singers and actors often refer to the entire power source complex as their "support" or "diaphragm." The anatomy of support for phonation is especially complicated and not completely understood. Yet, it is quite important because deficiencies in support frequently are responsible for voice dysfunction.

The purpose of the support mechanism is to generate a force that directs a controlled airstream between the vocal folds. Active respiratory muscles work in concert with passive forces. The principal muscles of inspiration are the diaphragm (a dome-shaped muscle that extends along the bottom of the rib cage) and the external intercostal muscles (located between the ribs). During quiet respiration, expiration is largely passive. The lungs and rib cage generate passive expiratory forces under many common circumstances, such as after a full breath.

Many of the muscles used for active expiration also are employed in "support" for phonation. Muscles of active expiration either raise the intra-abdominal pressure, forcing the diaphragm upward, or lower the ribs or sternum to decrease the dimensions of the thorax, or both, thereby compressing air in the chest. The primary muscles of expiration are "the abdominal muscles," but internal intercostals and other chest and back muscles also are involved. Trauma or surgery that alters the structure or function of these muscles or ribs undermines the power source of the voice as do diseases, such as asthma, that impair expiration. Deficiencies in the support mechanism often result in compensatory efforts that utilize the laryngeal muscles, which are not designed for power functions. Such behavior can result in impaired voice quality, rapid fatigue, pain, and even structural pathology such as vocal fold nodules. Current expert treatment for such vocal problems focuses on correction of the underlying malfunction rather than surgery whenever possible, including attention to the psychological concomitants of the condition.

Physiology

The physiology of voice production is extremely complex. Volitional production of voice begins in the cerebral cortex (Figure 2–5).

The command for vocalization involves complex interactions among brain centers for speech as well as other areas. For singing, speech directives must be integrated with information from the centers for musical and artistic expression, which are discussed elsewhere (Sataloff, 2017b). The "idea" of the planned vocalization is conveyed to the precentral gyrus in the motor cortex, which transmits another set of instructions to the motor nuclei in the brain stem and spinal cord. These areas send out the complicated messages necessary for coordinated activity of the larynx, thoracic and abdominal musculature, lungs, and vocal tract articulators, among other structures. Additional refinement of motor activity is provided by the extrapyramidal and autonomic nervous systems. These impulses combine to produce a sound that is transmitted not only to the ears of the listener but also to those of the speaker or singer. Auditory feedback is transmitted from the ear through the brain stem to the cerebral cortex, and adjustments are made within milliseconds that permit the vocalist to match the sound produced with the sound intended, integrating the acoustic properties of the performance environment. Tactile feedback from throat and other muscles involved in phonation also is believed to help in fine tuning vocal output, although the mechanism and role of tactile feedback are not understood fully. Many trained singers and speakers cultivate the ability to use tactile feedback effectively because of expected interference with auditory feedback data from ancillary sound such as an orchestra or band.

Phonation, the production of sound, requires interaction among the power source, oscillator, and resonator. The voice may be compared to a brass instrument such as a trumpet. Power is generated by the chest, abdominal, and back musculature and a high-pressure airstream is produced.

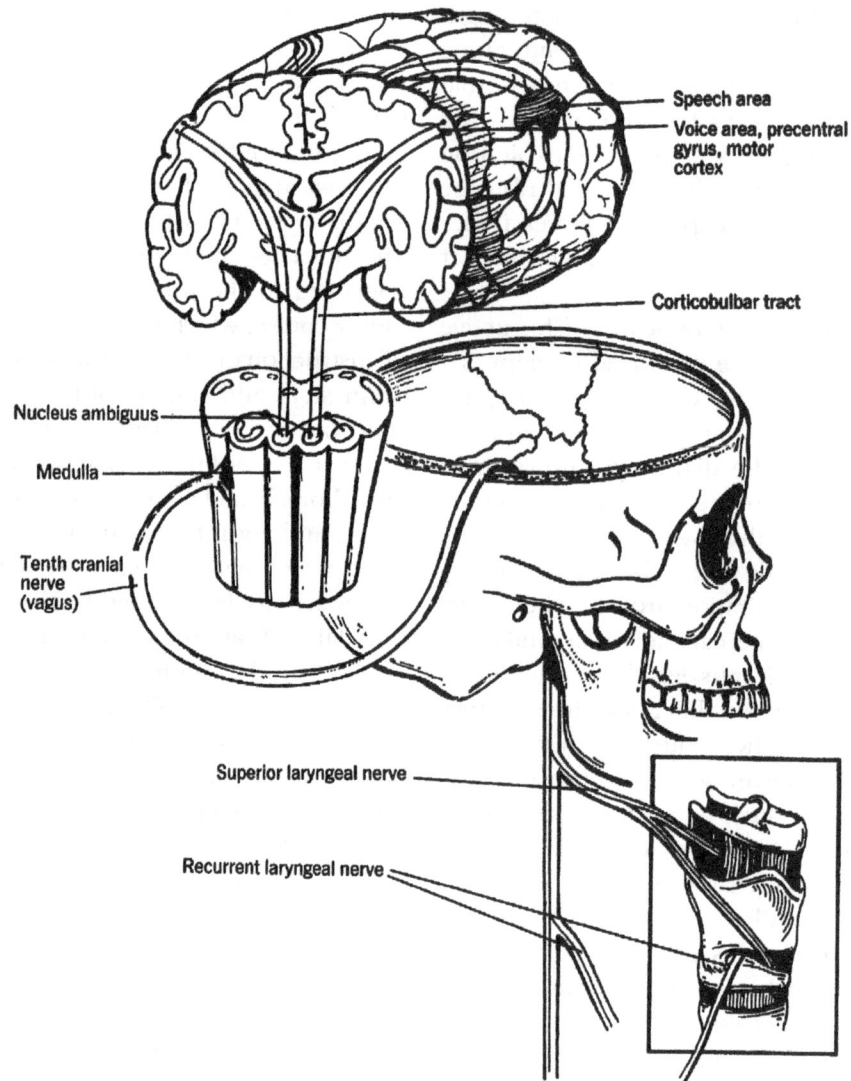

Figure 2–5. Simplified summary of pathway for volitional phonation.

The trumpeter's lips open and close against the mouthpiece producing a "buzz" similar to the sound produced by vocal folds when they come together and move apart (oscillate) during phonation. This sound then passes through the trumpet, which has acoustic resonance characteristics that shape the sound we associate with trumpet music. If a trumpet mouthpiece is placed on a French horn, the sound we hear will sound like a French horn, not a trumpet. Quality characteristics are dependent upon the resonator more than on the oscillatory source. The nonmouthpiece portions of a brass instrument are analogous to the supraglottic vocal tract.

During phonation, the infraglottic musculature must make rapid, complex adjustments because the resistance changes almost continuously as the glottis closes, opens, and changes shape. At the beginning of each phonatory cycle, the vocal folds are approximated and the glottis is obliterated. This permits infraglottic air pressure to build, typically to a level of about 7 cm of water for conversational speech. At that point, the vocal folds are convergent (Figure 2–6A). Because the vocal folds are closed, there is no airflow. The subglottic pressure then pushes the vocal folds progressively farther apart from the bottom up and from the back forward (Figure 2–6B) until a space develops (Figures 2–6C and 2–6D) and air begins to flow. Bernoulli force created by the air passing between the vocal folds combines with the mechanical properties of the folds to begin closing the lower portion of the vocal folds

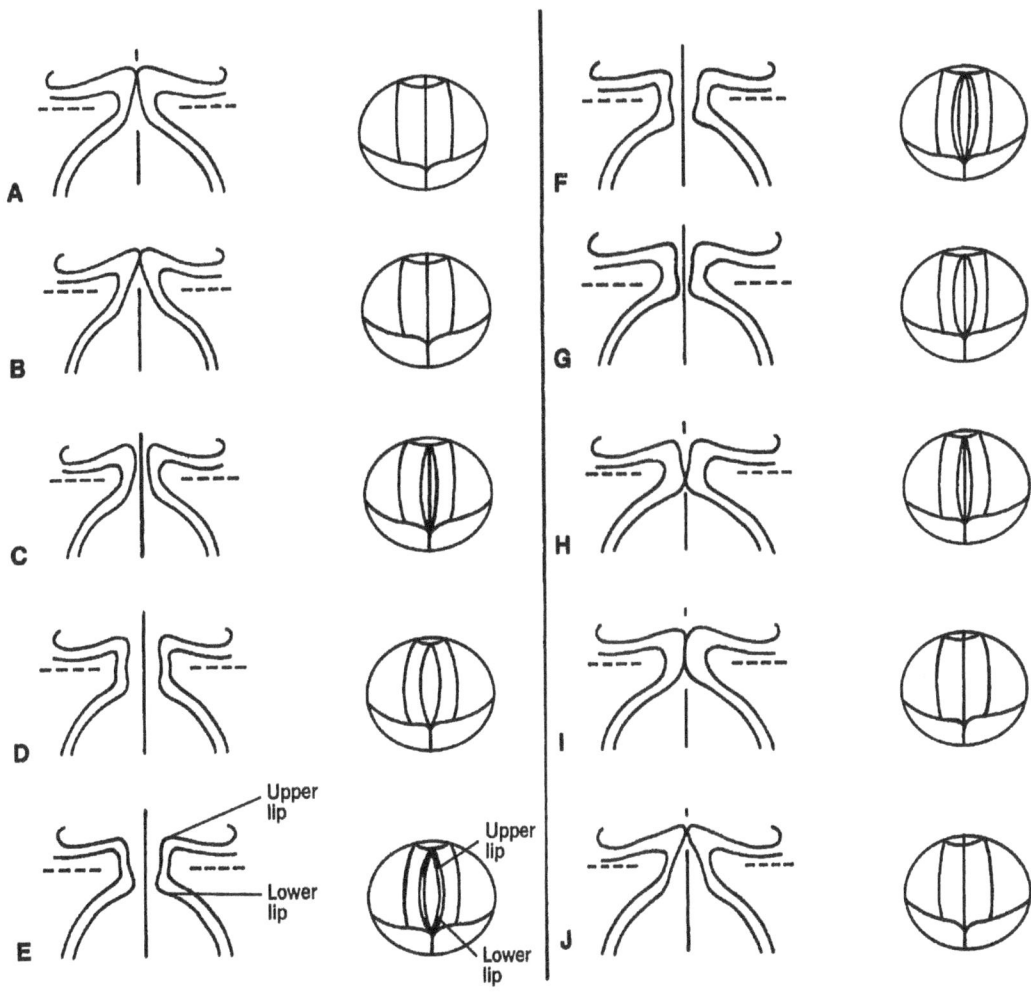

Figure 2–6. Frontal view (*left*) and view from above (*right*) illustrating the normal pattern of vocal fold vibration. The vocal folds close and open from the inferior aspect of the vibratory margin upward and from posterior to anterior.

almost immediately (Figures 2-6E to 2-6H) even while the upper edges are still separating. The principles and mathematics of Bernoulli force are complex. It is a flow effect more easily understood by familiar examples such as the sensation of pull exerted on a vehicle when passed by a truck at high speed or the inward motion of a shower curtain when the water flows past it.

The upper portion of the vocal folds has elastic properties that also tend to make the vocal folds snap back to the midline. This force becomes more dominant as the upper edges are stretched and the opposing force of the airstream diminishes because of approximation of the lower edges of the vocal folds. The upper portions of the vocal folds are then returned to the midline (Figure 2-6I), completing the glottic cycle. Subglottal pressure then builds again (Figure 2-6J), and the events repeat. Thus, there is a vertical phase difference. That is, the lower portion of the vocal folds begins to open and close before the upper portion. The rippling displacement of the vocal fold cover produces a mucosal wave that can be examined clinically under stroboscopic light. If this complex motion is impaired, hoarseness or other changes in voice quality may cause the patient to seek medical evaluation. The frequency of vibration (number of cycles of openings and closings per second, measured in hertz [Hz]) is dependent on the air pressure and mechanical properties of the vocal folds, which are regulated in part by the laryngeal muscles. Pitch is the perceptual correlate of frequency. Under most circumstances, as the vocal folds are thinned and stretched and air pressure is increased, the frequency of air pulse emissions increases and pitch goes up. The myoelastic-aerodynamic mechanism of phonation reveals that the vocal folds emit pulses of air, rather than vibrate like strings.

The sound produced by the oscillating vocal folds, called the voice source signal, is a complex tone containing a fundamental frequency and many overtones, or higher harmonic partials. The amplitude of the partials decreases uniformly at approximately 12 dB per octave. Interestingly, the acoustic spectrum of the voice source is about the same in ordinary speakers as it is in trained singers and speakers. Voice quality differences in voice professionals occur as the voice source signal passes through their supraglottic vocal tract resonator system (Figure 2-7).

The pharynx, oral cavity, and nasal cavity act as a series of infinitely variable interconnected resonators, which are more complex than that in our trumpet example or other single resonators. As with other resonators, some frequencies are attenuated and others are enhanced. Enhanced frequencies are radiated with higher relative amplitudes or intensities. Sundberg (1987) showed long ago that the vocal tract has four or five important resonance frequencies called *formants* and summarized his early findings in a book that has become a classic. The presence of formants alters the uniformly sloping voice source spectrum and creates peaks at formant frequencies. These alterations of the voice source spectral envelope are responsible for distinguishable sounds of speech and song. Formant frequencies are determined by vocal tract shape, which can be altered by the laryngeal, pharyngeal, and oral cavity musculature. Overall vocal tract length and shape are individually fixed and determined by age and sex (females and children have shorter vocal tracts and formant frequencies that are higher than males). Voice training includes conscious

Generation of Vocal Sound

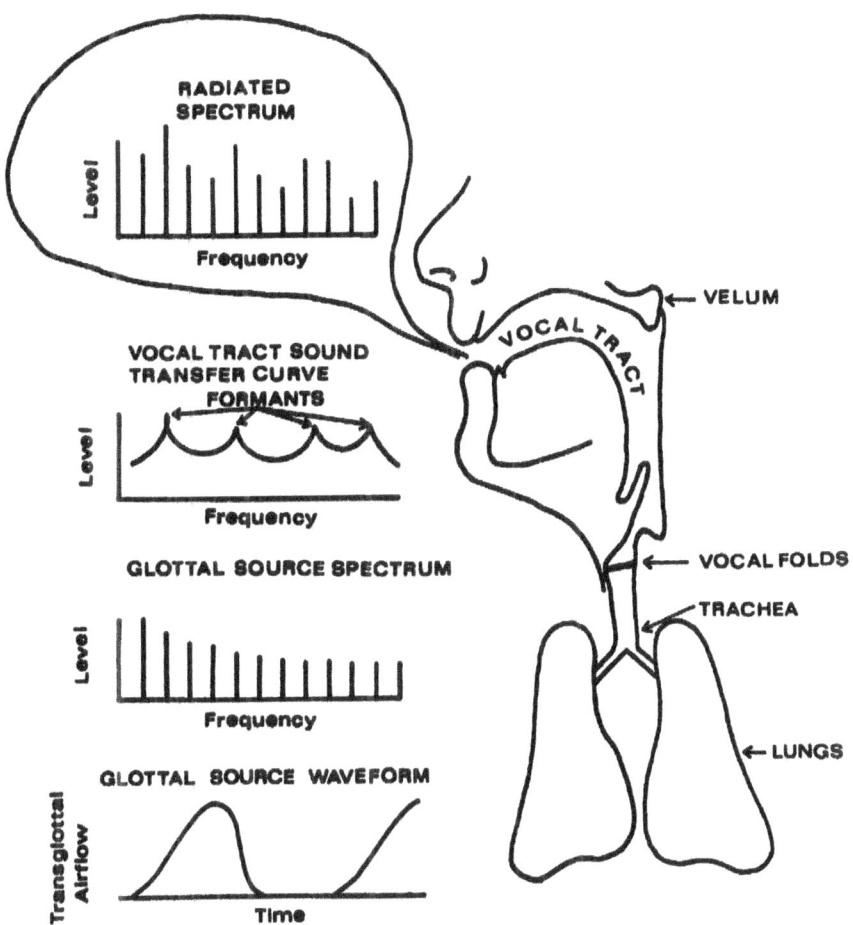

Figure 2–7. Determinants of the spectrum of a vowel (oral-output signal).

physical mastery of the adjustment of vocal tract shape.

Although the formants differ for different vowels, one resonant frequency has received particular attention and is known as the "singer's formant." This formant occurs in the vicinity of 2300 to 3200 Hz for all vowel spectra and appears to be responsible for the "ring" in a singer's or trained speaker's ("speaker's formant") voice. The ability to hear a trained voice clearly even over a loud choir or orchestra is dependent primarily on the presence of the singer's formant (Sataloff, 2017b). Interestingly, there is little or no significant difference in maximum vocal intensity between trained and untrained singers. The singer's formant also contributes substantially to the differences in Fach (voice classification) among voice categories, occurring in basses at about 2400 Hz, baritones at 2600 Hz, tenors at 2800 Hz, mezzo-sopranos at 2900 Hz, and sopranos at 3200 Hz. It is frequently much less prominent in high soprano singing (Sataloff, 2017b).

The mechanisms that control two vocal characteristics are particularly important: fundamental frequency and intensity. Fundamental frequency, which corresponds to pitch, can be altered by changing either air pressure or the mechanical properties of the vocal folds, although the latter is more efficient under most conditions. When the cricothyroid muscle contracts, it makes the thyroid cartilage pivot on the cricothyroid joint and increases the distance between the thyroid and arytenoid cartilages, thus stretching the vocal folds. This increases the surface area exposed to subglottal pressure and makes the air pressure more effective in opening the glottis. In addition, stretching of elastic fibers of the vocal fold makes them more efficient at snapping back together. Hence, the cycles shorten and repeat more frequently, and the fundamental frequency (and pitch) rises. Other muscles, including the thyroarytenoid, also contribute (Sataloff, 2017b). Raising the pressure of the airstream also tends to increase fundamental frequency, a phenomenon for which singers must learn to compensate. Otherwise, their pitch would go up whenever they tried to sing more loudly.

Voice intensity corresponds to loudness and depends on the degree to which the glottal wave motion excites the air molecules in the vocal tract. Raising the air pressure creates greater amplitude of vocal fold oscillation and therefore increases vocal intensity. However, actually it is not the oscillation of the vocal fold, but rather the sudden cessation of airflow that is responsible for initiating an acoustic signal in the vocal tract and controlling intensity. This is similar to the mechanism of acoustic signal that results from buzzing lips. In the larynx, the sharper the cutoff of airflow, the more intense the sound (Sataloff, 2017b). In the evaluation of voice disorders, an individual's ability to optimize adjustments of air pressure and glottal resistance is assessed. When high subglottic pressure is combined with high adductory (closing) vocal fold force, glottal airflow and the amplitude of the voice source fundamental frequency are low. This is called *pressed phonation* and can be measured clinically through a technique known as flow glottography. Flow glottogram wave amplitude indicates the type of phonation being used, and the slope (closing rate) provides information about the sound pressure level or loudness. If adductory forces are so weak that the vocal folds do not make contact, the vocal folds become inefficient at resisting air leakage and the voice source fundamental frequency is low. This is known as *breathy phonation*. *Flow phonation* is characterized by lower subglottic pressure and lower adductory force. These conditions increase the dominance of the fundamental frequency of the voice source in the perceived sound. Sundberg showed that the amplitude of the fundamental frequency can be increased by 15 dB or more when the subject changes from pressed phonation to flow phonation (Sundberg, 1987). If a patient habitually uses pressed phonation, considerable effort will be required to achieve loud voicing. The muscle patterns and force that are used to compensate for this laryngeal inefficiency may cause vocal damage.

Conclusion

The structure and function of the voice are extremely complex and incorporate essentially all body systems. Singing teachers and their students need to understand basic anatomy and physiology of the voice not only so that they have the vocabulary to think and talk about the voice but also so that they have adequate intellectual tools to analyze and articulate what they hear in a voice. Such knowledge also helps them understand what they are really trying to accomplish when using traditional pedagogical language (imagery) in their studios.

References

Hirano, M. (1975). Phonosurgery: Basic and clinical investigations. *Otologia (Fukuoka), 21*, 239–442.

Sataloff, R. T. (2017a). *Neurolaryngology*. Plural Publishing.

Sataloff, R. T. (2017b). *Professional voice: The science and art of clinical care* (4th ed.). Plural Publishing.

Sundberg, J. (1987). *The science of the singing voice*. Northern Illinois University Press.

3

Skills for Learning to Sing Music

Ronald Burrichter

Introduction

When conversation arises about singing, the statement, "I can't sing" followed by various and often colorful examples of the reason the individual holds this perception is very common. One of the most frequently heard observations is, "I can't read music!" This is perceived as justification for why an individual is unwilling to express themself through song. The mystery of the printed page of music can seem as daunting to the aspiring vocalist as a beginning reading text is to the new student in kindergarten. The ability to understand the printed page of musical notation can unlock for the singer a new world of joy and personal fulfillment in much the same manner that the kindergartener enjoys exploring the new world of books. "I learn differently." "I don't need to read the music." "Just play it for me a couple of times and I've got it!" This concept would equal the growing student believing that they could always rely on audiobooks for their learning and personal growth, an obvious misconception. Whether wanting to sing in the church or synagogue, to sing with the local community choir, to join the Barbershop Harmony Society (or nearly any other singing venue), the ability to correctly interpret the written symbols on the page will be the key to success and an essential element for lifelong singing enjoyment.

Musicianship Skills

Skills in any area of life are rarely automatic gifts from birth. We marvel as children experience the excitement of being able to crawl as they begin to sense their need for independence. With the continued learning process of walking comes the need to "childproof" the house as we delight in the growth that leads to running, jumping, and the many other marvels of childhood development. Skills build as the growth process continues into adulthood and beyond. The scope of personal success increases as the practice of skill development in life is maintained and welcomed. The development of musical skills follows a similar pattern, but is often limited, slowed, or avoided altogether when a thorough and supportive introduction to the understanding of those skills is not present. A child frequently learns to take their first steps when loving hands are inviting them to advance. The beginning musician builds their skill set and love of music when musicianship skills, the basic understanding of reading the score and bringing it to life in the voice or instrument, are presented with simplicity and supportive experiences. Let us explore some of these basic musicianship skills.

Singing and Rhythm

Where do we begin? The structure of music begins with rhythm. Rhythm allows the mind to organize the thought processes necessary to produce the appropriate pitch as well as the appropriate vowel or consonant, to produce them at the exact appropriate moment, and to synchronize those processes with other singers or the collaborative musical source. There are numerous systems available for understanding rhythms, and the curious singer can find abundant information about these methods through their computer. This author has found the use of what is commonly called "count-singing" to be a consistent aid in understanding the concepts of rhythm. The ability of the singer to divide the beat mathematically in a consistent manner can add a much-needed level of simplicity to the understanding of rhythm. As we explore this tool, we must first be certain that the terms used are universally understood. The aspiring singer who has already studied these fundamentals may wish to advance through this section, refreshing in their minds the meaning of these terms to avoid misunderstandings as we move further ahead. Students of music education may be interested in incorporating the concepts into future lesson plans.

Basics of the Printed Page

The mystery of the printed page begins as we view the five horizontal lines growing out of the bracket on the left side of the page, referred to as the *staff* (Figure 3–1). The treble and bass staves together are referred to as a *system*. Placed vertically on these horizontal lines at regularly spaced intervals are vertical lines with the space between the lines called a *measure* or *bar*.

To the right of the bracket that starts the staff you see two numbers stacked upon

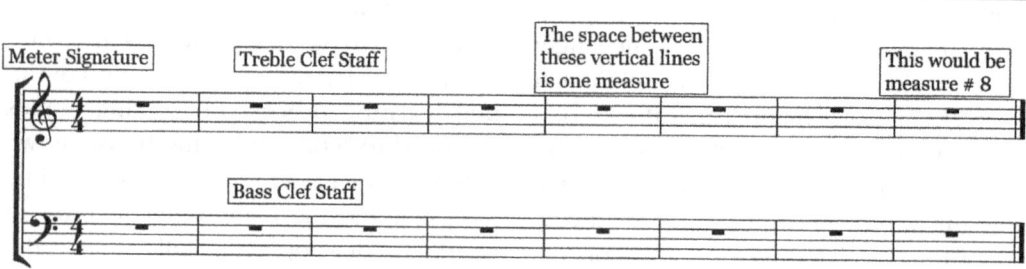

Figure 3–1. Basics of the printed page.

one another. This is called the *meter signature* or the *time signature*. The top number informs you of the number of pulses (or often called "beats") within each measure. A "beat" might be compared to the "ticking" of a time piece—the regular and consistent "ticking" that we associate with our watch or clock. If the top number of the meter signature is 4, there would be four "ticks" in each measure, three "ticks" if the top number is 3, and so forth. The speed of the "ticks" will vary according to the demands of the composer and the music, but the regularity of the clocklike "ticking" as the foundation for rhythm is important. The bottom number explains the note value that receives the pulse (beat). Figure 3–2 shows and names the various note values used most commonly in music.

You will notice that Beat 3 in the music is replaced with the syllable "T," ensuring that the accuracy of the beat is maintained. While notes are frequently beamed together as you see in Figure 3–2, they are frequently seen with "flags" rather than beams, as you see in Figure 3–3.

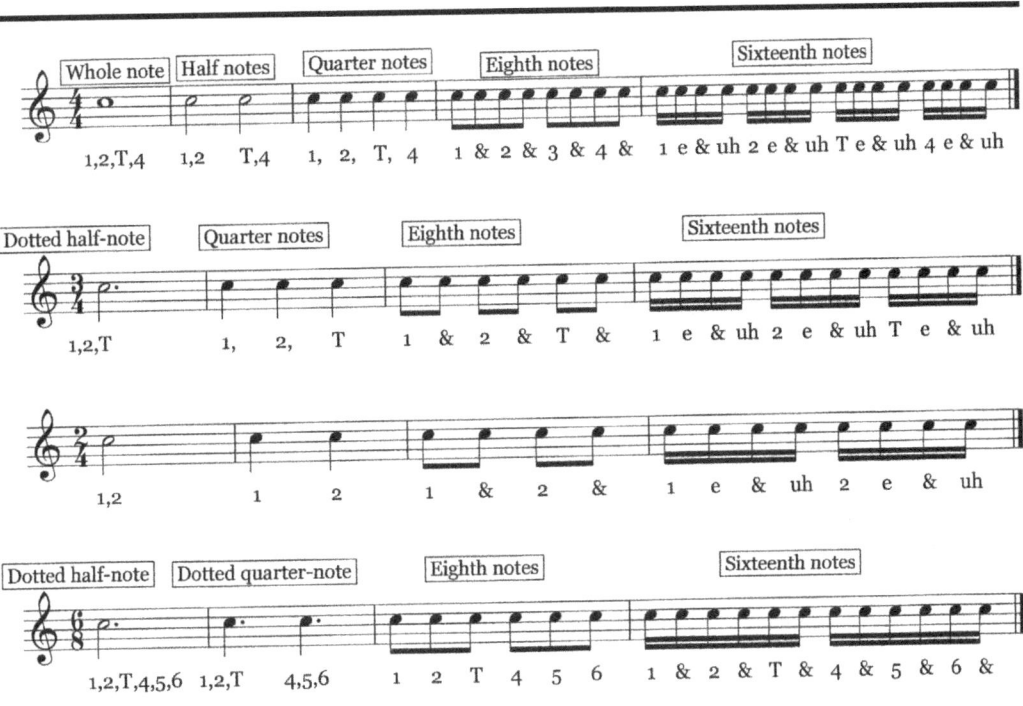

Figure 3–2. Basics of 4, 3, 2, and 6 beats per measure count-singing.

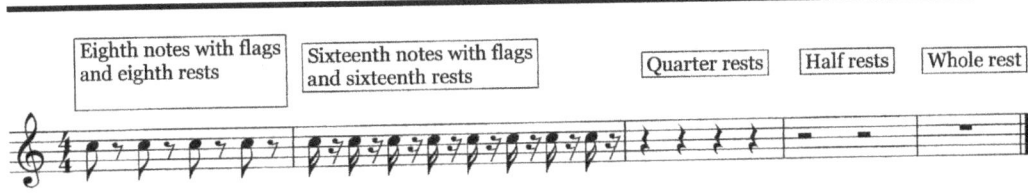

Figure 3–3. Basics of rhythmic symbols.

In more advanced music, one may see notation with three or four beams connecting the notes or "flags" attached to the stems connected to the note heads (32nd or 64th notes), but these are not common and need not concern us at this stage. Look carefully at the meter signature to be sure you understand how many beats or pulses there are in each measure. A meter signature of 3/4 would tell you that there are three beats per measure and the quarter note is the unit to be counted. A meter signature of 2/4 means two beats per measure with the quarter note being the unit counted, 5/4 would mean five beats per measure, although you would find this signature in more advanced repertoire. A meter signature of 3/8 would tell you that there were three beats per measure but that the eighth note was to be the note value receiving the beat. Through using the mathematical structure described, the musician can solve most rhythmic puzzles and understand how to "count-sing."

Other Rhythmic Tricks

The implementation of basic concepts of rhythmic structure is crucial to musical success. Solutions to this challenge are many, such as attaching rhythmic syllables to commonly used patterns. Four 16th notes might become "Mi-ssi-ssi-ppi" or "Mon-ti-cel-lo"; two eighth notes might be called "Hap-py" or "Dad-dy"; a pattern of four 16th notes followed by two eighths (a frequent pattern in music) might become "Mi-ssi-ssi-ppi Steam-boat." A triplet pattern (three notes on one beat) might become "Straw-ber-ry" or "Cho-co-late." The possibilities are as varied as the imagination creating them, but the success of any technique comes from the accuracy of the pattern offered and the visual connection between the clever words used and how they trans-late into the notes on the page. Saying the words is of no consequence if the connection to the printed page is not understood and the words are seen as a tool rather than a goal or a crutch.

Some people find the use of physical elements some help in understanding how rhythm is constructed or divided. Assuming you are using a measure of 4/4 time as an example, consider placing 16 toothpicks, matchsticks, or paper clips on the table in front of you. Place the objects in four groups of four objects each placed upon one another (creating a single pile). This would represent the pattern 1, 2, T, 4. Next, split each group of four objects into eight groups of two objects each. This would represent the rhythmic pattern 1 & 2 & T & 4 &. Next, make four groups of four objects each, which becomes 1-e-&-uh, 2-e-&-uh, T-e-&-uh, 4-e-&-uh. One can group the objects together to represent different rhythmic patterns if desired.

Another alternative would be to cut a paper into 16 squares, writing a large 1, 2, T, 4 on four squares, a lowercase "e" on four squares, an uppercase "&" on four squares, and a lowercase "uh" on four squares. These paper squares can now be placed in groupings like those described previously but with the added assistance of seeing the syllables used in count-singing. Similar visual aids could be developed for triplet patterns and rhythmic patterns that use the eighth note as the unit of pulse. Figure 3–4 offers other examples.

Some musicians find it helpful to tap their shoulder or breastbone in rhythm to feel physically the pulse of the music. Caution must be taken when using this method to avoid allowing the beat to become uneven, to wait to make contact until one is more comfortable with the rhythm. Figure 3–5 offers examples of rhythmic patterns frequently used in song. When the singer builds their mental library of these

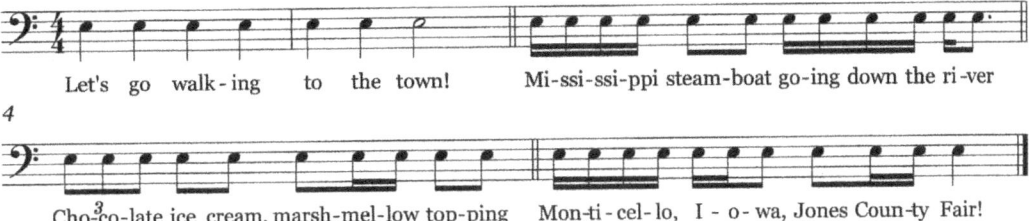

Figure 3–4. Text examples for rhythmic patterns.

Figure 3–5. Recognition of rhythmic patterns.

and other commonly used patterns, they can perform the rhythm more quickly and with a higher level of accuracy, thereby becoming more comfortable with the music reading process.

A clear understanding of the fundamentals of rhythm allows the musician's mind to process the reading task in an orderly manner, avoiding some confusion caused by "multitasking"—reading the rhythms and identifying the pitches at the same time.

Singing and Note Learning

While understanding rhythm is a challenge for some, that challenge pales when compared to the task of bringing sound to the mysteriously organized black dots on the printed page. The often-used term "sight-reading" strikes fear into the hearts of many musicians and especially into the minds of singers since singers have no physical mechanisms to manipulate in response to recognition of the black dots on the printed page. They must rely on the message from the brain to the vocal folds to produce the sound represented by the dot. The ability to do this "at sight" is a much-heralded skill obtained by some. The goal of *reading music*, whether "at sight" or through study, is very achievable by patiently developing an understanding of the "musical map"—a skill that can be enjoyed for a lifetime by nearly everyone. In much the same manner children learn to read the printed page, the singer can learn to recognize the "sound interval" to be sung to realize the distance between the black dots. For example, a printed version of the familiar song "Three Blind Mice" is printed in Figure 3–6.

Notice the placement of the notes on the staff as you sing the melody aloud. The first note ("Three") is on a line, followed by a note on the adjacent lower space, followed by the longer note on the next line down ("mice"). You have just learned how to read music! The connection made through your brain linking the location of the printed notes with the sounds you have sung is the beginning of your adventure in reading the score. Notice that the next measure is the same, so repeat it as you concentrate on the relationship between the sound and the notes. The third measure is similar in appearance except that the descending pattern ("See") begins on the next line above the beginning pitch in measure one and ends on the same pitch (and visual location) as the very first note of the selection ("Three"). "They all" starts on the same pitch as "See" and jumps to the notes placed on the third space on the staff for "all" (counting from the bottom up). Notice that "ran" is the same pitch as "all." The melody then goes down the stairs and comes right back up ("after the") to land on the same pitch you sang earlier on "all." Now reverse what you sang on "They all" when you sing "farmer's wife." There are then two repetitions of the same melodic idea with a slight change in the rhythm ("Did you ever see such a sight in your life"). You now continue down the stairs and end on the same pitch you sang earlier on "mice."

Follow the same concept with "Mary Had a Little Lamb," "Row, Row, Row Your Boat," and other similar children's songs, patriotic tunes, religious melodies, or seasonal songs—always striving to connect the visual aspect of how the melody appears on the printed page with the melody you already know. You may be surprised how quickly the mystery of printed music may be solved.

Understanding Aural Skill Levels

Tone production and pitch accuracy are a combined result of mental signals and mus-

Figure 3–6. Recognition of melodic patterns.

cular responses. In the same manner that all people have varying levels of athletic ability, individuals will have varying levels of pitch accuracy and pitch awareness. The singer who has "absolute pitch" or "perfect pitch" (terms frequently used interchangeably), meaning that they can identify or reproduce a pitch without the aid of an external source (piano, instrument, pitch pipe), is often viewed with envy by less experienced singers. In truth, singers who possess this rare gift sometimes admit that it is often burdensome because they must constantly be transposing music in their head to adapt to the tuning of the choir or the orchestra. Others develop what is commonly called "relative pitch" or "pitch recognition," having learned the sound of a certain pitch (usually A 440, as used in tuning the violin) and then relating the pitch they hear to the learned pitch. While these skills may be helpful, they are not essential for quality solo or choral singing.

"I can't match pitch" is another moan frequently heard from inexperienced singers. As mentioned earlier, all tone is produced by a message from the brain to the vocal mechanism. As is true with the other skills already discussed, this coordination can be developed by nearly everyone through careful and thoughtful practice. It is suggested that a singer needing help with this skill enlist the assistance of a trusted friend of similar vocal quality to serve as a mentor (soprano to soprano, tenor to tenor, etc.). The mentor would sing a specific pitch in the midrange of the voice, asking the singer to "match" that pitch. The singer should relax and concentrate on hearing the sung pitch in their head, not hurrying to reproduce it. The singer should then allow the breath to produce the sound as they imagined it in the mind at a medium-volume level. If the sound matches the note sung, a moment of listening to the combined "matched" tones should follow to confirm the sound of the "matched pitch" and reinforce the experience. A visual hand signal can be very helpful in confirming success for the singer. If the note generated does not "match" the sung tone, the singer should retain their tone and the mentor would bring the sung tone to the singer, allowing the singer to experience a "matched pitch" and recognize the unified sound. Often, the mentor using an open hand as a symbol of the pitch and asking the singer to match the example will help the matching process. Gentle up and down hand signals to the singer indicating that the pitch should go higher or lower may also be helpful. This exercise should be done in a quiet environment that is free from distractions because of the high degree of concentration required. This training requires intense concentration and is best done only for a short period of time. Frequent, patient repetition of the training over time will bring success. Soon the singer will be following the mentor in singing simple melodies and gaining confidence in their pitch awareness. The recognition of the problem and the identification of available tools bring positive results.

Strategies for Lifelong Music Learning

In a souvenir shop, this author recently saw a coffee mug printed with many sayings about music. One of the inscriptions read, "The more you love music, the more music you love." This certainly holds true for singing, and the more completely the singer has polished their musicianship skills beginning with their earliest singing experience, the more they will be able to enjoy their musical gift throughout their lifetime. Have you ever heard the old joke about how you know when singers have arrived at the door for rehearsal or performance? They can't find the key and don't know when to come in! This need not be a part of the experience for any vocalist who continues to stimulate their brain and their musical talent through active music making, be it in worship, community chorus, or other musical endeavors that challenge the vocalist. As the body ages, the need for active breath usage, attention to posture, the energetic and accurate enunciation of language, and the stimulation of brain function are all fostered and promoted by active singing. As the mind continues to be sharpened by undertaking new challenges, learning a foreign language, doing crossword puzzles, and other similar activities, so active singing appears to promote improved memory skills, heightened cultural awareness, and strengthened social connections. Continued focus on learning new music and new vocal techniques allows one to venture forward in exploring the magic of brain stimulation through singing alone and with others. Persons who sing joyfully in their vehicle as they drive home from work are not only leaving their job behind them but also freeing their body to take a deep breath. They feel the freedom of expression found in song and the satisfaction discovered through self-expression. A favorite melody captures the merit of lifelong singing when it implores the following:

Sing your way home at the end of the day.

Sing your way home, drive the shadows away.

Smile all the while, for wherever you roam,

It will lighten your day, it will brighten your way,

When you sing your way home.

Strong skills bring broad smiles and increased opportunities to enjoy singing activities.

Conclusion

A patient, careful, exacting introduction and development of basic music reading skills offers the singer a lifetime of exciting and stimulating musical experiences. The multitude of brain functions needed to facilitate singing complement the vibrant use of the mind. The merit of lifelong singing is voiced prominently by the many community choirs, church or synagogue choruses, retirement home choirs, and a multitude of other outlets that provide vocal opportunities for people of all ages. Musicianship skills promote active and successful participation in such endeavors for those who have patiently and continuously developed their talent and brain.

Discussion Questions

1. What do you perceive as the major challenges to reading the musical score? How would you meet these challenges?
2. Explain the importance of rhythm in music.
3. Explain the terms: staff, system, time signature, and measure.
4. Why should "T" be used in count-singing? What does it replace?

5. Name three simple songs that you can use as an example of what the printed page looks like for a song you already know. Locate those songs. Sing the examples carefully and notice the location of each pitch notated on the staff.

Resources for Further Reading

Music Learning

Carlson, R. (2019). Sight-reading insights from professional choral singers: How they learned and implications for the choral classroom. *Choral Journal, 60*(1), 8–21.

Henry, M., & Hamann, K. (2020). *Level up: An interactive system for vocal sight-reading*. GIA Publications.

O'Toole, P. (2003). *Shaping sound musicians: An innovative approach to teaching comprehensive musicianship through performance*. GIA Publications.

Schnebly-Black, J., & Moore, S. (1997). *The rhythm inside: Connecting body, mind, and spirit through music*. Rudra Press.

Online Resources for Music Learning

http://www.earbeater.com (customizable ear-training exercises)

http://www.musictheory.net (basic online theory for iPad and iPhone)

http://www.openmusictheory.com (an online music theory course)

http://www.teoria.com (basic music theory and aural/reading skills)

http://www.musicalmind.org (ear-training exercises, including solfege, dictation, and chord recognition)

https://trainer.thetamusic.com (ear-training games)

http://www.tonedear.com (basic ear-training exercises)

Choral Singing

Blocker, R. (Ed.). (2004). *The Robert Shaw reader*. Yale University Press.

Mussulman, J. (1979). *Dear people . . . Robert Shaw*. Indiana University Press.

4

Skills for Learning to Sing Text

Brenda Smith

Text distinguishes singing from every other form of music making. Whether you are singing classical or popular music, your delivery of text is central to your performance. Inspired by a poem or lyrics, a composer or singer/songwriter devises a singable, musical framework. In short, instrumentalists perform abstract melodies and singers sing texts set to music.

To sing expressively in any genre, you will delve into the sounds of language and the deeper meaning of words. In preparing a solo or choral score, you will grapple with pronunciation and articulation, grammar and syntax, and textual analysis. Expect to expand your horizons as you discover the vast range of texts and topics that have inspired song.

(Note: Your Class Voice plan may not include singing in any language besides English. This chapter contains introductory information for singing in English, Italian, German, and French. If the languages outside of English are not of interest to you or your classmates, feel free to skip over the passages describing foreign sounds.)

The Italian Language and Singing Skill

Since the 17th and 18th centuries, Western classical singers have based their singing style upon an Italian ideal called "bel canto" or beautiful singing. Singers of many genres seek "classical" vocal training. The term "classical" usually means the ability to sing evenly throughout the vocal range. As you have learned, an evenness of vocal quality is not only pleasing to the ear, but it improves the audibility of text for the listener. Because the singing style in the Western world was first introduced in Italy, beginning singing skills are taught using the five basic Italian vowels: "ah" [a], "eh" [ɛ], "ee" [i], "aw" [ɔ], and "oo" [u]. (The bracketed symbols are phonetic equivalents from the International Phonetic Alphabet or IPA.) We refer to the five basic Italian vowels as "pure" vowels, meaning they are single sounds that require no manipulation of the jaw or lips to create. Because of the ubiquitous presence of these vowels, spoken Italian language has a "musical" quality. When you listen to native Italian speakers, you will notice a lilt or a sense of "melody" in their speech.

When you speak or sing an Italian text, you notice how gently the elongated vowel sounds meld into one another. A melody from an Italian song is a seamless ribbon of vowels, punctuated by crisp consonants. The interpretive power of Western vocal music derives from its "legato" line, the steady flow of undulating tone that changes vowel and pitch imperceptibly. It has a mesmerizing effect, drawing the listener's ear and emotion to the climax of each phrase.

International Phonetic Alphabet

To learn to sing texts in any language, singers use the International Phonetic Alphabet (IPA) as a standard pronunciation guide. The IPA is used around the world for a wide variety of purposes. Perhaps you recall a teacher asking you to say "ah" as in "father." IPA offers [ɑ] as a symbol instead of a word for quick reference. Knowledge of IPA can be valuable to you in many situations outside of singing. For example, if you are introduced to a new acquaintance or a new word, you can note the proper pronunciations in IPA symbols for future reference. Many printed and online resources are readily available to help you learn the phonetic symbols. A listing of basic symbols and sounds in English appear later in this chapter.

Tricks for Learning IPA

Begin by associating each of the IPA symbols with sounds you know in English. For each symbol, think of a word in English that contains the sound. Memorize one word for each IPA symbol and practice using the word to recall the sound. Because singing involves sustaining vowel sounds, strive to master the vowels before moving to the consonants.

Consonants, either single or clusters, are classified by their method of production. Some are "voiced" [v], meaning that the voice is needed to make the sound, and others are "voiceless" [f]. Some consonants are "nasal" while others are "trilled." Each single consonant or consonant cluster has a unique symbol to remind you of its production and sound.

Once you have learned the IPA symbols for sounds in English, you can apply the symbols to help you recall sounds in other languages. The IPA does not teach to you "speak" a language, rather it helps you remember how to pronounce it. The IPA is a pronunciation tool used to notate sounds you have already heard spoken or sung by another voice.

The Value of the International Phonetic Alphabet

Taking a fresh look at sounds you utter every day can be illuminating. It is likely that you will discover more efficient, effective ways to sing or speak text. The more you use the symbols of the International Phonetic Alphabet, the more skillful and confident you will be as a singer, teacher, and choral conductor. If you portray a character role in musical theater, you may need to perfect the dialect appropriate to the time and setting of the plot. The IPA symbols can be of tremendous value for the recall of any deviations from common English pronunciation. The IPA is in current use as a rehearsal tool for private voice coaching as well as choral, operatic and musical theater rehearsals. No matter what genre you choose to sing, you will wish to be heard, understood, and expressive. Using the principles described in this chapter, you will gather the tools to analyze the sounds of words and deliver them consistently and beautifully.

Learning the IPA in English

If you wish to learn the International Phonetic Alphabet, begin by associating vowel sounds in English with the corresponding IPA symbols. Select a word that works for you or substitute another one that you are more likely to remember. Make it fun! (Note: The IPA is a set of symbols for sounds, not spellings. In some cases, there is more than one spelling that produces the same phonetic sound.)

Vowel Sounds

IPA Symbol	English Word Equivalents
[ɑ]	father, cot, otter
[æ]	cat, task
[e]	chaos, chaotic
[ɛ]	met, thread
[i]	seen, scene
[ɪ]	chin, grim
[ɨ]	lily, pretty (unstressed syllable, similar in sound to [ɪ])
[ɔ]	awe, moth
[o]	obey, oblation (the letter "o" in an unstressed syllable only)
[u]	fool, rule
[ʊ]	book, pull
[ə]	afraid, alone (also known as a "schwa")
[ɜ]	bird, learn (an "r-colored" vowel, appears only in English)
[ʌ]	done, sun

Classification of Vowels: Open and Closed

Generally, vowels are classified as "open" or "closed." An "open" vowel is formed without any *conscious* effort of the tongue, lips, jaw, or palate. The five basic open vowels in English are [ɑ] as in "father, [ɛ] as in "met," [ɔ] as in "awe," and [u] as in "fool."

A "closed" vowel is one formed by a manipulation of the tongue, lips, jaw, or palate. In other words, one "closes" the space in some way. For example, the sound of the written letter "a" as in "chaos" is closed and its IPA symbol is [e]. Another is [i] as in "seen." When the written letter "o" appears in an unstressed syllable as in "obey," the sound is closed and has the IPA symbol of [o].

Diphthongs

Diphthongs are vowel combinations made up of two sounds. In English, they are spoken or sung with emphasis on the first of the two sounds. As you see, the diphthongs are made by combining single sounds and symbols you learned previously.

IPA Symbol	English Word Equivalents
[aʊ]	brown, shout
[ɔɪ]	boy, boil
[aɪ/ɑɪ]	light, mile
[eɪ/ɛɪ]	sale or sail
[oʊ]	so or sew

Diphthongs Influenced by "r." Only in English there are diphthongs that are influenced by the presence of the sound of "r." For sake of tuning and tone in singing, the sound of "r" before a consonant or at the end of a word is silent or only minimally expressed.

IPA Symbols	English Word Equivalents
[ɛə/ɛɚ]	air or heir or ere
[ɪə/ɪɚ]	ear, tier, mere
[ɔə/ɔɚ]	ore, or, o'er; four, war
[ʊə/ʊɚ]	sure, tour
[ɑə/ɑɚ]	are, mar

Note: The chart indicates two possibilities for the pronunciations. The IPA transcription given on the left represents the vowel sound of the diphthong with a silent "r." The IPA transcription given on the left allows for a slight acknowledgment of the "r" sound.

Triphthongs

Triphthongs are vowel combinations made up of three sounds. In English, they are as follows:

IPA Symbols	English Word Equivalents
[aɪə/aɪɚ]	choir, fire
[aʊə/aʊɚ]	hour, flower

Note: As illustrated previously, two options for pronunciation are given. The second transcription implies a slight acknowledgment of the "r" sound while the first one indicates a silent or minimal use of "r."

The Letter and the Sound of "Y"

The letter "y" functions as a vowel in the middle of words and is expressed in one of several ways. Consider the letter "y" in words like "rhyme" [aɪ]/[ɑɪ] or "rhythm" [I]. The letter "y" appears sometimes at the end of a word or in an "-ly" ending. To improve tuning and word accent, singers are encouraged to deemphasize the sound by singing [ɪ] instead of [i]. The symbol [i̽] is used to indicate that the sound [ɪ] should be understated.

The sound of the letter "y" is associated with the symbol [j] and is called a "glide." The symbol [j] is used to indicate an additional sound that occurs in a word like "music" ['mjuz:ɪk].

English Only Sounds

Please note that the sound associated with [æ] as in "cat," [ɚ] as in "er" endings, [ɜ] or [ɜ˞] as in "learn," [i̽] as in "ly" endings, or [ʌ] as in "sun" are specific to English and do not occur in other languages. All these sounds present tuning issues. Rely on your instructor or coach to help you modify the vowels to create more beautiful, accurate sounds.

Wordless Singing

Words are sometimes inadequate to express emotions or feelings. In the world of vocal jazz, improvisation on a single vowel is called "scatting." Singers who scat use a vowel or a sequence of vowels to imitate instrumental passages. In some operas, composers include opportunities for singers to demonstrate vocal prowess. At the end of certain arias, the orchestral part sustains an unstable harmony while the singer improvises passages of vocal "fireworks." Such passages are called "cadenzas" because they occur at cadential or concluding points. For these moments of vocal freedom, most opera singers choose a favorable vowel sound that will facilitate the exhibition of their vocal skill and ecstasy.

Consonants

Single Consonants

In the International Phonetic Alphabet, simple consonant sounds are indicated by their corresponding alphabetical letter, as follows:

[b], [d], [f], [g], [h], [k], [l], [m], [n], [p], [r]*, [s], [t], [v], [w], [z]

Did you notice that there is no [c] in the International Phonetic Alphabet? The letter "c" is used to spell sounds that are pronounced as a "k" [k] or an "s" [s].

*The letter "r" has many expressive qualities. It can "influence" diphthongs, as you learned previously. It can be rolled/trilled or flipped/tapped depending on its use.

Consonant Clusters

Consonant clusters create new sounds to master. Remember: Some are voiced and others are unvoiced, sometimes called "voiceless." These sounds occur in other languages as well.

IPA Symbol	English Word Equivalent
[j]	you, use
[ŋ]	sing, song
[ŋk]	bank, sink
[ŋg]	angle, finger

[ʃ]	shun, caution
[ʒ]	measure, vision
[tʃ]	chant, march
[dʒ]	gem, jam
[θ]	breath, think
[ð]	breathe, this
[ʍ] or [hw]	when, what

Note: The sounds [θ] as in "breath," [ð] as in "breathe," and [ʍ] or [hw] as in "when" appear only in the English language. Non-native English speakers find these sounds difficult to execute.

Articulation of Consonants

The more you understand how consonants are formed, the easier it will be to produce them efficiently. The following is a list of the voiced and unvoiced or voiceless consonants and consonant clusters in English. Read through the list from left to right. Notice the involvement of your voice or its absence as you pronounce each pair. Next, practice words that begin with each consonant or cluster.

Voiced Spelling/Symbol			Unvoiced or Voiceless Spelling/Symbol		
b	[b]	bob	p	[p]	pop
d	[d]	did	t	[t]	toot
g	[g]	go	k	[k]	kick
l	[l]	lull			
m	[m]	maim			
n	[n]	noon			
v	[v]	vie	f	[f]	fee
w	[w]	woe	wh	[ʍ] or [hw]	whew

Voiced Spelling/Symbol			Unvoiced or Voiceless Spelling/Symbol		
y	[j]	you			
z	[z]	zoo	s	[s]	sue
h	[h]	ha!			
ch	[tʃ]	chew	sh	[ʃ]	shoe
th	[ð]	breathe	th	[θ]	breath

Next, speak the nasal consonant [ŋ] as in "si<u>ng</u>." Compare it with the sound of [ŋk] as in "sa<u>nk</u>" or [ŋg] as in "hu<u>ng</u>er." Do you sense that the symbol combinations depict the sounds you made? Notice also how IPA symbols help you understand the differences between sounds such as [ʒ] as in "mea<u>s</u>ure" or "presti<u>g</u>e" and the cluster [dʒ] as in "he<u>dg</u>e" or "<u>g</u>em" or "<u>j</u>am."

Consider how you create or "articulate" each consonant. Is your tongue involved? If so, is it the tip or the back of the tongue? Where does the tongue go when you move it? Does air rush over the roof of your mouth? Do you use your soft palate or your lips or some combination of these elements? In principle, a consonant is formed when an articulator (tongue, lip, teeth, palate, etc.) interrupts the flow of air as it moves through the vocal tract. The "point of articulation" refers to where the interruption takes place. Consonants formed by your lips, such as the letter "b" [b] or "p" [p], are called "bilabial" consonants. (Note: To avoid unnecessary pressure, singers strive to articulate bilabial consonants at the midpoint of the lips on the inner surface.) If the interruption occurs at the level of the teeth, such as the voiceless/unvoiced "th" [θ], it is called a "dental" consonant. When lips and teeth are involved as in the letter "f" [f], we call the point of articulation "labiodental." The area between your teeth and your hard palate, known as the "alveolar ridge," is where the tip of your tongue creates the letters "d" [d], "l" [l], "n" [n], and "t" [t]. Practice where on the alveolar ridge each of the four consonants works most efficiently. When you say the "y" [j] in the word "yes," notice where the tongue contacts an area slightly in front of your hard palate. In expressing the voiced sound [ʒ] in the word "mea<u>s</u>ure," the outer edges of the tongue touch the hard palate. You use your soft palate to the sounds of "k" [k] and "ng" [ŋ], respectively. The letters "m" [m] and "n" [n] are called "nasal consonants" because they both involve the structures of the nasopharyngeal region. Investigate the various points of articulation and practice finding the quickest, easiest ways to achieve a clear, crisp delivery of each sound.

Singing Versus Speaking Vowels and Consonants

The process of singing a vowel or consonant is different than speaking a vowel or consonant. In speech, you do not sustain vowels for several beats or carry them over three octaves. Both activities occur regularly when we sing.

Whether singing or speaking, strive for a relaxed jaw and a released, active tongue. Remember that singing or speaking on one tone is very tiring for the voice. Keeping "melody" in your speech is a healthy concept. With guidance and practice, you will achieve proficient, economical, and articulate diction in speech and song.

Using the International Phonetic Alphabet as a Tool

Study the lists of symbols and sounds previously provided. For each symbol, select one word you are certain to associate with the symbol. Practice the symbols and your word-to-symbol associations. Be sure each symbol reminds you instantly and accurately of the proper sound. Compare closely your penmanship with the symbol shapes provided in the previous lists. Make flashcards and test yourself. Quiz yourself to determine if you have memorized one equivalent word for each symbol. Once mastered, the International Phonetic Alphabet (IPA) is a useful, lifelong pronunciation tool. (Note: Sample quizzes and answer sheets are available in the online companion website to this textbook.)

Phonetic Transcriptions and "Rhyming Vowels"

In a dictionary or a phonetic transcription, you will find phonetic spellings of *spoken* language. Having learned that each vowel has its own tone quality, singers modify spoken vowels for the sake of beautiful singing tone. To ensure exquisite tuning, singers also learn to "rhyme" vowels, making words that rhyme—or almost rhyme—sound exactly alike. This process is especially useful when singing in English. As noted previously, English contains many sounds that are not inherently "singable," such as [ʌ] as in "but" or [ɜ] as in "learn."

The following is an excerpt from one of the earliest British songs composed by Thomas Morley (1557–1602) for a theatrical performance of William Shakespeare's play *As You Like It*. The second excerpt is taken from an American Appalachian folk song. Read silently and aloud the IPA transcription for each in the spoken version. When you repeat the words in the sung version, you will hear and feel a difference in the flow, audibility, and "singability" of the words. Remember to minimize the sound of the letter "r" before a consonant and at the end of words to enhance your tone quality. In the sung phonetic spellings given in the following examples, you will find a colon inserted where the "r" would appear in words like *corn, color,* and *her* to encourage sensitivity to this concept. Note: The pronunciation examples for spoken English were gathered from equivalents found in the *Oxford Diction of Pronunciation for Current English* (Upton et al., 2001).

British English Example

It was a lover and his lass, who o'er the green cornfield did pass.

Spoken ɪt wʌz ə lʌvər ænd hɪz læs hu ɔɚ ðʌ grin kɔɚnfild dɪd pæs

Sung ɪt waz ɑ lavə ænd hɪz læs hu ɔə ðɑ grin kɔ:nfield dɪd pæs

American Appalachian English Example

Black is the color of my true love's hair. Her lips are something rosy fair.

Spoken blæk ɪz ðə kʌlɚ ɔv maɪ tru lʌvz hɛər hər lɪpz ɑr sʌmθɪŋ roʊzi fɛər

Sung blæk ɪz ðɑ kɑl̯a: ɑv̱ maɪ tru lavz hɛə hə: lɪpz ɑə sɑmθɪŋ roʊzi fɛə

Sounds in Languages Other Than English

With each language you discover sounds that are very familiar as well as some that are unique. There will be many cognates: words that derive from a similar source. For example, "*luna*" in Italian means "moon" and is a cognate with "lunar" in English or "*amor*" (Italian) and "*amour*" (French) mean "love" and is reminiscent of "amorous" in English. In German, *Haus* and *Maus* look and sound like their English cognates "house" and "mouse."

Do not forget that the *imitation of sounds* is the foundational principle of the International Phonetic Alphabet. To sing or speak in other languages, listen to the sounds pronounced first by an accomplished singer or speaker. Imitate and repeat the sounds you hear until you are confident that your pronunciation is identical to the model. Use the IPA symbols to notate the sounds for instant recall and for practice.

Because each language has its own characteristic sound ideal, there are subtle differences in the vowel/consonant shapes and sounds. The IPA symbols are not exact equivalents but rather "points of departure" for achieving comparable sounds. Listen to the difference between *Haus* in German pronounced [hɑos] and *house* in English pronounced [haʊs]. Though similar, the German *Haus* [hɑos] is a much rounder sound than its English equivalent *house* [haʊs]. Both words feel and sound slightly different. The IPA will assist you in creating the subtle changes required for perfect singer's diction.

Sounds in Italian, German, and French

If you choose to sing repertoire in languages other than English, see the following short list of IPA symbols and their sounds you would encounter in the Italian, German, and French languages.

[a]	Italian, German, French "bright ah"
[ʎ]	Italian: *gli* (the)
[ç]	German: *ich* (I)
[x]	German: *ach* (Ah!)
[y]	German: *für* (for); French: *sur* (on)
[ʏ]	German: *Glück* (luck, pleasure)
[ø]	German: *schön* (pretty); French: *feu* (fire)
[œ]	German: *möchte* (want to); French *fleur* (flower)
[ã]	French only: *ensemble* (group)
[ɛ̃]	French only: *jardin* (garden)
[õ]	French only: *garçon* (boy)
[œ̃]	French only: *un* (one, a), *humble* (humble)
[r]	rolled/trilled "r" (extended)
[ɾ]	tapped/flipped "r" (brief)

As you see, each language has its own one-of-a-kind sounds that must be mastered. Though Italian and German language both have diphthongs, they are treated differently than in English. German and French contain "mixed vowels," sounds that blend two vowels to make a new one. The German language contains the consonant sounds [ç] and [x] known as the "ich-laut" and the "ach-laut." In French, you find four nasal vowels [ã], [ɛ̃], [õ], and [œ̃] that give the language its character and color. Italian and German double consonants are handled in specific ways. In English, the letter "r" may be silent or sounded, while in Italian, German, and French, it is always acknowledged in one manner or another such as "trilled" or "flipped." In Italian and French, consonants are often minimized to encourage the forward flow of the language. German words are rich in consonants, all of which have expressive roles to play in communication. In German, words that begin with open vowels are never elided but rather set apart. Do not fret about the details. As you learn a language, you gather fresh perspectives on culture, music making, and world history. There are many resources in print, online, recorded as speech and as song to assist you in your study and practice of singer's diction.

Diction in Context

The Sufi poet and mystic, Jalaluddin Rumi wrote, "Poems are rough notations for the music we are" (Barks, 2003). Most songs are multidimensional creations based on poetry or lyrics. Singer's diction involves more than the accurate pronunciation of a text. To sing in any language meaningfully, you must grasp the song's poetic essence. Study the expressive elements of the text including vowel colors and consonant articulation. Using the inflection suggested by the musical setting, read each text silently and aloud. Allow the sound of the words to "speak to your heart." Let this lyric reading reveal to you the expressive qualities you wish to deliver to an audience.

Conclusion

Singing distinguishes itself from other art forms because it is based on text. Learning to divide and conquer a poetic text is a part of being an accomplished singer. The International Phonetic Alphabet (IPA) is the basic tool for identifying and remembering the proper pronunciation in the languages you will sing.

Discussion Questions

1. What are the important elements of "singer's diction"?
2. What is the International Phonetic Alphabet (IPA)? Who uses it?
3. Why are the IPA symbols taught first in one's native language? How is the IPA used?
4. How is singing a text different than speaking it?
5. What does it mean to "rhyme" vowels? Why rhyme vowels in singing?

Resources for Further Reading

Grubb, T. (1990). *Singing in French: A manual of French diction and French vocal repertoire.* Schirmer Books.
LaBouff, K. (2008). *Singing and communicating in English: A singer's guide to English diction.* Oxford University Press.
Odom, W. (1997). *German for singers: A textbook of diction and phonetics* (2nd ed.). Schirmer Books.
Paton, J. G. (2004). *Gateway to Italian diction.* Alfred Publishing.
Retzlaff, J., & Montgomery, C. (2015). *Exploring art songs lyrics.* Oxford University Press.
Smith, B. (2021). *Diction in context: Singing in English, Italian, German, and French.* Plural Publishing.

References

Barks, C. (2003). The music we are. In *Rumi: The book of love: Poems of ecstasy and longing* (pp. 25–31). Harper One.
Upton, C., Kretschmar, W., & Konopka, R. (2001). *Oxford dictionary of pronunciation for current English.* Oxford University Press.

5
Singing Solo

Brenda Smith

Have you ever wondered why we sing the way we do? In this chapter, you will learn how singing in the Western world developed from its earliest roots in the sacred tradition to the current trends on the Broadway stage. You will become familiar with the terminology used by singers and teachers of singing.

The Singing Art in the Western World

The art of singing in the Western world evolved from the practice of reciting texts. Reading or chanting of sacred texts had long served as a means of meditating, educating, and lifting human minds and spirits. As the ceremonies of the early church developed, the chanting of hymn texts, psalms, and liturgies became an essential element. The assembly of worshippers increased and required the expansion of the ecclesiastical spaces into massive, vaulted areas. Instinctively, the monks began to "call out" the sacred texts, elevating the pitch of their voices in the process. (Technically speaking, they elongated the vowel sounds and crisply articulated the consonants.) The expansive acoustics of cathedral naves amplified and unified the monks' voices. Their utterances circulated like ribbons of undulating tone, wrapping the congregation in an otherworldly aura of text amid candlelight and incense. Though created by a coincidence of sound and acoustics, the result was profound. Performers and listeners alike recognized and developed the expressive potential of this "elevated" text delivery. By this means, vocal music in the Western world became rooted in the repetition of meaningful texts.

In Renaissance Florence (ca. 1580), a group of highly cultured Italian literary, visual, and musical artists along with philosophers and politicians met to invent an art form that would capture the essence of human creativity. The group, later called the *Florentine Camerata*, invented a means of combining all the arts in one singular presentation that we now call "opera," literally meaning "a work." (You may already know the word "opus," meaning a composition or set of works composed at the same time. Opera and opus derive from the same root.) The earliest operas were based upon Greek myths and Roman legends—literature that illuminated valuable and timeless moral lessons. The myth or legend was rewritten into the format of a play with roles clearly delineated for dramatic purposes. Then and now, the texts assigned to be sung by the operatic characters are assembled in a "little book" or *libretto*. The action is delivered as a vocal recitation or *recitative*. A recitative is sung by a single voice over a simple harmonic foundation. The simplicity of the form allows the audience to hear and comprehend the dramatic circumstances. A character's reactions to the dramatic action are expressed in an "aria." To remember the term, consider that the commentary on the action is "aired" by a character in an "aria." An opera aria is based upon a limited amount of emotive text set to music with frequent repetitions. An aria reveals the inner nature of a character while allowing the opera singer to demonstrate vocal skill and artistry. Characters sing together with one another (duets, trios, quartets, and larger units) in what is known as an *ensemble*. The basic forms of opera (recitative, aria, and ensemble) are the building blocks of music dramas of all types.

In the earliest operas, the human voice was used to "elevate" the text using aspects of the voice to convey the emotional response of the characters to the dramatic plot. The singers who performed in these early operas had been trained as young boys and men in the ecclesiastical style of singing. They adapted their vocal technique to deliver text expressively on the opera stage. In the process, the expression of text became the principal goal of Western singing. Instrumental forms derived from their vocal counterparts as "songs without words." It is important to remember that operetta, musical theater, art songs, popular songs, and folk songs developed from the same ideals.

Bel Canto, Legato, and the Even Scale

How did the Western ideal of singing as a means of text expression become a vocal technique? By the seventh century, choir schools called "schola cantorum" were established to train boys and men in the skills required for liturgical singing. Chanting was an oral tradition, transmitted by skilled singers who served as mentors for younger students of singing. The basics of singing such as relaxation, posture, breathing, and resonance were taught by example. What the early pedagogues demonstrated and taught became known as "bel canto" or "beautiful singing." It is a singing style based on a seamless flow of breath with a consistency of vocal quality called "legato" singing.

Legato singing occurs when the voice moves imperceptibly from pitch to pitch and vowel to vowel, carried on a constant stream of breath energy. The continuous threads of melody and text mesmerize the listener. As the poet Elizabeth Bishop (1911–1979) wrote: "There is a magic made by melody" (Hollander, 2001, p. 11). Legato singing is a fundamental goal for every student of singing and a feature of good vocal training. To sing in this connected "legato" manner, every tone you produce must be aligned with the tones before and after it. Through vocal exercises, feedback, and repetition, you learn to sing every note and every vowel evenly throughout your range. With an "even scale" as a skill in your vocal toolbox, you can perform texts that are easily intelligible and appreciated by your listener.

Range, Registration, and Tessitura

How exactly do you achieve an even scale with which to sing legato, you ask? The basics of singing are foundational for building the skills you need for legato singing. With training and practice, you will curate a collection of vowel sounds that match throughout your vocal range. Human voices can utter many more tones than the human ear can hear. For singing, most of us are confined to about two and a half to three octaves of notes (pitches). Your *range* encompasses the highest to the lowest pitches you can produce healthfully—in other words, without strain or force. Your vocal range is likely to expand with training.

Your range has distinct regions or "registers" in which certain tones are created similarly and have comparable tone qualities. The notes within a register bear similar tone quality because of the vocal fold vibrations and vocal tract adjustments required to produce them. Tones made within a single register sound alike but are distinct from those made in other registers of your range. In principle, vocal *registration* refers to the notes you sing, those that lie above and below your speaking voice, and those that lie in a region in which you could either sing or speak. The terms used to classify the registers can be very confusing. Some pedagogues refer to "head," "mixed" or "middle," and "chest" register, with the mixed or middle register being the area in which the voice can sing and speak. To access notes for singing above or below the mixed or middle register, subtle changes occur in the positioning of the vocal mechanism. To maintain stability, you learn to balance breath energy with tone and vowel quality.

For many young singers, instability at a point of transition between the registers can be disconcerting. In vocal pedagogy writings, an area of transition is often termed a "passaggio" or passage. The transition occurs because the vocal instrument, the larynx, must shift slightly to produce a particular note. Leverage is required to stabilize the vocal mechanism. Since the singer cannot see the larynx in transition, it is difficult to gauge how much breath energy and what vowel and tone adjustments are needed for a seamless passing from note to note. Through trial and error, singers develop successful strategies that yield an even scale.

With training, you too will learn to negotiate the points of transition between your vocal registers. Most singers agree that notes above the speaking range need less weight of sound but require an increase of breath energy. Conversely, notes below the speaking range are easier to achieve by decreasing breath pressure. In the same way that instrumentalists develop efficient fingerings to access keys on a horn or keyboard, singers learn to adjust breath pressure and tonal weight to unify vocal registers throughout their range.

As you select and prepare vocal repertoire, it is wise to consider the *tessitura* of the piece, meaning "where the melodic material lies." A song or aria of modest range might have a "difficult" *tessitura,* if most of the notes you are expected to sing lie unusually high or extremely low in your vocal range. Vocal repertoire in which the melody glides gently throughout your vocal range is said to be in a moderate *tessitura* and would, in general, be more comfortable to sing.

Fach is the German term for "classification" and is used to specify the voice part of a singer (soprano/alto/tenor/bass). You may be curious about your voice classification. Ask a voice teacher, choral conductor, or vocal coach to help you determine what area of your voice works with the most ease. The part you sing in a choral group or the role you accept in a musical production should relate favorably to your vocal timbre, range, and sense of ease. Voice classification is necessary for professional singers who contend for roles but not as essential for a young singer.

The terms "range," "registration," and "tessitura" are closely related and are frequently used interchangeably. It is not uncommon to find a specific key or style that fits your voice best. Range, registration, and tessitura are issues that you and your teacher use to select and prepare the vocal repertoire most appropriate to your vocal gifts and goals.

Messa di Voce or "Measuring" the Voice

In the world of *bel canto* singing, *messa di voce* or "measuring the voice" is a useful skill that enables you to explore the notes in your range, to sing expressively, and to evaluate the health of your vocal instrument. *Messa di voce* involves evenly increasing and decreasing volume (*crescendo* and *decrescendo*) on an individual sustained tone. Figure 5–1 is an example of how *messa di voce* is indicated in a musical score.

"Measuring" voices began as a practice of voice pedagogues in the early choir school tradition. It was used to determine

Figure 5–1. Example of *messa di voce*.

the maturity and stability of a boy's voice and technique. In the mid-16th century, the technique was applied as a choral diction device in the masses and motets of Giovanni Battista Palestrina (1525–1594). The composer placed stressed syllables of a text on long note values that fell on strong beats of measures. When the singers performed the musical notes with *messa di voce* technique, the stressed syllables received emphasis, causing them to emerge dynamically from the texture of the singing. This manner of performance was musically appealing and spiritually impactful. The listeners clearly heard and understood the sacred words that the singers beautifully expressed. Listen to an excerpt from the "Gloria" movement of Palestrina's *Pope Marcellus Mass* to understand the original purpose of this potent vocal skill.

Additional Uses for Messa di Voce

Messa di voce exercises are very effective in developing vocal skill and for strengthening and stabilizing your voice. As you "measure" breath energy and tone, you will achieve an even scale throughout your vocal range.

Messa di voce is used as a therapeutic measurement tool, too. Vocal pedagogues and medical professionals recommend *messa di voce* exercises as a means of evaluating vocal readiness and health. Arguably, if you are unable to produce a *messa di voce,* it might be an indication of vocal fatigue or infirmity.

Tone Quality and Vibrato

The term "tone quality" is used to describe the aesthetic standard for speaking and singing voices. "Vocal quality," "resonance," and "timbre" are other words used to describe vocal sound production. It might be said that tone quality or vocal quality refers to clarity and beauty, while timbre speaks to the "color" of vocal tone ("light" or "dark," "brassy" or "flutelike," for example). None of these terms is exact nor is there a universal way to quantify the sound of a human voice.

When a voice fails to function properly, medical professionals evaluate its vocal quality as one factor leading to an appropriate diagnosis. If a voice is weak, breathy, or hoarse, it may be classified as having a "poor vocal quality." The source of the vocal problem may be functional or pathological. Only a thorough examination by a qualified medical team can confirm the causes for either breathiness or hoarseness.

Vibrato is a feature of tone quality that refers to a "shimmer" or pulsation within a vocal or instrumental tone. If you are an instrumentalist, you have been trained to produce or minimize vibrato to achieve specific musical effects. Vocal vibrato emerges as the result of physical maturity and vocal skill. We do not expect young, untrained singers to present with a steady, even vibrato. Once vibrato is evident in a developing voice, a voice teacher can guide a student toward its maintenance and use. The amount and rate of vibrato can be adjusted to meet aesthetic and musical demands. The vibrato rate, character, and evenness are factors that have an impact on vocal quality and tuning.

Conclusion

Singing in the Western world grew from the tradition of chanting texts. Consistency of sound and delivery made the texts easily audible. Singing set the standard for musical expression. Most instrumental forms imitated singing in style and form. How we sing could have been very different, had history taken other turns. Beautiful singing or *bel canto* is achieved through a steady use of breath and an evenness of tone. Over the centuries, voice teachers have trained their students to breathe and sing in ways that exemplify the original *bel canto* principles.

Discussion Questions

1. What role did text play in the creation of the art of singing in the Western world?
2. What is the difference between range, registration, and tessitura? What is an even scale?
   Define the word "legato" and explain its role in the concept of *bel canto* singing.
3. What is *messa di voce*? What are its uses?
4. Why is it difficult to classify a voice? How would you describe the sound of your voice?
5. How does vibrato relate to vocal tuning?

Resources for Further Reading

Kimball, C. (2006). *Song: A guide to art song style and literature* (2nd ed.). Hal Leonard Corporation.

Pleasants, H. (1966). *The great singers.* Simon and Schuster.

Smith, B. (2020). Vibrato and the older singer. In M. Howe (Ed.), *A user's manual for the aging voice* (pp. 91–101). Compton Publishing.

Stark, J. (1999). *Bel canto: A history of vocal pedagogy.* University of Toronto Press.

Toft, R. (2013). *Bel canto: A performer's guide.* Oxford University Press.

Reference

Hollander, J. (Ed.). (2001). *Committed to memory: 100 best "poems to memorize* (p. 11). Riverhead.

6
Singing With Others

Brenda Smith and Ronald Burrichter

Singing Together in Choirs

In learning to play tennis, one spends time alone hitting the ball into a wall and striking it when it bounces back. This helps to develop the skill of handling the tennis racket but soon becomes boring and the need to hit the ball to another individual becomes important. The young football player does their individual drills to build skills but yearns to be on the field with the team to continue their joy of the game. In a similar manner, singing alone is a wonderful experience that lifts the spirit and expresses emotion, but the special feeling of joining with others in making music brings a lift to the step, a lilt to the spirit, and a joy to the heart. Whether floating the soprano melody, carefully tuning the alto harmony, spinning the lyric sound of the tenor, or supporting the harmony with the warmth of the bass foundation, choral singing is a unifying and uplifting experience.

Choral groups come in all sizes and sing many different styles of music. Most music education programs require voice majors to participate in a choral ensemble. Instrumental music education majors may not be required to sing in a choir but are likely to play in a band or orchestra that accompanies a choral performance. Collegiate choral groups of all kinds are populated with non-music majors who seek to include music in their academic lives despite career interests in other areas. In adult life, many singers become active amateur choristers if the demands of professional and family life allow. Countless professional singers claim the choral art as their introductory singing experience. There is much to learn about vocal technique from singing with others in a choral ensemble. Let us explore the history of choral singing, what skills it trains, and what to expect as you age.

A Brief History of Early Choral Singing

Ever wonder where the designations *soprano*, *alto*, *tenor*, and *bass* came from? They are terms used to categorize the first choral singers in the Western world. Singing in the Western world evolved from the recitation of spoken text in the sacred ceremonies of the early church. The first organized singing was called "monody" because one part sang a single melody *a cappella*, meaning unaccompanied (literally "for the chapel"). The music featured gifted male singers singing alone as well as groups of singers performing in unison. These young men were "holding" the main melodic material and were therefore called "tenors" from the Latin word "tenere," meaning to hold. Always keep in mind that the tenor part "held" the melody. You will discover that the tenor line dominated choral writing for centuries and still plays a very significant role in any choral composition.

With time, as the voices of some young men matured, their voices dropped in range, forcing them to sing in a different acoustical relationship with their tenor colleagues. The lower voices created a harmonic foundation or *basis* for the music making. "Basses" were those who sang the bottom line. As younger, unchanged voices joined the ranks of choral groups, they sang "at an altitude" above the tenor line and were referred to as "altos." The youngest singers sang "superior" to the altos and became known as "sopranos." The framework of soprano-alto-tenor-bass became the structure or skeleton underlying musical form for centuries to come.

This liturgical singing style was intended to glorify God and was later called *bel canto* or "beautiful singing" because of its ethereal, otherworldly sound. An evenness of tone production was the hallmark of the singing. The term "legato" was given to the steady undulation of text-laden melodic lines that were acoustically amplified by the grand architecture of the sacred spaces. (Earlier in this textbook, *legato* is defined as the imperceptible change of vowel and pitch within a melodic context.) This skill relies upon a stream of air that is steady and energized. It is the powerful means by which singing or playing expresses musical meaning.

In summary, Western world music making has its origins in the choral experience. Whether you play an instrument or sing a song, your goal will be the same, namely, to create a "singing" line.

Unison Singing

"The most basic and vital aspects of the choral art are to be learned from unison singing" (Ehmann, 1968, p. 152). Beginning with the traditions of Gregorian chant, unified singing of a single melody with peers has been foundational to Western singing technique. Unison singing involves all the singers singing "as one voice." To "blend" your voice with others in unison singing, you must listen very carefully and match vowels and pitches exquisitely. The slightest variation in vowel or pitch causes a single voice to emerge from the unified character of the melody.

Unison singing builds many skills you will use when you sing alone or as a member of a section in a choral ensemble. As you practice singing unison with others, you will build strong vowel and pitch tuning skills. You will learn to understand how musical phrases are shaped and enjoy being an integral part of expressing them with others.

Identical to solo singing, choral singing requires personal discipline. If the conductor does not suggest how the choir should sit or stand, remember what you have learned about the basics of singing so that you do not put your vocal instrument at risk of injury. Relax, assume a singer's posture, breathe deeply, and create beautiful vocal tone. Choral rehearsals last much longer than solo singing practices and can fatigue your body, mind, and voice. Be sure to warm-up your voice before rehearsal and cool it down afterward.

When rehearsing unison singing with others, allow yourself to respond physically to the musical lines. The use of hand gestures to imitate the shapes of phrases helps members of an ensemble unify their musical ideas. As you combine your voice with others, sense the release of your breath and tone. This lyric release of your sound guided by energized breath is essential to *legato* singing.

Choral Breathing

Unison singing allows you to learn "choral breathing"—a skill that allows you to take a momentary, discreet breath before returning imperceptibly to the corporate choral tone. Unlike solo singing, choral singing does not require any chorister to complete a long phrase on one breath. Choral breathing is a practice that permits you to come and go from a long phrase without stress or embarrassment. To breathe "chorally," select an unaccented beat or syllable, relax, and breathe. Repeated notes are especially advantageous points for departure and reentry. While you are breathing chorally, listen intently to the voices around you so that you can return to the unison sound at the same dynamic level and vowel quality of your peers. The practice of choral breathing is a feature that distinguishes solo singing from singing with others. Choral breathing helps keep every singer "in the game" without strain. The choral breath that refreshes the singer also enriches and enlivens the corporate choral tone. (Please note that the technique called "choral breathing" has also been called "staggered breath." This author prefers the term "choral" because it helps a chorister remember to stay alert and active in the choral moment. The process of "staggering" breath is sometimes dictated by the conductor, creating an assignment for the chorister. The concept of choral breathing is based upon the individual singer's need for breath.)

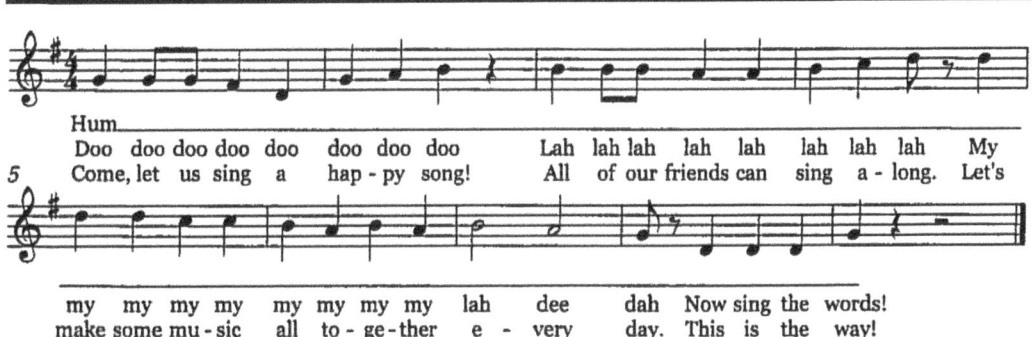

Figure 6–1. Unison melody example.

Canons

Canon singing is the team sport of unison singers. A canon, also called a "round," is a unison melody that offers contrapuntal possibilities. The melody unfolds into harmony when individual voices or groups enter at designated intervals. Because of its repetitive nature, a canon is perhaps appreciated more by its singers as an act of choral solidarity than by its listeners in a performance. Canonic singing fortifies the singer's vocal, rhythmic, and harmonic skills.

When singing a canon, the ensemble first presents the theme in unison. There are two important reasons for this manner of performance. Singing the canon once through in its simplest form unifies the singers and prepares them for the canonic version. The unison singing of the theme familiarizes the listeners with the musical material to follow when the canonic version begins. Canon singing teaches vocal independence while singing with others. "Holding your own" in a canon requires vocal and musical discipline. As described in unison singing, you must "rhyme" the vowels and maintain the rhythm, tempo, and dynamic levels, while tuning the intervals throughout the counterpoint. Canons are uniquely designed to reveal harmonic mysteries as the canonic lines overlap. The conclusion of a canonic theme begins the theme's repetition, giving a sense of unending melody.

Figure 6–2. Unison melody example as a canon.

Suggested Canons for Class Voice Use

The following is a brief list of canons, also called "rounds," that you may enjoy including in your Class Voice work.

> The following are also recommended: "Are You Sleeping?" (French origin); "Dona nobis pacem" (Palestrina 17th century); "Hey, Ho! Nobody at Home!" (Pammelia 1609); "If Your Voices Are Tuned" (early American/Lowell Mason); "Make New Friends" (traditional); "Music Alone Shall Live" (German origin); "Oh! How Lovely Is the Evening!" (German Origin); "Row, Row, Row Your Boat" (anonymous, 19th century); "There Was an Old Man From Calcutta" (British origin); "Viva la musica!" (Michael Praetorius); "White Coral Bells" (traditional); and "Why Shouldn't My Goose Sing as High as Thy Goose?" (anonymous).
>
> The following are the sources for these and additional canons/rounds:
>
> Archibeque, C., & Hannaford, K. (Eds.). (1993). *Canons for choirs.* Santa Barbara Music Publishing.
> McKay, D. P. (Ed.). (1990). *Sound before sense.* Bourne Music Publishing.
> Terri, S. (Ed.). (1974). *Around the year in rounds.* Alfred Music Publishing.
> Weber, S. (Ed.). (1994). *Rounds galore.* Astoria Press.

Two-Part Singing

Two-part choral settings are the choral equivalent of a vocal duet. Two-part choral settings may feature a melody with a contrasting line; the second voice serving as a harmonic accompaniment to the principal melody. Some two-part settings are built around two separate but complementary melodies. Two-part arrangements come in various combinations of like and unlike voices such as soprano and alto (SA)/tenor and bass (TB), soprano and tenor (ST)/alto and bass (AB), among others.

Two-part choral settings are especially useful repertoire for choirs of untrained singers and of older singers. Unlike canon singing, each part has its own character and melodic concepts. The singers within a part remain independent of the countermelody. As a singer, singing two-part choral music challenges you to tune vowels and pitches within your section and with the countermelody while maintaining rhythmic accuracy. If you are a choral conductor, two-part choral settings create satisfying artistic results from a simple musical setting and are fine repertoire for inexperienced choristers (Figure 6–3).

The Singing Life of Choral Singers

Singing Soprano in a Choir

If you sing soprano in a choir, your part will often contain the melody. Though the part may be accessible and tuneful, it is almost always exposed. Thorough preparation will be your best strategy for success. Whether you are singing solo or choral repertoire, it is always important to learn your part carefully. Use your musicianship skills to hear the music and count the rhythms with accuracy. Do not rely on your ear alone. Seek vocal technical guidance if you need it. To help your choral conductor place your voice appropriately in the choir, be mindful of your voice classification,

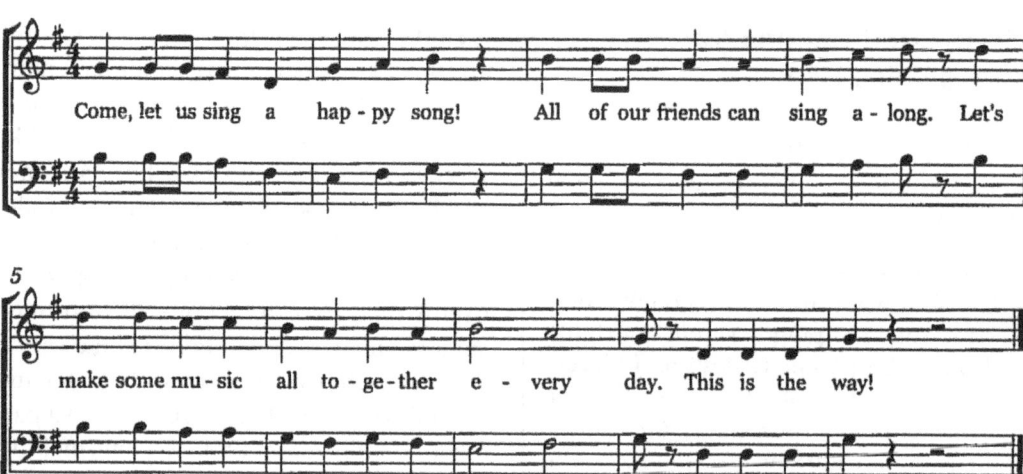

Figure 6–3. Unison melody example in a two-part arrangement (SA/TB).

range, and registration. If you are a first soprano, challenge yourself to sing the second soprano part from time to time. The discipline of exquisite vowel and pitch matching will keep your mind alert and your skills sharp.

It is not uncommon for a choral soprano part to contain passages of sustained high or repeated notes at the upper extension of your range. Do not feel compelled to sing every note. Use your choral breathing skills to relax your voice and body. To save your vocal strength, sing passages in high tessitura down the octave in rehearsal. If you are studying voice privately, take your choral scores to your voice lesson and ask your teacher how to negotiate difficult choral passages.

As a choral soprano, discipline yourself to sit or stand tall in rehearsal and performance as you would in a solo singing situation. Resist any sense of competition with your vocal peers and rest your voice when possible. Remember that high notes are acoustically advantaged over lower ones. Sing lyrically and enjoy your role within the soprano section.

Singing Alto in a Choir

Arguably, the alto part is the most difficult to sing in any choir. Choral alto parts generally cover a very limited vocal range and lie within the register transition between mixed and chest voice. Singers who identify themselves as mezzo sopranos or contraltos (altos) are praised for the warmth of their vocal timbre. Such voices are also coveted because the text they deliver is easily intelligible, since their musical lines are situated in the speaking voice range. Choral alto parts, however, are often monotonous vocal lines. The altos frequently sing the crucial note that tunes and balances the harmonies of the whole choir. So, you see, as an alto—no matter your age or level of vocal training—you have a lot of responsibility on your shoulders.

Complaints of vocal and mental fatigue among choral altos are very common. If you sing alto in a choir, challenge yourself to sing each successive repeated note slightly higher than the one before. Be vigilant about tuning your notes to the bass line as often as possible so that you remain active mentally and musically. Approach your middle and lower voice from a "head voice attitude" by keeping lyricism throughout your range. During your warm-up routine, make it a habit to exercise the upper as well as the middle and lower areas of your voice. Always cool it down after rehearsal.

Singing Tenor in a Choir

As mentioned earlier in this chapter, in the Western world, the earliest organized singing was done by men. The chanting by monks of psalms, prayers, liturgy, and hymns flowed into the lyric lines that evolved into Gregorian chant. For centuries thereafter, the tenor part carried the thematic material in choral polyphonic music. The powerful acoustical advantage of the treble quality of the tenor voice kept the melody prominent above other choral parts soaring through the grand, vaulted cathedrals used for worship.

Your tenor voice lies primarily in the head voice register, an important factor since the tenor part generally stays in the upper part of the tenor vocal range. It is important for you to find this head register early in your singing experience and to embrace it as the natural and healthy production of your sound. Stretching the neck, tightening the jaw, or locking the abdominal wall will impede free vocal production. Since the tenor part occasionally dips into the upper baritone range, learning to mix the head voice into the lower quality of the bottom range is important.

Tenor voices are rare, but you should not let this concern you in the choral setting. The acoustical advantage of your head voice coupled with the natural resonant "ring" of your voice makes it possible for fewer tenors to balance the choir.

The tenor part lies in a "harmonic vacuum" between the pitch being sung by the basses and the altos, frequently a space of an octave or more. It is through this intervallic "hole" that your part floats, aided by the acoustical advantage and resonant power.

The "lyric release" of your sound, meaning an easy flowing tone that rides on energized breath, should be your goal. You may sometimes be encouraged to "push out that tone" or "cover" the quality of the upper range. This frequently leads to vocal strain and fatigue, distorted quality, and intonation problems and should be avoided. Where prolonged upper voice singing is required, conductors might consider rewriting your vocal line or revoicing the chord and allowing a few alto voices to double your tenor part. Asking any voice or choral section to sing more loudly for balance purposes should be avoided. Revoicing a vocal line can accomplish the same result while saving voices. This principle is especially true for the tenor part.

Singing Baritone or Bass in a Choir

Everyone recognizes that a building without a solid foundation is not a safe structure. An automobile with poor tires is not safe to drive because the tires are the foundation upon which the vehicle rests. The SATB choral ensemble without a firm baritone/bass section to establish the musical foundation will surely struggle in many ways. Yes, there are instances where the baritone and bass part are separated, but in much choral music, the lowest notes are given to the "basses," in which case baritones and basses are viewed as one. When a distinct bass I and bass II division occurs, each individual part must take musical responsibility for critical tuning and matched vowels.

What are the challenges for you as a baritone choral singer? You may be required at times to venture into the tenor range for upper pitches. At other times, you will join your low bass colleagues for passages in a lower vocal range. Keeping your lyric head voice "spin" in the upper range without stretching the neck or using falsetto, almost as a tenor would, is essential for the upper range. Your lower notes will be produced more easily if you avoid tucking your chin and pressing down with your head. Keeping a "velvet halo" around your tone at all volume levels is a valuable goal. In the awareness that the baritone/bass section is regularly responsible for the foundation of the tuning and accurate rhythmic shape of the music, pay careful attention to both factors as you sing with your colleagues in support of the other choral voices.

If you are a bass singer, do you face the same challenges? Yes, except that the challenges occur about a third lower in the vocal range. Basses are adept at allowing their lowest notes to "rumble" as they sing at or below the bottom of the bass clef staff. Imagine the structure of an ensemble as an "acoustical pyramid." For example, consider the changes in sound qualities from the double basses to first violins in an orchestra or the tuba to the flute section of a wind ensemble. Allow your rich bass voice to climb the "acoustical pyramid" toward a lighter baritone quality as your bass line ascends. Avoid attempting to maintain the "rumble" quality as pitches go higher. Every singer, including the bass and baritone, needs to allow the vocal weight and quality of their voice to change as the melody moves through the vocal registers. As you place the stones for careful tuning under the choir, be very aware of keeping the accurate pulse of the music.

Choral Singing and Tuning

"What is so special about choral music?" you might ask. For many people, the joy they experience in joining their voices together with others is magical and inspirational. From the earliest chanting by monks and tribes to today's sophisticated choral ensembles, the merging of voices together has had special meaning. The unison singing of the crowd at a soccer match lifts the crowd and inspires the players. The singing of a national anthem by a crowd stirs our deepest patriotic feelings. Singing "Happy Birthday" as a group brings a smile to every face. Singing together in an organized ensemble is artistically gratifying and socially unifying. The satisfaction and joy found in working together to express text through the medium of melody and harmony fuels choral singing.

Challenges of Choral Singing

The challenges of choral singing are as diverse as the singers in the ensemble, but certain challenges are ubiquitous, namely, tuning, tone quality, rhythmic accuracy, and text clarity. As stated in Chapter 3, rhythm is the underpinning of musical expression. Even the most beautiful choral tone sung precisely in tune does not convey the musical idea of the composer if the harmonies do not align rhythmically. Without rhythmic accuracy, words become unintelligible gibberish. True music making by a choral ensemble occurs only with exact rhythmic precision. Count-singing helps choral singers understand and practice rhythmic accuracy.

Voices are highly diverse. Helping choral singers achieve a healthy, collective tone quality that blends individual voices requires a skilled conductor and willing choral singers. Realizing that singers cannot hear themselves, the choral conductor must weave the individual colors together into one fabric. Robert Shaw's frequent declarations to his choirs that no voice should ever emerge from the "sleeve" of the choral sound is an excellent concept that applies to volume, vowel color, tuning, motion (vibrato), and tone quality. Relentless pursuit of a unified tone (often called "choral blend") by each choir member produces an excellent choral result.

An audience member attending an instrumental concert does not expect to be told a story. A listener is moved by the beauty and power of the ensemble. The crowd leaving the choral concert will be unhappy if the text sung by the choir is indiscernible. If the choir enunciates clearly and precisely, important words of the text emerge and are audible. Presenting the text with such clarity is the mark of a well-presented choral concert.

All singers must tune every note they sing. When a new choral work is introduced, time must be taken to allow the choir to experience and integrate the sound of each tuned chord. This author calls this process the development of a "harmonic road map." Use of it shortens rehearsal time for concert preparation. Vowels must match or chords will not tune. When the entire choir sings precisely the same vowel, overtones are generated that enrich the choral tone. It is the skilled choral conductor who assists a choir in experiencing the tuning process and the rewards this tuning brings.

Score Marking

"A short pencil (or stylus) is better than a long memory" is an axiom that holds great truth for you as a choral singer. During rehearsals, instrumentalists and orchestral players are accustomed to entering into their music the information from the conductor. You should duplicate that practice in the choral setting. Note that a pencil (or stylus if using an iPad or tablet) is preferred because changes may be necessary later. By its nature, singing involves "multitasking." With a few words or symbols jotted into the music score at the appropriate location, you need not "remember" the instructions given at the previous rehearsal, only read what you wrote at previous rehearsals.

As a choral conductor, you can code your request in any manner that is helpful to your singers. The important factor is that the codes are entered into the music, freeing the choir members to achieve greater precision and expression together. Accents, staccato and tenuto marks, breath marks or breath "bridges," and other expressive codes can be dictated by the conductor from the podium to save time and ensure clarity. Elements of phrasing, tuning, and diction can also be noted. For example, a pitch regularly sung a bit sharp could be marked with a downward arrow and the converse for a flat pitch. The letter "r" in English which is treated gently at the ends of words or before a rest such as "Mother" [ˈmɑðˌə] or [ˈmɑðˌɚ] can receive a slash mark to indicate caution. The letter "r" in a word like "purple" [ˈpɜːpəl] should be silent before a consonant. If a conductor wishes for a syllable or consonant to be delayed, a bracket can be a good visual reminder. See the word "pur-ple" below. A few examples of score marking

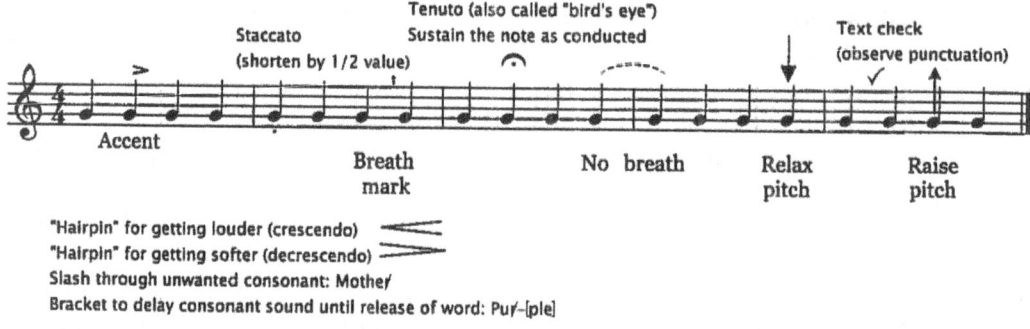

Figure 6–4. Score marking examples.

symbols are offered in Figure 6–4 to stimulate creative habits.

Conclusion

Though solo singing brings personal recognition, choral singing offers a satisfaction unlike any other pursuit. No matter your age, ability, or taste, there is a choral group for you to join at any age. Wherever your career may take you, there is a vocal ensemble that will welcome you.

Choral experiences will help you develop your singing and musicianship skills, acquaint you with expansive musical forms, and offer you the satisfaction of teamwork. The sound ideal of choral music is one of unity, allowing you to relax and share music making. You abandon your own vocal ego for the sake of a corporate identity and share the rewards of group success. From the preparation and presentation of choral music, you will gain insights that transfer directly to solo singing and teaching situations.

Lifelong choral singers report that the choral art contributes positively to well-being and confidence in all seasons of life. Notice the vocal changes that occur as you age and seek qualified assistance. For every age, there is an ideal choral genre that will suit your taste and skill. From children's choirs to show choir, barbershop to symphonic choir, church or synagogue, glee club to senior citizens choir, an appropriate ensemble awaits your participation.

Discussion Questions

1. Define the following terms: soprano, alto, tenor, and bass.
2. What does the term "bel canto" mean? Why is "legato" singing an important goal and how is it achieved?
3. Why are unison singing and canon singing useful skills for singers? How is canon singing different from part singing? From solo singing?
4. What are the elements that need to be marked in a vocal score?
5. How does score marking assist singers? Teachers? Conductors?

Resources for Further Reading

Meredith, V. (2007). *Sing better as you age: A comprehensive guide for adult choral singers.* Santa Barbara Music.

Olson, M. (2010). *The solo singer in the choral setting: A handbook for achieving vocal health*. The Scarecrow Press.

Smith, B., & Sataloff, R. (2012). *Choral pedagogy and the older singer*. Plural Publishing.

Smith, B., & Sataloff, R. (2013). *Choral pedagogy* (3rd ed.). Plural Publishing.

Reference

Ehmann, W. (1968). *Choral directing* (p. 152) (G. Wiebe, Trans.). Augsburg Publishing House.

7
Skills for Mastering Repertoire

Brenda Smith and Ronald Burrichter

How do you master a new song or aria? In this chapter, you will find detailed information about planning warm-ups and cool-downs and learning songs or arias. We also suggest best practices for practicing, memorizing, and performing repertoire with confidence. The chapter includes an overview of vocal repertoire from folk song to art song and arias as well as a listing of resources for further study.

Warm-Ups and Voice Building

You "build" the vocal instrument each day by establishing the basics of singing. Our voices, bodies, minds, and spirits are tossed about throughout the day in "non-singer-friendly" ways. Each of us needs to release physical tensions, ground our posture, and engage our breath if we wish to use our voices in a healthy way. Class Voice warm-ups introduce different ways to prepare for your singing day. Select the most effective exercises to incorporate into your own daily practice.

Relaxation and Posture

Each warm-up period begins with initiatives to release tension and establish a "singer's posture" in which your weight is balanced and your body is tall and buoyant. Organize the relaxation portion of your warm-up to fit the level of tightness and the degree of mental stress you feel. Relaxation involves centering your mind, releasing physical tensions, and calming your spirit. A tall, erect posture places your vocal instrument in the optimum position for efficient breath use and phonation. In class, once a singer's posture has been introduced and perfected by everyone, a verbal reminder should be sufficient. For more information, review the explanations and examples in Chapter 1.

Breathing and Resonance

In the following text you will find plans that create a basic structure for connecting breath to tone. Remember that no set of notes will "warm up" a voice. Your understanding of the rationale and your mindful delivery determine the worth of any pattern. The five-step plan described in the following sections is a systematic plan for arriving at beautiful tone production. There are four sample exercise routines at the end of this section. Let's begin by addressing each step separately.

Step 1

Warm-ups for singing are intended to move the vocal instrument from its speaking posture to the singing one. We speak in a narrow range of notes. Singing necessitates access to notes above and below the speaking range. *Step 1* (Exercise I) unites your breath with notes above and below the speaking voice, providing ease of onset. Figure 7–1 is one example.

Begin with gentle glides and slides from slightly above the speaking voice to the midrange of the voice using lip trills, chewing while humming, trilling with tongue between lips (known as "raspberries"), or phonating through a straw. Such exercises, useful in both warm-up and cool-down procedures, are known as "semi-occulted vocal tract" (SOVT) exercises. "Semi-occulted" refers to the partial closing of the mouth during phonation. SOVT exercises connect air to tone without jaw tension. Straw phonation, a very popular and effective tool in vocal pedagogy, is another semi-occulted vocal tract (SOVT) exercise along with nasal consonants ([m], [n], and [ŋ]) and fricative consonants ([v], [z]). "Due to the growing body of research demonstrating improvement in vocal efficiency, SOVT exercises have become standard protocol in teaching singing" (Ragan, 2020, p. 74). As you get to know your voice better, you will find specific SOVT procedures that suit you best. Besides their value as vocal technical tools, SOVT exercises have many therapeutic applications, too.

Note: If the lip trill is difficult to access at first, try placing your fingers on either side of your lips to create a slight pucker. This might free your facial muscles. You might also try lip trilling without pitch. The sound resembles a horse's bray. When you sense that the breath is connected, allow a pitch to enter the flowing lip trill. Notice the gentle onset of your voice. With practice, lip trills will become second nature.

Step 2

The basic "pure" Italian vowels facilitate ring and resonance in your voice. *Step 2* (Exercise II) will remind you of the difference between spoken vowels and sung vowels (Figure 7–2). Wiggle your jaw and tongue as you sing a series of Italian "pure" vowels on one pitch. Let your breath be steady and energetic. Do you sense that some vowels are naturally more resonant or free than others? Take note of the most resonant and free ones. Let them be your guides. As you repeat the pattern at higher

Exercise I.

Lip trill
Chewing hum

Figure 7–1. Sample warm-up sheet I, exercise I. All exercises should be transposed up and down as needed.

and lower pitch levels, make the necessary adjustments until you feel that all the vowels "live" in the same place with your tongue and jaw completely relaxed. Use *messa di voce* to assist you in finding exactly the right amount of breath engagement.

Step 3

Step 3 (Exercise III) helps you connect breath energy with more pitches over a larger range (Figure 7–3). Do not carry weight from the first note to the second but allow the voice to glide on the breath. Tune carefully as you descend to the tonic pitch. Any exercise pattern that incorporates a slide (or slur) will help you connect your breath energy to your sound.

Step 4

Step 4 (Exercise IV) contains extended scale patterns (Figure 7–4). Note that the patterns

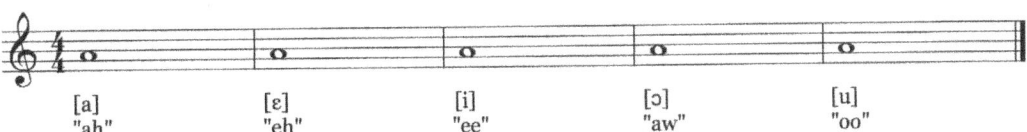

Figure 7–2. Sample warm-up sheet I, exercise II. All exercises should be transposed up and down as needed.

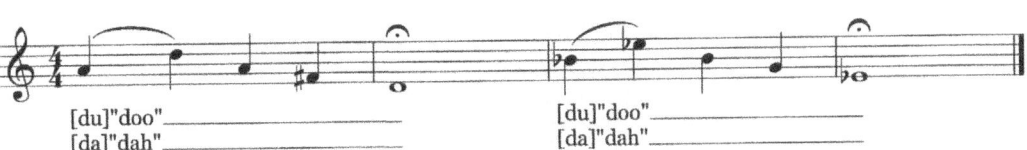

Figure 7–3. Sample warm-up sheet I, exercise III. All exercises should be transposed up and down as needed.

Figure 7–4. Sample warm-up sheet I, exercise IV. All exercises should be transposed up and down as needed.

for step 4 use a voiceless consonant before a combination of the vowels [i] and [a]. The voiceless consonant is intended to invite breath engagement. In the example, you would extend the [f] until you feel breath connection before moving to the vowels. Why the vowels [i] and [a]? The [a] vowel always needs the focus so easily achieved by [i], while [i] benefits from the warmth of the [a]. When paired together, they act as helpers to one another. Match the two vowels as you move between them. Notice that step 4 patterns repeat or elongate the highest note, allowing you opportunities to adjust tone and air. As you practice, you will build skills and develop confidence. Balance your breath energy until you produce a ringing, vibrant tone. A long scale is a good fourth step to expand the range of your vocal control.

Step 5

Step 5 (Exercise V) is the "skill teaching" exercise, be it staccato, agility, or some other vocal challenge (Figure 7–5). This step helps you train the skill(s) that you need for the repertoire you will be singing in your practice time or classwork.

(The following four exercise sheets [Figures 7–6 through 7–9] indicate in the International Phonetic Alphabet [IPA] which vowel sounds to use. For students who are less familiar with IPA, a colloquial equivalent is given.)

Voice class warm-ups demonstrate an orderly way to eliminate any physical cramp or mental strain, align your body, access your breathing mechanism, and connect your breath and voice. The design of a vocal warm-up is very intentional, giving you the foundation for a beautiful, healthy vocal tone. Each warm-up procedure teaches you one way to prepare for singing. At the end of the course, you will have accumulated numerous exercises for your use as a singer, teacher, or choral conductor.

Cool-Downs

Plan to include a brief cool-down regimen as a conclusion of your music making. Warm-ups prepared your voice to sing. Cool-downs bring your voice back to its speaking posture (Figure 7–10, see p. 83). "In a recent study, singers' subjective data clearly indicated a perceived sense of vocal well-being in both their singing *and* speaking voices after utilizing a vocal cool-down protocol" (Ragan, 2020, p. 166).

Sigh through your range on a lip trill, chewing hum, or "raspberry" or use any of the SOTV exercises described previously. Transpose your chosen pattern by half step

Exercise V.

Figure 7–5. Sample warm-up sheet I, exercise V. All exercises should be transposed up and down as needed.

Exercise I.

Exercise II.

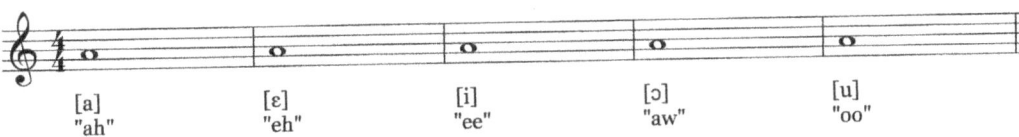

Exercise III.

Exercise IV.

Exercise V.

Figure 7–6. Sample warm-up sheet I, exercises I to V. All exercises should be transposed up and down as needed.

(semitone) until you have arrived at your normal speaking range. Chant a few words on pitch to be sure your voice feels released and ready for speech. Cool-downs do not need to be as extensive in length as warm-ups but should not be neglected.

Exercise I.

Exercise II.

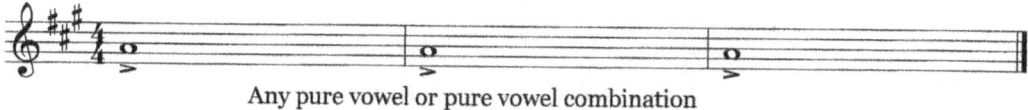

Exercise III.

Exercise IV.

Exercise V.

Figure 7–7. Sample warm-up sheet II, exercises I to V. All exercises should be transposed up and down as needed.

Exercise I.

Lip trill
Chewing hum
Single vowel
Alternate between [u] "oo" and [i] "ee"

Exercise II.

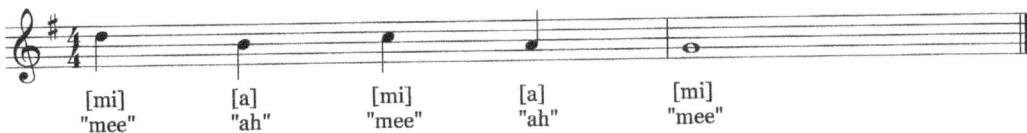

Exercise III.

Once on solfege syllables
Repeat on [du] "doo", [da] "dah", or [di] "dee"

Exercise IV.

Messa di voce

Use any pure vowel combination

Exercise V.

Figure 7–8. Sample warm-up sheet III exercises I to V. All exercises should be transposed up and down as needed.

Exercise I.

Exercise II.

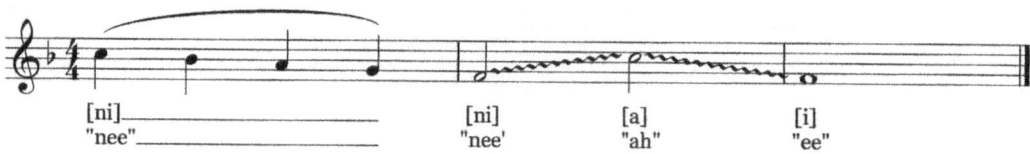

Exercise III.

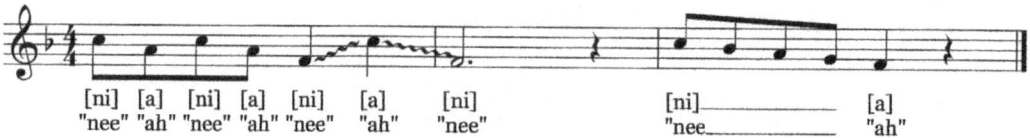

Exercise IV.

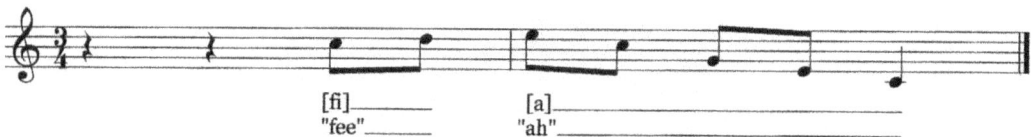

Exercise V.

Figure 7–9. Sample warm-up sheet IV, exercises I to V. All exercises should be transposed up and down as needed.

Cool-Down Example I.

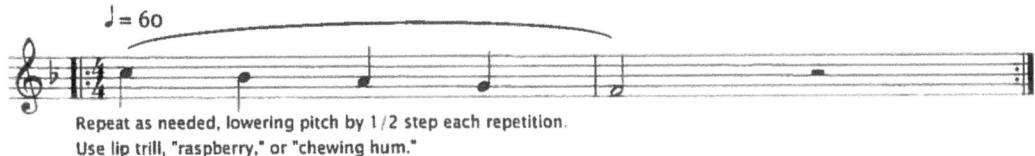

Repeat as needed, lowering pitch by 1/2 step each repetition.
Use lip trill, "raspberry," or "chewing hum."
Inhale through the nose on each rest.

Cool-Down Example II.

Repeat 3 times smoothly on "ah," descending by 1/2 step each repetition.
Breathe through the nose on rests.

Cool-Down Example III.

Repeat 3 times, lowering the pitch 1/2 step with each repetition. Inhale through the nose on each rest.

Cool-Down Example IV.

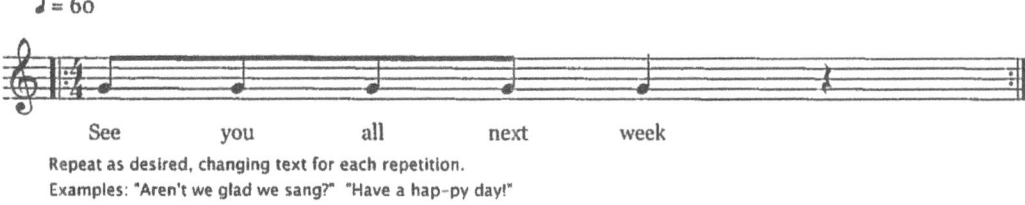

Repeat as desired, changing text for each repetition.
Examples: "Aren't we glad we sang?" "Have a hap-py day!"
Make your own!!

Figure 7–10. Cool-down examples I to IV.

In voice class, you will become familiar with best practices for preparing your voice and repertoire. Make room in your daily schedule for a short regimen of vocal warm-ups in the morning and cool-downs after each singing activity. Search for voice practice time among the other important tasks on your daily schedule.

Solving Vocal Problems in Repertoire

Vocal exercise patterns generally outline triads, arpeggios, and scale passages. Warm-up sessions train flexibility, tone quality, vowel consistency, and even registration. When you sing vocal repertoire, the challenges are much different. Melodic material is not necessarily scalelike or triadic. You may find certain rhythms, phrase lengths, or text underlay to present vocal obstacles. Identify the difficulties inherent in a passage and equip yourself with the skills required to succeed.

What musical shapes create vocal obstacles? Repeated notes, descending intervals or phrases, chromatic passages, and leaps of more than a third typically require vocal technical strategies. Find passages that present these shapes. Simplify the passages and create exercises to incorporate in your warm-up routine. Once the song is performance ready, the skills you learned are also reliable tools for future use.

Repertoire Learning Skills

Why is it wise to develop a method for score study and song preparation? The vocal instrument distinguishes itself from all human-made instruments because the voice is guided by neurological signals. You have probably had the experience of learning a song "by ear." You may have listened to it passively while riding in a car or watching a movie. Though you may have mastered the text and melody, you may not have addressed the song's vocal technical issues. For the voice to work efficiently, the details of music and text must be learned mindfully. You must "train" your mind to guide your voice and body.

We begin with the mechanics of score preparation. Text is what sets vocal repertoire apart from all other musical genres. We will investigate ways to understand and pronounce the text in its musical setting. Because learning music requires practice, we explore strategies for practicing vocal music. An orderly method of learning to sing a song or aria is the best way to prevent performance anxiety. If you know your song or aria completely and you know how you came to know it, there is little to fear about presenting it for the enjoyment of others.

Let's move to the practical side of learning a song or aria. If you are a choral conductor, this information will be significant to you as you plan rehearsals and train your choirs.

Learning a Song: Step 1 Is the Text

Concert attendance brings a sense of appreciation for beauty and artistry to the average concert attendee. One expects to hear the beautiful and soaring sounds of the strings supported by the other orchestral instruments when one attends an orchestra concert. The merging of the many instrumental timbres of the symphonic band are the aural treat experienced when one attends the band concert. What does the concertgoer expect when attending the choir concert or song recital that is unique to the world of singing? Text!

While the orchestra or band might paint a tone poem, the listener has no expectation regarding the delivery of intelligible words. Those attending a choral concert or voice recital will surely leave disappointed if they have not been able to understand the words that were sung, even if the text is in a language that they do not speak themselves. The famed choral and orchestral conductor Robert Shaw often explained to choristers that it was not their responsibility to interpret text for the listener. He believed that the choir should present the words with such clarity that the listener could decide the meaning of the text personally. This concept mandates that singers enunciate the text clearly, produce vowel sounds precisely, and punctuate carefully within the composition's rhythmic context. In so doing, they allow the text to be embraced by the music as prescribed by the composer.

A song composition is the result of an encounter between a composer and the words of a poet or lyricist. The impetus for a song is a text. A composer engages with the thoughts and emotions depicted by the poet or lyricist. The phrases of the text have musical elements within them. Lyric poetry has meter and rhythm as well as a certain lilt or melody. The composer reads and recites the poem or lyrics enough times to grasp its shape and content. Melody punctuated by the poem's rhythm begins to emerge within a harmonic context.

Because an opera or *oratorio* is based upon a "libretto" or script, its music must suit the character and voice part assigned to each role. (An oratorio is a sacred drama that is presented in concert version without stage movement. You are probably familiar with Handel's *Messiah*. It is an oratorio, a work in operatic form that deals with a religious topic.) Generally, *operettas* (small operas) and musical theater derive from a more collaborative process. Working as a team, the lyricist and the composer often create text and music simultaneously. The operetta team Gilbert & Sullivan and the musical theater team Rodgers & Hammerstein are well-known examples.

As you prepare a new score, take note of the compositional process. Study the relationship between the poet, librettist, or lyricist and the composer. You may find clues that help you answer your musical or interpretative questions. Each revelation will build your confidence as you approach your performance of the work.

Word Mastery

What, then, is the core of text delivery? Vowels framed by consonants carry the message of any language and the majesty of the human voice. As a student of singing, you and your teacher will strive to find the vowel sound that allows the beauty of your voice to emerge. It is a constant quest. Unless you are singing a text written in a dialect, it is essential that you avoid regional "street language" pronunciation. To preserve the clarity of text and promote beautiful tone, sing as long as possible on the principal vowel of any diphthong and delay its "vanish" or "glide." Singers frequently find that focusing on the purity and color of the vowel they are singing is of more help to them than attempting to deal with their vocal or vowel "placement." (Placement is a vague term that confuses many singers.)

Avoid the "quick fix" of aligning syllables with notes and calling it song. Involve yourself deeply in the preparation of your music. The following suggestions are offered to assist you in preparing a song:

- Type out the text of the song as if you were typing a letter. Print it. Do not type passages repeated in the music. Study the sentence structure in its prose form. Read it aloud as you would a letter or the lines of a play rather than in column form (as in a poetry book).

- Create a phonetic transcription of the text using the International Phonetic Alphabet (IPA) symbols. It does not matter whether the text is in English or in another language. It is important to choose the best vowel and match it to its rhyming partner(s) in the poem. Do this task mindfully. The act of "rhyming" ensures perfect tuning. Identify the rhyme scheme by following down the right side of the text. Be sure to use the same vowel symbols for words that rhyme.
- Be certain to look up the definition of any words you do not know, including musical terms (frequently in Italian). If the song is in a language other than your own, leave enough space between lines to allow for a word-by-word translation. Do NOT trust the poetic "singable" translations that would allow you to sing a foreign language song in English. Many editions offer a poetic translation of the song for study purposes. This poetic translation, while helpful, does not replace the need for a word-by-word translation that gives you the exact meaning of every word sung.
- Read the text aloud until it flows naturally. Observe the punctuation. Avoid allowing your voice to drop in pitch at the end of sentences. When preparing a song in a language you have not mastered, read it aloud until the words are completely familiar and easy to say properly.
- Express the meaning of the text in your own words. Think what the words mean, then put them into your own vocabulary, into "singer speak" phrases or normal conversational language.
- When completely fluid with the spoken text, read the words in the rhythm of the music. (Always observe the punctuation.) After feeling the flow of the text on the rhythmic pulse, add the text to the melody. As you merge the text and melody, be patient. Go slowly. Avoid practicing mistakes that will be difficult to correct later.
- Look carefully at the words and use the vowels to "vowel sing" the song. ("Vowel sing" means sing it on the vowels of the words only, without consonants.) This will build your awareness of the pure vowel needed for good singing. It also strengthens your ability to sing a legato line.
- Transform your legato singing into an intelligible, lyric expression of text by adding the consonants efficiently.
- Celebrate your accomplishment!

Understanding Vowels

What sounds carry the singing voice? Vowels! Singers, voice teachers, and choral conductors must communicate clearly about vowels. Vowel sounds can be challenging to discuss using words. Words fail us when we attempt to define or modify the sounds we hear. It is possible to inspect a trumpet or a clarinet. Fingerings and embouchure formation can be observed and discussed. The voice, answering only to the brain and hidden within the body, is more mysterious and difficult to quantify. The result is often the use of terms that leave the singer without specific direction or even confusion.

Perhaps you have been told to sing a "taller vowel" or a "more vertical vowel" that might improve tone quality or resonance. How "tall" or "vertical" should a vowel be, you ask? As you experiment to find the answer, it is likely you will increase pressure on the back of your tongue but not achieve a better vocal sound. Try instead to associate a word with the desired vowel sound. (Be careful to choose a word that is relatively free from local dialect or color.) Using common words to demonstrate a desired vowel sound is an approach that fosters clear communication between student and teacher, singer and vocal coach, or chorister and choral conductor.

The following is a set of examples:

- [ɑ] as in October, octopus, Oscar
- [ɛ] as in Eskimo, feather, pledge
- [i] as in evil, please, speak
- [ɔ] as in awkward, awesome, claw
- [o:ʊ] as in dope, open, pole
- [u] as in cool, food, moon

Use these guiding words as specific, ready tools. They are easily understood and readily achieve clear agreement regarding the appropriate vowel sound to sing. If necessary, say the word in a sentence to confirm it. Think carefully about the vowel to be sung, the length of time you sing it in the rhythmic context of the song, and where you release it. Terminology such as "vertical, tall vowel"; "forward"; and "not so far back" is vague and bewildering, while [i] as in "please" is clear and useful.

Materials for Score Preparation

It has been said that a dull pencil is better than a sharp mind. When you address a new song or aria, grab a writing tool to record every facet of your preparation. Let the score remind you of what you have learned and what you intend to do. You may prefer to scribble on an iPad screen or take painstaking notes on paper. Do what is convenient for you. Most importantly, realize how active your mind must be for your vocal instrument to work well. Write down small but essential details such as breath marks, pronunciation symbols, and word-by-word translations where you can see them readily. This method relieves stress and ensures good results.

Because text is the essence of song, begin by writing in the symbols from the International Phonetic Alphabet (IPA) into your score. Highlight the *time signature*, noting any *meter* changes within the song or aria. Note all dynamic marks and any articulation indications such as *staccato*, *tenuto*, or accents. If you find a *fermata*, note the poetic punctuation under it. In vocal music, a *fermata* generally, but not always, implies a breath after the conclusion of the word. Remember that a *fermata* indicates a note value that is longer than the written one. In most choral contexts, a *fermata* implies a doubling of the note value. Be sure to mark the poetic punctuation and your breath marks. Compare your breath marks with the phrase marks of the music. Compromises between poetry, music, and breathing are, at times, inevitable.

Establishing the Context for a New Song

Learning a new song can be a daunting task. Once you understand the text and its musical setting, strive to learn more about its context. As a performer, you are the vessel through whom the poet, librettist, or lyricist, and composer speak to the audience. If you gather information about the creative team behind the song/aria and the style period in which they worked, you will equip yourself to be their outstanding, confident representative.

How should you go about researching a song? The following is one example of what to look for and how to compile what you learn. Use this example to design your own method. Then, follow the maxim, "Plan your work and work your plan."

- Research the composer and the poet.
    - When did the composer live?
    - What was the musical period of the composer's life?
    - Were there factors in the composer's life that influenced their musical ideas?
    - What instruments would have accompanied this song?
    - Did the composer write other songs?
    - Did the composer write in other genres?
    - What was the composer's most significant composition?

Similar questions should be answered about the poet, although some poets may be more difficult to research due to the quantity and importance of their output. (To assist you in your research, you will find standard reference materials listed at the end of this chapter.)

Collect the information you gather for ready reference in the future and file them away for use in the preparation of program notes for concerts. Preserve materials you gather from attending performances. Most concert programs include notes that guide the audience to specific details of the music and text. This information can be useful to you in future voice study and program building. The following is a sample fact sheet that you might adapt to suit your needs.

Sample Fact Sheet for Vocal Repertoire

FACT SHEET FOR VOCAL REPERTOIRE

NAME _____

Title of song or aria _____

Composer name and dates _____

Poet name and date (if known) _____

Historical style period of music _____

Did the composer compose in other genres? Yes No

   If yes, which genres?

For what is the composer best known?

Is there a personal connection between the composer and the poet?

Is the occasion for the work known? Yes No

   If yes, what was it?

In the space below, summarize the meaning of the poem in one sentence.

What is the most important single phrase of the poetry, in your opinion?

Listen to at least two recordings of your selection.

List below performer and accompanist.
Indicate which was the most meaningful to you and why.

1. Performer _____ Accompanist _____

2. Performer _____ Accompanist _____

3. Performer _____ Accompanist _____

The performance that was most meaningful was _____ because:

In the space below, cite your sources for future reference.

Musical Preparation

What is the best way to learn a new song? Divide and conquer the musical tasks. Here is an example:

- Learn the notes without rhythm and, then, address the rhythm without notes.
- Combine the two tasks by count-singing the notes and rhythm. Abide by the breath marks you indicated in your preparation of the text.
- Sing the musical phrases on one vowel instead of the text, being careful to sing accurate notes and rhythms. (To avoid boredom, select a different vowel for each new phrase.) Be careful to breathe as planned, beginning with gentle inhalation and concluding each phrase with a thorough exhalation of any unused air.
- Recite the poem as "elevated speech" with an acute ear to the rhyming vowels.
- Confirm what vowel works best vocally as well as phonetically.
- Extract the vowels of the words and chant them phrase by phrase.
- Sing each phrase on the vowels only. Be intentional about the vowel and its function in the poetic word.
- Add the consonants efficiently and precisely.

You have now established a vocal foundation for the singing of the text. Avoid any jaw or tongue tension as you sing from vowel to vowel. Slowly increase the tempo to match your skills. Agile passages work best if they are learned deliberately. The tempo advances easily when the music is well learned.

Practice Strategies

Practicing is one of the most complicated of skills for singers. Because singers do not hear their voices as their listeners do, a singer cannot rely upon aural feedback in a practice room. Singers, when they practice, strive to replicate the "sensations" of resonance experienced in the most recent lesson or rehearsal, not the "sounds." Keeping a practice log has proven its worth. The practice log begins with the goals and practices determined by the teacher and student during a voice lesson. The practice log can be used to pace the student's vocal and musical progress until the next lesson. Provided are three templates of sample practice logs for your consideration.

Sample Practice Logs

Sample One

WEEKLY PRACTICE/LISTENING LOG

Name: _____ Week of _____

Day One: Time of Practice Sessions _____ _____
          Location   _____ _____

Repertoire Addressed:

Goals Met: 1.
            2.
            3.

Goals for Next Practice Session:

Day Two: Time/Location of Practice Sessions _____

Repertoire Addressed:

Goals Met: 1.
            2.
            3.

Goals for Next Practice Session:

Day Three: Time/Location of Practice Sessions _____

Repertoire Addressed:

Goals Met: 1.
            2.
            3.

Goals for Next Practice Session:

Day Four: Time/Location of Practice Sessions _____
Repertoire Addressed:

Goals Met: 1.
             2.
             3.
Goals for Next Practice Session:

Day Five: Time/Location of Practice Sessions _____
Repertoire Addressed:

Goals Met: 1.
             2.
             3.
Goals for Next Practice Session:

Day Six: Time/Location of Practice Sessions _____
Repertoire Addressed:

Goals Met: 1.
             2.
             3.
Goals for Next Practice Session:

Coaching Session: Date _____
Goals Set and Met: 1.
                    2.
                    3.

Weekly Evaluation of Preparation

Repertoire for Lesson: 1.

                               2.

                               3.

                               4.

Good News and Questions for Lesson:

Listening: Work _____   Performer _____

Comments:

Sample Two

PRACTICE PLAN

Name _____ Week _____

Day   Time   Place   Exercises   Repertoire

Monday

Tuesday

Wednesday

Thursday

Friday

Saturday/Sunday

Report on Rehearsal With Collaborative Pianist/Coach

Questions and Comments:

Sample Three

WEEKLY PRACTICE/LISTENING LOG

Name _____ Week of _____

DAY ONE:

Where and when did I practice?

Which selections and texts from the weekly plan did I address in my practice time(s)?

What goals did I set for my practice?

1.   2.   3.

What were the results of my practice(s) today?

What are my objectives and plans for my next practice session?

DAY TWO:

Where and when did I practice?

Which selections and texts from the weekly plan did I address in my practice time(s)?

What goals did I set for my practice?

1.   2.   3.

What were the results of my practice(s) today?

What are my objectives and plans for my next practice session?

DAY THREE:

Where and when did I practice?

Which selections and texts from the weekly plan did I address in my practice time(s)?

What goals did I set for my practice?

1.   2.   3.

What were the results of my practice(s) today?

What are my objectives and plans for my next practice session?

DAY FOUR:

Where and when did I practice?

Which selections and texts from the weekly plan did I address in my practice time(s)?

What goals did I set for my practice?

1.   2.   3.

What were the results of my practice(s) today?

What are my objectives and plans for my next practice session?

DAY FIVE:

Where and when did I practice?

Which selections and texts from the weekly plan did I address in my practice time(s)?

What goals did I set for my practice?

1.   2.   3.

What were the results of my practice(s) today?

What are my objectives and plans for my next practice session?

DAY SIX:

Where and when did I practice?

Which selections and texts from the weekly plan did I address in my practice time(s)?

What goals did I set for my practice?

1.   2.   3.

What were the results of my practice(s) today?

What are my objectives and plans for my next practice session?

COACHING SESSION: Date _____ Time _____

What selections from the weekly plan did I choose to rehearse?

1.   2.   3.

What did I achieve?

What did I sing by memory at my coaching session?

What should I work on next time?

CHECKLIST FOR MY LESSON:

What selections from the weekly plan am I prepared to sing at my lesson?

- _____ Do I have my recording device ready?
- _____ Do I have the IPA transcription and word-by-word translations written in my scores?
- _____ Have I highlighted the breath, dynamic, and tempo markings in my scores?
- _____ Do I know what the words to my songs/arias mean?
- _____ Do I know the context for the songs/arias I am singing?
- _____ Have I investigated the composers? The poets?
- _____ Have I completed the fact sheet for the songs/arias I will sing?
- _____ To whom did I listen this week? Whose performance was my preference? Why?

What skills will I hope to accomplish in my lesson?

What questions do I have for my instructor?

Practice Styles

Learning to practice efficiently and effectively is essential to success in singing. Our voices tire easily. It is very important to achieve an understanding of practice goals and methods. No two people practice in the same way, or in the same place, or for the same length of time.

Here are a few tips:

When? Make practicing a regular part of your weekly schedule. You may choose to rest one day per week. Use the time to study your music and its component parts silently. Remember: Before rehearsals, lessons, or classes that require voice use, do not forget to warm up your voice and to cool it down afterward.

Where? Find a place free of distractions so that you can settle quickly into a practice routine. If windows in practice room doors allow the mind to wander, affix a piece of notebook paper to the window frame during the practice period. Turn off all cell phones and distracting devices. Let practice time be an escape from worldly thoughts—a private time between you, your voice, and your music.

What? Begin each session with a warm-up and end it with a cool-down. Singers use muscles throughout the body to produce and support tone. These muscles must be activated and stretched gently, then relaxed.

How? Warm-up periods include
- Relaxation
- Posture
- Breath
- Resonance

Cool-down periods include
- Sighing from upper range back to speaking range
- Release of any tension in extremities, throat, and head
- Thorough exhalation

Remember: No pattern of notes or series of vowels will help you with any vocal skill training unless you understand the purpose of the exercise. Be sure you thoroughly understand the *why* and the *how* of each exercise. Use the recording of your lesson or the notes from class to remind you of your achievements and objectives for the week. Decide before the practice session what you would like to accomplish on any given day. Also, keep in mind that not all practice activities must take place in a practice room. Rhythms, poetic translations, and phonetic readings can be accomplished anywhere, anytime.

- Practice repertoire from simple to complex in the attitude of "divide and conquer."
  - Approach difficult passages only when adequate preparation has been made.
  - When learning new repertoire, master all notes and rhythms with complete accuracy before adding text and interpretative ideas or nuance.
  - Speak the words in rhythm while playing the bass line.
- Begin early to seek strategies for memorization.
  - Note phrases that repeat, sequences, alliteration, and poetic logic.
- Make each step of your practice a preparation toward a confident, musical performance.
  - Stand tall.

- Breathe deeply.
- Concentrate.

The Role of Mindfulness and Joy in Practice

Keep in mind that the overall result of practice time is equal to your level of awareness. Memorize the sensations that correspond to beautiful tone, accurate tuning, proper pronunciation. In practice time, quality succeeds over quantity. At the conclusion of a practice session, evaluate your results. Ponder what has improved. Write down any questions or observations that you wish to remember. Make notes to remind yourself of the starting point for the next practice session. Do not expect perfection. Some singing days are better than others. It is often said that learning is not always linear. At the conclusion of a less productive session, sing through a favorite song or aria to give yourself a positive send-off. Reward yourself for work well done!

Most importantly, never lose your love of singing. Consistent, regular practicing will bring you skills needed for greater communication with your audiences, deeper understanding of the art form, and increased facility with your voice. Your love for singing grows incrementally with your skills for efficient, effective practicing.

Performance Anxiety and Musical Preparation

Have you experienced performance anxiety? If so, how would you characterize it? Is it a necessary evil? A motivating factor? A paralyzing force? "When a singer freezes or commits a blunder in a big performance moment, anxiety is either the root cause or the outcome" (Emmons & Thomas, 1998, p. 147). Call it performance anxiety or stage fright, an uncomfortable public performance is unpleasant. "Every performer, in order to be an outstanding and well-educated musician, must understand the basic facts about performance anxiety: what really causes it, how it affects the nervous system, and what techniques are most effective in managing it" (Cornett, 2019, p. 59).

How you practice and prepare for your performances really matters. Barry Green, author of *The Inner Game of Music*, has long advocated for slow learning and meticulous practice of solid techniques as a means of ensuring a productive presentation.

> The voice is a peculiarly troublesome instrument. It's stressful enough working for that perfect performance with any instrument, but the more I have learned about the singer's world, the clearer it has become to me that singers experience a whole *world* of vulnerability that pianists, percussionists, and other instrumentalists simply never have to face. (Green, 2003, p. 220)

Performing is an exciting experience but it should not be a fear-filled one. In her writings, Barbara Conable, a teacher of Alexander Technique and body mapping to singers, reports having observed musicians of many types suffering physical discomfort as well as mental anguish in performance. Conable describes a hierarchy of performance anxiety that begins with the slightly uneasy feelings called "butterflies" and moves to self-consciousness, emotional responses involving judgement, and ends with completely debilitating fright. Facing your fears and your physical or emotional responses to them is a first step toward finding strategies to alleviate unpleasant performance worries. Turning anxious feelings into productive ones can be done by changing your mindset and adjusting practice patterns. (For more information, see *What Every Singer Needs to Know About the Body, Fourth Edition* [Malde, Allen, & Zeller, 2020].)

Tips for Mindful Preparation

As you approach a new song, begin by preparing the score as described previously. Arrive at the practice room equipped with a practice plan that is organized from simple to complex. Celebrate each small success as you achieve each element. Allow plenty of time for learning the music and vocal demands of a song. When notes, rhythms, and texts are thoroughly familiar, memorize methodically. Note the rhyme scheme and textual meaning.

In preparation for a performance, create a subtext and integrate it into your practice and performance plans. What role does the introduction play? Visualize the scene and breathe into its landscape and pathos. Plan how you will build the drama of the song to its climax. Keep the poetic situation alive throughout the postlude.

Take advantage of a full-length mirror to watch yourself. Rehearse a mock performance of your song. Practice every element. If a video camera is available, record your mock performance. Begin by stepping away and walking on, if possible. Take a poised bow to your imaginary audience and then settle yourself into your singer's posture. Pause to collect your thoughts. You may wish to lower your head as you recall the song's form and innermost meaning. Practice assuming a smiling countenance. Lift your head and greet your audience with a positive, grateful expression.

Rehearse how you will indicate your readiness to your collaborative pianist. Will you turn your head and/or use a hand gesture? Are you more relaxed if your collaborative pianist "reads" your readiness from your demeanor? Imagine vividly the performing space, the lights, and the audience. Select certain phrases of your song that you will address to individual listeners. At the song's conclusion, greet the audience's imaginary applause and acknowledge your collaborative pianist's work. Relax and evaluate how your mock performance looked and sounded. To help you feel "in control" of your performance, develop a checklist for your evaluation. Here are a few performance aspects you might consider.

- Was your breathing steady and relaxed? If not, when was it tense and/or constricted?
- Did you remain buoyant in your posture?
- Did you feel tingling or tightness in your body? If so, when and/or where?
- Was your mouth dry or moist?
- Was the meaning of the text always in your mind? If not, what distracted you?
- What phrase/s did you perform best?
- What passages should you revisit?
- What would you change?

Acknowledge what you enjoyed about your performance. Devise constructive ways to intervene where negative results obtained. For subsequent performances, determine new ways of problem solving. The act of performing is a "dynamic" and everchanging circumstance. If you have a mindful, well-rehearsed performance plan, you will be less vulnerable to distractions.

Performing and Mental Toughness

Otolaryngologist Dr. Jean Abitbol states:

> Stage fright, this irrational fear that strikes one just before coming on stage, has many psychological causes. It can be brought on by simple superstition, by the fear that we won't be good enough or by any anxious anticipation, by an unfortunate cat-whistle at a previous performance, and so on. It can't exist in the absence of the public, even if the public is just one person. (Abitbol, 2016, p. 134)

Stage fright is real, but it is not inevitable. You have the power to manage your performance anxiety. It was Ralph Waldo Emerson who said that concentration is the secret to strength. Clearing the mind of unnecessary and unattractive thoughts helps every human being regain an equilibrium of spirit.

Many performers report journaling, meditation, and even self-hypnosis as a means of mitigating performance fears. Eastern practices such as yoga, *qigong*, or *t'ai chi ch'uan* might prove beneficial to you. Alexander Technique, the Feldenkrais Method, and Laban Movement Analysis are specifically designed to meet the stresses artistic performers face. There are many popular breathing routines like alternate nostril breathing or triangular or circular breathing that can slow the mind and center it. Mindfulness training is another method intended to help erase negativity and increase creative thinking. Find the method or practice that suits you best for situations on and off the stage.

Mental toughness derives from careful, incremental learning and repetition. Include small milestones in your learning plan and rejoice when you reach each one of them. Peak performing experiences do not occur by chance. They are built on layers of solid preparation. As you approach a performance, make it your mantra to say, "I know *what* I am about to present, and I know *how* I know it." This kind of mindful training will make outstanding performance experiences the reward for your hard work.

Physical Factors and Performance

Unlike any human-made instrument, the vocal instrument requires nourishment and rest. As you prepare for a balanced, productive performance, monitor your physical health. Much has been written about the benefits of a healthy diet, regular exercise, and consistent sleep for overall singer well-being. As a student, you may be required to perform in class during a busy academic week. Plan your work, your sleep, and your meals carefully. Water is a key ingredient to vocal ease. Hydrate, hydrate, hydrate! Limit caffeine and other stimulants. Increase nourishing food. Exercise moderately. Enjoy regular sleep and indulge in frequent naps. Heed the words attributed to the English Renaissance lutenist and singer John Dowland (1563–1626) in the song "Weep You No More, Sad Fountains": "Sleep is a reconciling, a rest that peace begets." Physical fitness, good dietary habits, and sufficient rest contribute to successful performing.

Singing and Sharing the Stage

W. Timothy Gallwey, author of *The Inner Game of Tennis* and related titles, noted:

"Since both sports and music are commonly performed in front of an audience, they also provide an opportunity for sharing the enjoyment of excellence as well as the experience of pressures, fears, and the excitement of ego involvement" (Green & Gallwey, 1987, p. 7). Singers rarely perform in a vacuum. They generally share the stage with a collaborative pianist, with other singers and/or instrumentalists, and maybe even a conductor. Allow the spirit of teamwork to increase your resolve and to build your confidence.

Conclusion

How you prepare for a performance has a great deal to do with how you, the performer, will experience it. Respect the texts and music you sing by preparing them carefully and practicing in an orderly way. There will always be something new and exciting for you to sing and share. Approach the stage with joyful anticipation.

Discussion Questions

1. Name the steps for learning a new song or aria. Why is it important to mark the score?
2. Why is it important to understand the context of a song or aria?
3. What is the purpose of a practice log? How will you design one for your use?
4. What elements make singing different from playing human-made instruments in performance?
5. What strategies will you use to enjoy your performances with minimal anxiety?

Resources for Further Reading

Practice Skills

Andrews, E. (2005). *Muscle management for musicians.* The Scarecrow Press.

Craig, D. (1993). *A performer prepares: A guide to song preparation for actors, singers, and dancers.* Applause Books.

Feindel, J. M. (2009). *The thought propels the sound.* Plural Publishing.

Helding, L. (2020). *The musician's mind: Teaching, learning, and performance in the age of brain science.* Rowman & Littlefield.

Klickstein, G. (2009). *The musician's way: A guide to practice, performance, and wellness.* Oxford University Press.

Sterner, T. (2012). *The practicing mind: Developing focus and discipline in your life.* New World Library.

Performance Anxiety

Caldwell, R. (1990). *The performer prepares.* Pst Inc.

Cornett, V. (2019). *The mindful musician: Mental skills for peak performance.* Oxford University Press.

Emmons, S., & Thomas, A. (1998). *Power performance for singers: Transcending the barriers.* Oxford University Press.

Green, B. (2003). *The mastery of music: Ten pathways to true artistry.* Broadway Books.

Green, B., & Gallwey, T. (1987). *The inner game of music: The classic guide to reaching a new level of musical performance.* Doubleday Pan Books.

Heirich, J. (2011). *Voice and the Alexander Technique: Active explorations for speaking and singing.* Mornum Time Press.

Malde, M., Allen, M. J., & Zeller, K. A. (2020). *What every singer needs to know about the body* (4th ed.). Plural Publishing.

McAllister, L. (2013). *The balanced musician: Integrating mind and body for peak performance.* The Scarecrow Press.

McGrath, C., Hendricks, K., & Smith, T. (2017). *Performance anxiety strategies: A musician's guide to managing stage fright*. Rowman & Littlefield.

Nelson, S., & Blades, E. (2018). *Singing with your whole self: A singer's guide to Feldenkrais awareness through movement* (2nd ed.). Rowman & Littlefield.

Ristad, E. (1982). *A soprano on her head: Right-side-up reflections on life and other performances*. Real People Press.

Sapolsky, R. (2004). *Why zebras don't get ulcers: The acclaimed guide to stress, stress-related diseases, and coping* (3rd ed.). Henry Holt and Company.

Solovitch, S. (2015). *Playing scared: A history and memoir of stage fright*. Bloomsbury.

References

Abitbol, J. (2016). *The power of the voice* (p. 134). Plural Publishing.

Conable, B. (2020). Appendix A: What to do about performance anxiety. In M. Malde, M. J. Allen, & K. Zeller (Eds.), *What every singer needs to know about the body* (4th ed., pp. 283–294). Plural Publishing.

Cornett, V. (2019). *The mindful musician: Mental skills for peak performance* (p. 59). Oxford University Press.

Emmons, S., & Thomas, A. (1998). *Power performance for singers: Transcending the barriers* (p. 147). Oxford University Press.

Green, B. (2003). *The mastery of music: Ten pathways to true artistry* (p. 220). Broadway Books.

Green, B., & Gallwey, T. W. (1987). *The inner game of music: The classic guide to reaching a new level of musical performance* (p. 7). Doubleday Pan Books.

Ragan, K. (2020). *A systematic approach to voice: The art of studio application* (p. 74, 166). Plural Publishing.

Ragan, K. (2020). A vocal cool-down for choral singers. In B. Winnie (Ed.), *The choral conductor's companion: 100 rehearsal techniques, imaginative ideas, quotes, and facts* (pp. 166–169). Meredith Music Publications.

8
Vocal Skills and Repertoire

Brenda Smith and Ronald Burrichter

What Singers Sing

Many successful professional singers in various genres attribute their vocal skill and longevity to "classical training." What does it mean to be "classically trained," you ask? What kind of music do students of classical music sing? The classical or "bel canto" learning objectives are to sing beautifully and deliver text intelligibly. With *bel canto* singing ideals as a vocal foundation, you can easily add the vocal skills required for other popular singing styles such as musical theater, jazz, and Contemporary Commercial Music (CCM). In the book *So You Want to Sing CCM (Commercial Contemporary Music): A Guide for Performers,* Robert Edwin wrote: "Breathing can and should be standardized throughout all styles" (Hoch, 2018, p. 126). No matter what you sing, the basics of classical singing will serve you well. The human voice functions best when the voice user is relaxed, well-positioned, and capable of a deep breath. The clear delivery of text is the expressive desire of every singer.

Learning repertoire in many historical styles and languages helps a student of singing increase vocal color and nuance. Musical styles and languages have their own sound ideals and manners of performance. The briefest exposure to classical vocal repertoire in English, Italian, German, and French broadens a singer's perspective on expressive possibilities.

Folk Songs

Who writes folk songs? Folk songs are conceived by the "folk" and passed from generation to generation by oral tradition. Folk songs are generally strophic in form and tend to relate a story, often concluding with a moral lesson. Through an acquaintance with folk songs, singers investigate other cultures and musical styles. Have you heard "O sole mio" sung by Luciano Pavarotti in the now legendary 1990 "Three Tenors" extravaganza from Rome, Italy? The song evokes the scenery and sentiment of the Neapolitan region of Italy. Similarly, each region of France has its own folk song tradition, reflecting local dialects and ways of living. Nationalism in 19th century Germany sparked interest in folklore and folk song. Johannes Brahms (1833–1897) arranged nearly 150 German folk songs for solo voice with piano. Ralph Vaughan Williams (1872–1958) is said to have collected more than 800 English and Scottish folk tunes. Benjamin Britten (1913–1976) also arranged folk melodies from the British Isles. Aaron Copland (1900–1990) gathered typical American folk melodies into two volumes entitled *Old American Songs*. By giving them a place in concert repertory, composers have preserved folk songs for posterity. Many folk songs are readily available in arrangements for solo voice and piano or choral ensembles.

Early Italian Songs and Arias

Selected Italian songs and arias from the 17th and 18th century are standard repertoire for beginning Classical singers. Why, you ask? Because early Italian songs and arias demonstrate the *bel canto* singing style in its purest form. Many of them were composed by singers and singing teachers. Based on the tenets set forth by the *Florentine Camerata*, the works are simple settings intended to elevate text through vocal and harmonic means. Unlike later operatic arias, the early arias were performed with a small instrumental ensemble. The melodies are generally limited in tonal and dramatic scope. The skills you learn by mastering one of them will be applicable to many other genres of vocal repertoire.

British and American Song

During the late Renaissance and early Baroque period, British vocal music was performed for the aristocracy as a kind of intellectual entertainment. The lute, a precursor of the guitar, was a favorite instrument used by singers to accompany themselves or others in strophic settings known as "lute songs." It is believed that the theatrical works of William Shakespeare included performances of songs and airs. Solo vocal repertoire can be found in the masques, oratorios, and early opera of 18th century England composed by Henry Purcell, George Frideric Handel, and their contemporaries. British art song composers in the 19th and 20th centuries drew upon many of the same poetic sources to create song repertoire. You will find many comparative settings of poetry by William Shakespeare, William Blake, A. E. Housman, and W. B. Yeats, among others.

The first "American" art song may have been written during Revolutionary War times by Francis Hopkinson (1737–1791). For many decades, British and European vocal styles dominated the American musical scene. As you study American art song, note the propensity for American composers to select poetic works by William Shakespeare, Christina Rossetti, and other English literary masters as the basis of their work.

Composers such as Aaron Copland, Leonard Bernstein, and Virgil Thomson traveled to France to study with Nadia Boulanger. Her influence is obvious in American art song repertoire of the mid to late 20th century.

German Lieder

In the early 19th century, the piano gained popularity as a fixture in the parlor of European homes. This development prompted the social practice of small, intimate gatherings for entertainment and friendly conversation. Composers set poetic texts to music as a means of sharing art and ideas. The German art song or *Lied* differs from a folk song because the Lied is based on a preexisting work of art, a poem.

Early 19th century Lieder was originally sung with piano before a small audience. Franz Schubert (1797–1828) is well-known for his "Schubertiades"—friendly get-togethers intended for the sharing of Lieder as points of departure for conversation. Illustrations from the time show Schubert at the piano surrounded by an enthusiastic group of friends engaged in reading texts and singing them. To Schubert, who composed more than 610 Lieder, the discussion of the text and the singing of it were of equal importance.

Composers including Franz Schubert, Robert Schumann (1810–1856), and Johannes Brahms (1833–1897) expanded the Lied form by grouping Lieder in a series known as a *Liederzyklus* or "song cycle." Originally, a song cycle was a set of songs meant to be performed consecutively. The texts of song cycles are frequently unified around a story line or single theme.

By midcentury, composers such as Hugo Wolf (1860–1903), Gustav Mahler (1860–1911), and Richard Strauss (1864–1949) orchestrated Lieder, bringing song repertoire to the public concert stage. Orchestrated Lieder present greater vocal technical challenges than those composed for piano accompaniment. (A few German Lieder are mentioned in this chapter for your consideration. A more extensive list is available in the online companion website to this textbook.)

French *Mélodie*

The earliest French art songs known as *mélodie* were also written for private audiences at social gatherings known as "salons." The *mélodie*, so named because of its characteristic flowing melodic lines, did not enjoy the same popularity as its German counterpart. The aesthetic life of the French aristocracy has always held the French language in high esteem. Theodore Zeldin wrote: "No foreigner should ever mock the French language, first because he does not understand it properly, and secondly because it has divine status in France" (Zeldin, 1996, p. 348). Though singing was appreciated, many saw little reason to interpret through music an already "melodic" spoken language. For that reason, there is less French vocal repertoire in total.

Early French art song followed the example of early German Lieder, adapting strophic texts to simple vocal settings. The French version of art song became more sophisticated through the contributions of Gabriel Fauré (1845–1924), Claude Debussy (1862–1918), and their contemporaries. Selecting texts of intellectual complexity, these composers designed cinematic accompaniments that give place for the singer's interpolation of the poetic text. The melodic line emulates the rhythm and range of spoken language. The independence of the vocal line from its harmonic context requires a thorough understanding of music and of vocal skill.

Should you choose to study a French art song or *mélodie,* remember the words of the American author and Francophile Edith Wharton (1862–1937) when she wrote:

> The artistic integrity of the French has led them to feel from the beginning that there is no difference in kind between the curve of a woman's hat-brim and the curve of a Rodin marble, or between the droop of an upholsterer's curtain and that of the branches along a great

avenue laid out by Le Nôtre. (Wharton, 1997, p. 39)

In other words, the melodic line undulates with elegance, potency, and grace like the wafting scent of a fine French perfume. (Examples of French vocal repertoire suggested for Class Voice are available in the online companion website to this textbook.)

Learning Vocal Skills Through Repertoire

Did you know that the selection of repertoire is crucial to your vocal success? Certain songs challenge us to develop specific vocal skills. Other songs offer us the opportunity to use or display them. Oddly enough, you may conquer a vocal problem by confronting it in a musical moment.

Vocal exercises dealing with vowel purity, tone quality, and/or agility are pathways to song. The union of text with melody in a harmonic context brings together your body, your mind, and your heart with your voice. You might say it is when "the rubber meets the road" for students of singing. Vocal repertoire has the capacity to evoke and fortify positive vocal habits. Text set to music touches human sensibilities and emotion, adding meaning to the music making.

In the following text you will find specific selections that have proven their worth in helping singing students address vocal technical obstacles. The listing is by no means exhaustive. The selections are age and size appropriate for beginning singers and adaptable for adult learners. Astute selection of repertoire will help you set intentional learning objectives and performance goals. Use the ideas to spark your creativity for Class Voice and for future singing experiences.

Suggested Vocal Repertoire and Lesson Plans for Class Voice Study

Class Voice helps you acquire fundamental skills for singing. In the following text you will find an explanation and a lesson plan for addressing each skill. Suggestions for vocal repertoire and comparative listening are included.

Breath Coordination and Gentle Onset

It could be said that singing begins when air meets intelligence. Singers coordinate breath energy with mental impulses determining pitch and vowel. In technical terms, this process is called "flow phonation." Many voice teachers use the term "singing on the breath" to mean that vocal fold vibration is governed by the flow of energized breath alone with no compensatory jaw or muscle tension. The result is a *gentle* onset of vocal sound. A hard attack or "glottal stop" puts your voice at risk of injury and is not aesthetically appealing. The achievement of a consistent gentle onset of sound requires practice. (This concept contrasts with the pressurized air required for the onset of wind instrument tone.)

By their nature and manner of performance, certain songs evoke a gentle onset of sound. Suggested songs in each category are provided in the following text.

Lullabies

Lullabies, songs that lull children to sleep, are a part of the folk tradition of most countries. A lullaby is an excellent vocal pedagogical tool for learning to breathe and sing gently and evenly.

8 ■ VOCAL SKILLS AND REPERTOIRE

> **LESSON PLAN FOR LEARNING A LULLABY**
>
> 1. Imagine a drowsy child resting peacefully in the presence of a trusted guardian.
> 2. Breathe deeply in a spirit of trust and calmness and exhale.
> 3. Inhale and sing the melody as a semi-occulted vocal tract (SOVT) exercise such as a lip trill or chewing hum.
> 4. Sing the melody on a single vowel such as "oo" [u].
> 5. Breathe thoroughly and calmly as you begin each phrase.
> 6. Continue to sing "on your breath" with a gentle onset as you sing the vowels of the words.
> 7. Add the consonants and allow your voice to flow easily and steadily.
> 8. Maintain a tall, buoyant posture and a consistent use of breath.

Sample Repertoire for Learning Lullabies

1. "All Through the Night" (Welsh folk song), also known as "Sleep My Child" and "Peace Attend Thee."
   Suggested listening: The song in its original Welsh ("Ar Hyd Y Nos") sung by baritone Bryn Terfel to glean a fresh perspective.
2. "Wiegenlied" by Johannes Brahms (1833–1897), best known in English as "Lullaby and Goodnight." The first verse derives from folk tradition and was published in *Des Knaben Wunderhorn* (*The Young Boy's Wonder Horn*)—a volume of folk poems collected by Achim von Arnim and Clemens Brentano.
   Suggested listening: "Wiegenlied" sung in German by Dutch soprano Elly Ameling. She regularly performed it as an encore concluding her art song recitals.
3. "Nana" (Spanish folk song) arranged by Manuel De Falla (1876–1946) and published in *Siete canciones populares* (*Seven Popular Songs*).
   Suggested listening: Compare the performances of mezzo sopranos Teresa Berganza and Marilyn Horne.

> Also recommended: "American Lullaby" by Gladys Rich, "Lullaby" by Cyril Scott, "Marias Wiegenlied" by Max Reger (available in German and English as "Maria's Lullaby"), "The Little Horses" by Aaron Copland, and "To a Little Child" by Clara Edwards.

For further understanding of the art form, listen to "Violin Lullabies" performed by violinist Rachel Barton Pine. The ease of the bow stroke is indicative of the gentle onset desired for singing.

Early Lute Songs

The lute song is one of the earliest forms of English song, dating from the 16th century. The lute is a plucked stringed instrument related to the mandolin and guitar. (For more information about lutes, visit http://www.lutesociety.org.) Because of it limited acoustical properties, the lute was used for music making in small, intimate social gatherings. Lute song singers generally accompanied themselves. Most lute songs are strophic in form and convey stories or commentary. Much like a lullaby, the singer is in command of the onset of each phrase.

> **LESSON PLAN FOR LEARNING TO SING LUTE SONG**
>
> 1. Prepare the musical score, marking breath opportunities and repeated passages.

2. Read the text of the first verse silently, noting the punctuation and musical pauses.
3. Assume a seated posture with your feet placed squarely in front of you and your back tall.
4. Imagine a lute lying in your lap with its long neck and fingerboard.
5. Elevate your left arm and hold the imaginary neck and fingerboard at the ready.
6. Exhale and take a deep, refreshing breath.
7. Sing the melody as an SOVT exercise such as a lip trill or chewing hum. Exhale, relax, and take a deep, refreshing breath.
8. Sing the melody on a single vowel such as "oo" [u]. Exhale and relax.
9. Breathe thoroughly and calmly as you begin each phrase.
10. Sing the phrases on the vowels of the words.
11. Continue to sing "on your breath" with a gentle onset.
12. Add the consonants, allowing your voice to flow steadily as you "tell" the story.

Sample Repertoire for Learning Lute Songs

1. "Come Again, Sweet Love" by lutenist/singer John Dowland (1563–1626)

    Notice how each phrase ends with a sense of pause for reflection. The pauses will help you with achieve an easy onset of sound for each subsequent phrase.

    Suggested listening: Listen to an online performance of this selection by countertenor Alfred Deller and/or soprano Barbara Bonney.

2. "Have You Seen but a White Lily Grow?" by Anonymous

    Note how the ascending melodic scale passage. The music "paints" the meaning of the word "grow." As the pitch rises, the voice grows in volume and energy.

    Investigate the performance of soprano Valeria Mignaco with lutenist Alonso Marin. It will help you comprehend the freedom of expression a lute song affords.

3. "The Silver Swan" by Orlando Gibbons (1583–1625)

    The sensitive nature of the subject matter induces a gentle approach to text and tone. The composer also set the song as a choral work.

    Suggested listening: Compare a performance of "The Silver Swan" sung by The Gesualdo Six with a solo performance. Also, listen to "The Silver Swan" composed by American composer Ned Rorem sung by soprano Leontyne Price.

> Also recommended: "Fain Would I Change That Note" by Tobias Hume; "Underneath a Cypress Tree" by Francis Pilkington; "Flow, My Tears," "Flow Not So Fast, Ye Fountains," or "Weep You No More, Sad Fountains" by John Dowland; "When to Her Lute Corinna Sings" by Thomas Campion; and "When Laura Smiles" by Philip Rosseter.

Note: Were you to select "Weep You No More, Sad Fountains" by John Dowland as a class or solo project, it would be valuable to compare it to the musical settings by Roger Quilter and Rebecca Clarke (solo and choral). The two later settings reflect the intimate manner of performance of the original lute song version.

Folk Songs

Folk songs are the responses of the "folk" to daily occurrences. Folk songs are often strophic in form because the texts relate stories of the human experience. Many are pensive in spirit, relating details of beautiful past events and lessons learned. Folk song singers find the guitar the perfect harmonic accompaniment. Comparable to the lute song, a folk song is sung with text sensitivity and ease, making it a useful teaching tool for breath and tone coordination.

> **LESSON PLAN FOR LEARNING TO SING A FOLK SONG OR ART SONG**
>
> 1. Read the text aloud with attention to the strophic form (verse with chorus).
> 2. Express the text as prose in your own words.
> 3. Recite the chorus at three different volume levels and tempi, varying your tone of voice with each repetition.
> 4. Assume a singer's posture, relax, and exhale.
> 5. Inhale and sing each phrase separately as a SOVT exercise such as a lip trill or chewing hum. Take time to exhale and relax between each phrase.
> 6. Sing each phrase on a single vowel such as "oo" [u] or "ah" [a]/[ɑ]. Exhale and relax.
> 7. Chant the words, elongating the vowel sounds and delivering the consonants crisply.
> 8. Sing the song on the vowels of the words, observing the rhythmic values accurately.
> 9. Sing the song on the words without accompaniment with a gentle onset to each phrase.
> 10. Sing the song with the accompaniment, preparing each breath in a timely manner.

Sample Repertoire for Learning Folk Songs

1. "O Waly Waly" arranged by Benjamin Britten (1913–1976)

    This folk song has been set by many composers, but Britten's is the most useful for the purpose of developing an easy onset of sound. The accompaniment imitates the rowing of oars and allows the singer much freedom to begin each phrase. The beautifully sad nature of the text and musical mood encourages a relaxed, sincere delivery of the text.

    Suggested listening: Compare performances by tenors Ian Bostridge and Peter Pears.

    Note that the performance by Peter Pears is accompanied by Benjamin Britten.

2. "The Lass from the Low Countree" by John Jacob Niles (1892–1980)

    Written "in the style of a folk song," the text and setting depict the social struggles of rural Appalachian American life. The singer tells a story with a serious moral lesson. The repetitive form offers opportunities to articulate the text nimbly and colorfully.

    Suggested listening: Compare performances by soprano Hope Koehler and the late contralto Maureen Forrester. Consider the contrasting approaches to the repeated, concluding phrases of each verse.

3. "In stiller Nacht" arranged by Johannes Brahms

    Brahms arranged many German folk songs for solo voice and for quartet or choir. "In stiller Nacht" ("In Still of Night") is a popular folk song readily available in German or English. With poignant text set to lush harmony, the song induces calm breathing and warm tone.

Suggested listening: Compare the solo performances of soprano Lucia Popp and mezzo soprano Christa Ludwig with the choral version performed by the Atlanta Master Chorale under the direction of Dr. Eric Nelson.

> Also recommended: "Black Is the Color of My True Love's Hair" arranged by John Jacob Niles, "Danny Boy" arranged by Fred Weatherly, "Long Time Ago" arranged by Aaron Copland, and "The Ash Grove" arranged by Benjamin Britten. Though not a folk song arrangement, "Linden Lea" by Ralph Vaughan Williams is a song in folk-style composed on poetry by William Barnes. "Linden Lea" would be another excellent choice.

Note: The volumes of *Old American Songs* arranged by Aaron Copland, *Folksong Arrangements* arranged by Benjamin Britten, and the folk song collections of Ralph Vaughan Williams provide additional resources.

Art Songs

Using tonality and musical gesture, art song composers strive to capture the inner spirit of the poem. Musical figures in the accompaniment evoke images of textual elements such as blossoms fluttering, water splashing, or moonlight glistening. Word accent and harmonic treatments trigger emotions in the singer as well as the listener. Art songs can be superb vehicles for positive vocal technical improvement.

Sample Repertoire for Learning Art Songs

1. "Drink to Me Only With Thine Eyes" attributed to Ben Jonson (1572–1637)

    Ben Jonson wrote two poems entitled "Song to Celia." (Please note that "Celia" is a common name for a female in pastoral poetry.) Jonson included them in a group of miscellaneous poems under the heading *The Forest*, published in 1616. The second "Song to Celia" is best known in English-speaking circles by its first line, "Drink to me only with thine eyes." The text was first set to music anonymously by an 18th century composer. Roger Quilter (1877–1953) immortalized the setting by including it in the *Arnold Book of Songs* he published in 1950. The impetus for the poet's opening request derives from the information gleaned in the second verse. Celia, upon recently receiving a bouquet (rosy wreath) of flowers, chose to breathe upon them and return them to the sender. She hoped that her presence would remain amid the blooming flowers as an encouragement to the sender.

    Suggested listening: Compare the performances of baritone Robert Merrill with those of bass Paul Robeson. To grasp the popularity of the song, investigate recorded versions sung by Aretha Franklin and by Johnny Cash.

2. "O Fair to See" by Gerald Finzi (1901–1956)

    An excerpt from Christina Rossetti's collection entitled *Sing-Song: A Nursery Rhyme Book* (1872), "O Fair to See" is a text imbued with a reverence for the beauties of nature. In its tonality and phrase shapes, Gerald Finzi's musical setting (Opus 13, No. 2) depicts the words with a sense of wonder. The music and mood encourage a tenderly timed delivery of the text.

Suggested listening: Listen to the performance of tenor John Mark Ainsley accompanied by Iain Burnside. Note the gentle onset of sound that begins each phrase and the intensity of textual expression.

3. "Hands, Eyes, Heart" by Ralph Vaughan Williams (1872–1958)

    The words of this song were written by Ursula Vaughan Williams, wife of the composer, and exude devotion to the beloved. Set in a medium vocal range, the song provides a singer with ample time to breathe and express each phrase with assurance.

    Suggested listening: Compare performances of soprano Ruth Golden accompanied by Levering Rothfuss as well as mezzo soprano Glenda Maurice, accompanied by Graham Johnson. Notice how their vocal delivery emulates assurance and ease.

> Also recommended: "Come Ready and See Me" by Richard Hundley, "Orpheus with His Lute" by William Schuman, "Out of the Morning" by Vincent Persichetti, and "When I Have Sung My Songs to You" by Ernest Charles.

Note: Should you select "Out of the Morning" by Vincent Persichetti, you might wish to compare the settings by Richard Hundley or Ricky Ian Gordon, both of which use the first line of the Emily Dickinson text "Will there really be a morning?" as the title.

Legato and Phrasing

Legato singing, the imperceptible melding of vowel and pitch, is essential to bel canto singing style. The *Florentine Camerata*, the influential group of artists and philosophers who invented opera in 1584, advocated for the "elevation" of the voice as a means of sensitive, dramatic text delivery. Begin your study of legato technique with an Italian song designed to feature flowing melody.

> **LESSON PLAN FOR LEGATO AND PHRASING**
>
> 1. Create simple warm-up patterns using an Italian "pure" vowel ([a], [ɛ], [i], [ɔ], or [u]).
> 2. Speak and then sing the vowels of the text for the first phrase on a steady stream of air. Exhale and relax.
> 3. Repeat and intensify your breath energy by engaging you core muscles.
>   a. Imagine you are pulling a boat to shore. Use a hand-over-hand gentle motion at waist height. Extend arms fully in front of you and keep your elbows away from your body.
>   b. Under your instructor's guidance, use an exercise band of light resistance to help you engage your breath energy as you sing. (The band can be affixed to an object such as a table or piano leg. Your instructor will demonstrate for you how to tug gently on the band without compromising posture or developing bodily tension.)
> 4. Exhale at the end of each phrase and relax.
> 5. Using hand gestures, guide the phrases with gestures that follow the contours of the phrases.

6. Read the text silently as you add the consonants with crispness and efficiency.
7. As an exercise, chant each phrase, one at a time, on a single pitch of medium range. Exhale and breathe between each repetition.
8. Sing each melodic phrase with the text *a cappella*. Exhale fully after each phrase.
9. Sing the phrases with the bass line of the accompaniment only. (Be sure to maintain rhythmic and tuning accuracy.)
10. Sing the phrases with full accompaniment and expression.

Sample Repertoire for Learning Legato and Phrasing

1. "Amarilli, mia bella" by Giulio Caccini (1546–1618)

   A member of the *Florentine Camerata*, Giulio Caccini was a composer, singer, and voice teacher. There is no better way to understand the legato ideal than to sing an aria written to demonstrate the skill. Notice how the music follows the word accent of the language. The poet is pleading his case with a doubting lover, taking time and care to be convincing and steady. The character of the music encourages your effort to sing with an evenness of tone and energetic breath. "Amarilli, mia bella" has simple melodic material and "user-friendly" phrase shapes. Text setting allows coordinated breathing and invites gentle onsets of sound, serving as a vocal exercise that yields an artistic result. Other early Italian arias that are particularly effective in developing legato singing style and phrasing are "Alma del core" by Antonio Caldara and "Tu lo sai" by Giuseppe Torelli. For the more advanced student, "O del mio amato ben" by Stefano Donaudy would be a welcome choice.

   Suggested listening: Listen to performances by native Italian artists such as Cecilia Bartoli and Luciano Pavarotti. Compare the diction and interpretations of non-native-speaking Italian artists such as Joyce DiDonato and Ramón Vargas. What are the similarities? What are the differences?

2. "My Lovely Celia" by George Munro (1680–1731)

   George Munro was a keyboard player who composed popular song. Though from another historical era, its popular nature invites a sincere, steady legato singing style.

   Suggested listening: Compare the performances of mezzo soprano Dame Janet Baker with tenor Stuart Burrows to discern the sound ideal and manner of performance. The gentle lyricism of the song inspires the singer to a warm, steady vocal color.

3. "Fair and True" by Peter Warlock (1894–1930)

   This meditative reworking of a Shakespeare text offers an interesting union of word play and music. Peter Warlock's setting entangles intriguing harmonies with text that conveys sincerity and wisdom.

   Suggested listening: Listen to the performance of Norman Bailey accompanied by Geoffrey Parsons. Notice how the piano part provides an extra dimension to the melody.

Also recommended: "Beneath a Weeping Willow's Shade" by Francis Hopkinson, "Gentle Annie" or "Why No One to Love" by Stephen Foster, "My Own Country" by Peter Warlock, or "The Lamb" by Theodore Chanler.

Vocal Agility and Flexibility

Agility and flexibility in singing are learned through vocal exercises that train mental acuity. To sing fast-moving notes, a singer must think a new vowel for every note while maintaining an evenness of tone quality. Most of us master one skill at time. Take an agile passage and master the notes and then, the rhythm. When all notes and rhythms are accurate, sing the passage on one vowel before introducing the vowels of the text. For every note, no matter how short, give a fresh vowel impulse along with a clear pitch signal. Train these skills with care at a slow tempo. Allow the tempo to increase because you know the music, text, and vocal technique thoroughly. Here is an exercise that will help you add agility and flexibility to your skill set as you learn the selections suggested in the following text.

LESSON PLAN FOR VOCAL AGILITY AND FLEXIBITY

1. Glide through diatonic triads such as 5-3-1; 5-3-1-3-5-3-1; and 3-1-5-4-3-2-1. Sing the patterns as SOVT exercises on lip trills or chewing hums. As the pitches of the patterns descend, point upward with a finger or open palm. As the pitches ascend, point downward. Begin slowly and increase tempo. Use a light, lyric approach when singing the ascending passage. Follow by singing the gliding patterns on "oo" [u], sliding effortlessly from pitch to pitch. Exhale and relax.
2. Sing a series of five-tone scale patterns using "doo" [du] and "bee" [bi]. (Example: du-bi-du-bi-du-bi-du-bi-du on 1-2-3-4-5-4-3-2-1). As the pitches ascend, wiggle your knees to perpetuate flexibility in your body as well as your voice. Sing the pattern on the vowels only: "oo" [u] and "ee" [i]. Massage your jaw to avoid tension. Exhale and relax.
3. Create patterns to sing on "oo" [u] and "ee" [i] using phrases excerpted directly from the repertoire. (Use the same tools to achieve ease and agility. Sing lightly as you approach upper notes, keeping your knees and jaw relaxed and flexible.)
4. Learn the music slowly on tone syllables such as "la" [la] or "dee" [di]. Allow an increase in tempo when you feel equipped to sing faster. Be sure to keep a steady, relentless pulse. (Avoid slowing down during difficult passages and speeding up for easier ones.)
5. Sing the phrases on the vowels of the words being careful to acknowledge each breath mark and to relax before each inhalation.
6. Add consonants with intention and sing each phrase *a cappella* in its musical context. Sing the song with bass line only before singing it with its full accompaniment.

Sample Repertoire for Learning Vocal Agility and Flexibility

1. "When Daisies Pied" Thomas Arne (1710–1778)

    Thomas Arne was himself a singer, lutenist, and violinist. He was associated with Covent Garden and

Drury Lane Theatre in London as a stage director. The text of "When Daisies Pied" was excerpted from Shakespeare's *Love's Labour Lost*. The arpeggiated melodic material in the verse contrasts with the staccato and sighing shapes in the refrain, making it ideal for practicing two different vocal skills.

Suggested listening: Dame Joan Sutherland's 1960 performance with harpsichord demonstrated the lightness and flexibility required for this agile tune.

Note: John Rutter set this text in his "Birthday Madrigals." This lively, contemporary choral version will help you recognize the vitality inherent within the text.

2. "It Was a Lover and His Lass" by Thomas Morley (1557–1603)

The refrain "With a hey and a ho and a hey non ni no" is interspersed between textual elements, creating a burst of freedom and energy. Like any "tra la la" or "fa la la" refrain, the interjection trains quicker, more flexible singing skills. For a comparable example, see the "Heigh-ho! Sing heigh-ho!" refrain found in "Blow, Blow Thou Winter Wind" set by Roger Quilter.

Suggested listening: Several British composers set the text, "It Was a Lover and His Lass." Listen to a different setting and compare it with Thomas Morley's original setting. You can select from settings by Frederick Delius (1862–1934) in *Four Old English Lyrics,* Gerald Finzi (1901–1956) in the cycle entitled *Let Us Garlands Bring* (Opus 18, No. 5), Roger Quilter (1877–1953) Opus 3, No. 3, or "Pretty Ring Time" by Peter Warlock (1894–1930).

3. "Selve amiche" by Antonio Caldara (1670–1736)

From the opera *La constanza in amor vince l'inganno* (1710), the aria begins with a single statement and follows with melismatic passages in gentle sequences. Though a beautiful work for performing purposes, it is a perfect vocal preparation for agile singing. Every note in the melismatic passages must be sung with a fresh, well-chosen Italian vowel. Because of the moderate tempo, the aria teaches agility and flexibility that will be applicable to works sung at faster tempi.

Suggested listening: Listen to the aria "Selve amiche" sung by Italian mezzo soprano Cecilia Bartoli accompanied by pianist György Fischer and compare it with a performance by Korean-American coloratura soprano Kathleen Kim accompanied by guitarist Jong Ho Park.

> Also recommended: "I Attempt From Love's Sickness to Fly" by Henry Purcell, "Nel cor più non mi sento" by Giovanni Paisiello, "Pur dicesti, o bocca bella" by Antonio Lotti, "Spirate pur, spirate" by Stefano Donaudy, and "The Lass With the Delicate Air" by Thomas Arne.

Vocal Color and Text Painting

Vocal color is the expression that the singer gives text, be it sung or spoken. Think about the tone of your voice when you describe a beautifully satisfying experience. With what other colors do you explain an unfortunate event? In both cases, you have used vocal color to define and enhance the words. With vocal color, you "paint" the text.

LESSON PLAN FOR VOCAL COLOR AND TEXT PAINTING

The sound of your voice is the sound of your spirit. In this exercise, allow your voice to reflect various moods. The result will create a palette of vocal colors for text painting and expression. Use the explanations to create the following exercises.

1. Begin with a descending five-tone scale (5-4-3-2-1) singing on "my-ah-my-ah-my-ah-my-ah-my" [maɪ ɑ maɪ ɑ maɪ ɑ maɪ ɑ maɪ] with your happiest sound. Repeat the same example with your "sad" sound, giving careful attention to accurate tuning (Figure 8–1).

2. Sing the pattern 1-3-5-3-5-4-3-2-1 on "way ah way ah way ah way ah way" [wɛɪ ɑ wɛɪ ɑ wɛɪ ɑ wɛɪ ɑ wɛɪ] in your "happy" voice. Repeat it in your "disappointed" voice. Repeat the pattern in your "elated" or "jubilant" voice as if you had recently made a very pleasant acquisition (Figure 8–2).

3. Select a phrase from the song to be sung and exercise it in the same way using several different mindsets or attitudes.

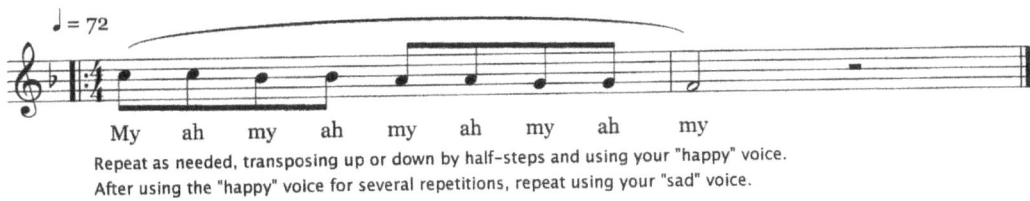

Figure 8–1. Example 1 for vocal color and text painting.

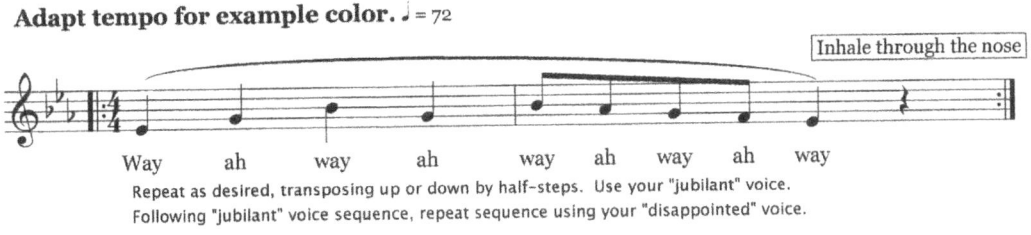

Figure 8–2. Example 2 for vocal color and text painting.

Sample Repertoire for Learning Vocal Color and Text Painting

1. "Down by the Salley Gardens" arranged by Benjamin Britten

William Butler Yeats published the poem "Down by the Salley Gardens" in 1889 as part of a collection called *The Wanderings of Oisin and Other Poems*. "Down by the Salley Gardens" has found a firm place in Irish tradition. Many composers have been drawn to create musical settings. The Britten version is perhaps most appropriate for the beginning singer.

Suggested listening: Contrast the settings by Benjamin Britten, Ivor Gurney, and George Butterworth, to name only a few. Each treats the text differently from a harmonic standpoint.

2. "O Mistress Mine" by Roger Quilter (1877–1953)

In Shakespeare's *Twelfth Night*, a clown named Feste sings a love song, "O mistress mine, where are you roaming, O stay and hear your true love's coming who can sing both high and low." This song appears in Act 2, Scene 3 and portrays the vigor and brevity of youth. Its robust presentation of thought and melody induces energetic expression.

Suggested listening: Compare Quilter's interpretation with a contrasting treatment of the same text found in the song cycle *Let Us Garlands Bring* by Gerald Finzi. How are the settings similar? How are they different?

3. "Silent Noon" by Ralph Vaughan Williams

The 19th century poet, Dante Gabriel Rossetti was a gifted visual artist. He belonged to a group called the Pre-Raphaelite Brotherhood comprised of young English artists united in their pursuit of a realistic expression of nature. They were inspired by the work of Italian painter and architect Raphael (1483–1520). In Rossetti's poem "Silent Noon," you find vivid description of nature and human feeling. The musical setting by Vaughan Williams features lush harmonies interspersed with a brief recitative. The tuneful melodic shapes, perfectly attuned to word accents, prepare the listener for the approaching hour when the "song of love" is heard. A student of singing who masters this song will glean vocal, expressive, and performance skills.

Suggested listening: Though Ralph Vaughan Williams's setting is the most familiar, "Silent Noon" was also set by American composers Frederick Shepherd Converse (1871–1940) and Henry Clough-Leighter (1874–1956). As you compare the settings, do you notice any elements that distinguish the music as British or American?

> Also recommended: *Cowboy Songs* by Libby Larsen, "Down by the Salley Gardens" by Rebecca Clarke, "If I Only Had a Moustache" by Stephen Foster, "Money O!" by Michael Head, "O Mistress Mine" by Amy Beach or by Theodore Chanler, "The Old Maid's Prayer" by Frederick Silver, "Tobacco" by Tobias Hume, and "When I Think Upon the Maidens" by Michael Head.

Range and Registration

Every singer wishes to have a full complement of notes. Developing an even scale from the lowest note of your range to the highest necessitates study and practice. Notes to be sung in the same range in which you speak need to be tempered in weight to accommodate the adjustments to be made for notes above and below the speaking range. Here are songs that can help you become familiar with the subtle changes that foster an even approach to range and registration.

LESSON PLAN FOR IMPROVING RANGE AND REGISTRATION

1. Begin with gentle sighs on "ah" [ɑ], "oh" [ɔʊ], and "oo" [u] at midrange. Vary the repetitions at slightly higher and lower pitch levels. Enjoy the release of voice and tension.
2. Sing five-note descending patterns at medium, medium high, and medium low range as SOVT exercises on lip trills, chewing hums, or the nasal cluster "ng" [ŋ] to connect your voice and breath.
3. Cup your hands around your lips to create an imaginary megaphone. Select a pitch in upper middle range and call out "Hel-lo!" Allow your voice to arch upward and descend steadily. Transpose to higher pitches using a lighter approach to each note of higher range.
4. Create patterns of ascending and descending fifths (1-5-1) to sing on "ah" [ɑ], "oh" [ɔʊ], and "oo" [u], bending your knees gently as you approach the upper note. Use your hands and arms freely in gestures that release tension. Remember to sing "through" the highest and lowest notes, not "to" them.
5. Sing 5-8-5-3-1 beginning at midrange on "ah" [ɑ] or "oh" [ɔʊ] or "oo" [u], gliding from 5-8-5-3-1. Release your knees as you approach the highest notes. Point to a distant wall, guiding your sound forward through the end of the pattern. Transpose to higher and lower keys. Repeat the pattern with text such as, "Oh, oh, oh, I know!" or "Ah, ah, ah, you see!"
6. Find a passage in your repertoire that contains an excursion into an upper or lower extreme of your voice. Use the methods described previously to address a difficult passage. Simplify its patterns and transpose them. As you feel more comfortable, increase the level of difficulty. When you have mastered the passage, decide with intention how you will address it within the context of the song or aria. Remember: Notes in upper ranges demand less weight and more steady breath energy. Notes in lower ranges rely more upon relaxation and a clear connection to your speaking voice.

Sample Repertoire for Improving Range and Registration

1. "Loveliest of Trees" by John Duke (1899–1984)

    The poem "Loveliest of Trees" was written by one of England's best-loved poets A. E. Housman. He was a gifted amateur who loved the tranquility of the rural countryside. Housman lived near the Severn River that crosses the region known as Shropshire. In a famous lecture entitled "The Name and Nature of Poetry," Housman reported that poetry, to him, was a kind of dialogue with himself. The poem attracted the attention of several composers. The setting by John Duke is well-known and offers you a chance to gather important vocal tools. The song opens with a descending triad invocative of a vocal exercise. The middle section of the song requires you to negotiate notes in your lower speaking range before you return to the opening theme.

    Suggested listening: Compare the setting by John Duke with those of George Butterworth, Ivor Gurney, and Vernon Duke. Each composer delivers the moral lesson of the poem in a slightly different musical way.

2. "Early in the Morning" by Ned Rorem (b. 1923)

In his 1959 essay "Writing Songs," Ned Rorem states: "The poem's rightness and the success of the resulting song come only with a sense of style and taste in determining the kind of music used with the kind of poem chosen" (Rorem, 1983, p. 301). "Early in the Morning" is one of Rorem's *14 Songs on American Poetry* (1961). The poet Robert Hillyer describes the memory of a distant summer morning spent in Paris, France. The text is rich with alliteration such as "hosing the hot pavement" and "dash of flashing spray." Such phrases invite vocal color and text painting.

Suggested listening: Compare the performances of mezzo soprano Susan Graham accompanied by Malcolm Martineau as well as baritone Nathan Gunn accompanied by Kevin Murphy. Note the freedom of expression in each performance and the clarity of diction. Be sure to wait for the final cadence and its very "Parisian" resolution.

3. "Beautiful Dreamer" by Stephen Foster (1826–1864)

Stephen Foster wrote some 200 songs. Some were intended for the stage and others were popularly called "parlor songs" because of their use as entertainment in parlors across America. "Beautiful Dreamer" is a typical example of a parlor song with its nostalgic, sentimental tone. Arguably, this song demonstrates best the composer's gift for easily flowing melody. The melodic material moves from upper middle to lower range before settling at midrange. If you abandon yourself to the song's graceful musical shape, you will learn how to negotiate your vocal range evenly. The compound meter of 9/8 facilitates the lyric lilt of each phrase.

Suggested listening: Compare performances of soprano Nadine Sierra accompanied by pianist Bryan Wagorn as well as mezzo soprano Marilyn Horne accompanied by Martin Katz. Notice the lyricism and ease in both presentations of this song. Also explore the many versions of the song performed by the popular artists of various genres and by choral groups.

> Also recommended: "Ah! May the Red Rose Live Always!" by Stephen Foster, "Here Amid the Shady Wood" or "As When the Dove" by George Frideric Handel, "i carry your heart" by John Duke, "It's All I Have to Bring" by Ernst Bacon, "Songs My Mother Taught Me" by Antonin Dvorak, and "There Is a Lady Sweet and Kind" by Norman Dello Joio.

Messa di voce

In Chapter 5, you learned that *messa di voce* or "measuring the voice" is a useful tool for exploring your range, singing expressively, and evaluating vocal readiness. *Messa di voce* involves evenly increasing and decreasing volume (*crescendo* and *decrescendo*) on an individual sustained tone. Because *messa di voce* originated as a *bel canto* singing skill, many early Italian arias require *messa di voce* as an expressive expectation. As you "measure" breath energy and tone to achieve *messa di voce*, you also stabilize your singing skill and develop evenness throughout your range.

LESSON PLAN FOR LEARNING TO SING MESSA DI VOCE

1. Chant at medium range a sustained "oo" [u] followed by "ah" [ɑ] followed by "oo" [u].
2. Sing the vowel pattern on one pitch at medium range sustaining each vowel for two quarter note beats at moderate tempo. Exhale.
3. Expand the vowel pattern to "oo" [u] to "aw" [ɔ] to "ah" [ɑ] to "aw" [ɔ] to "oo" [u] (Figure 8–3). Notice how your sound increased and decreased as the vowels changed. Exhale.
4. Sing one sustained pitch on "oo" [u], beginning gently and intensifying your breath energy to the center of the phrase; creating a hand motion that depicts the opening of a budding flower can help you increase the sound more steadily. Exhale.
5. Repeat on "ah" [ɑ]. Begin with your fingers touching as if you were making a heart. Allow the shape to open as the volume increases and recede as it decreases.

Sample Repertoire for Learning to Sing Messa di voce

1. "Ombra mai fu" from *Xerse* by George Frideric Handel (1685–1759)
   Born in Halle, Germany, G. F. Handel was trained as a harpsichordist, organist, and violinist. Handel developed an international reputation as a performer and composer. He spent much of his life in London, where he composed in many genres. For voice, Handel composed operas in both Italian and English. His oratorio *Messiah*—a large-scale work for soloists, choir, and orchestra on a Biblical theme—is probably familiar to you. This aria opens with an extended note specifically intended to feature an opera singer's mastery of the *messa di voce* skill.

   Suggested listening: Compare the performance sung by mezzo soprano Jennifer Larmore with that of countertenor Andreas Scholl. Notice how both performers use *messa di voce* to express the opening word "ombra" (*shadows* or *shade*).

2. "Music for a While" by Henry Purcell (1659–1695)
   Henry Purcell, himself a chorister of the Chapel Royal, composed secular and sacred vocal music (both solo and choral), stage works, and instrumental music. His opera *Dido and Aeneas* (1689) is believed to be the first enduring English operatic work. He wrote it for amateur singers at a boarding school for girls. He created songs and arias that were inserted into plays such as *King*

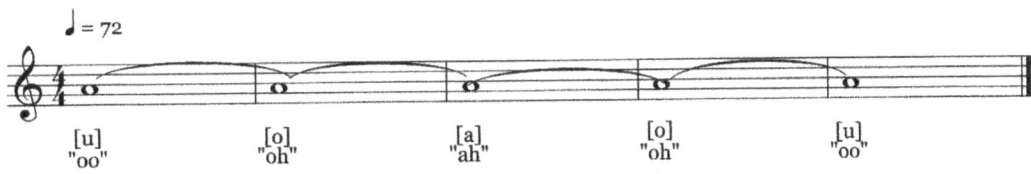

Figure 8–3. Exercise example for *messa di voce*.

Arthur and *The Indian Queen*. He also adapted works by Shakespeare such as *The Fairy Queen* based on *A Midsummer Night's Dream* and *The Tempest*. "Music for a While" derives from the Greek epic drama *Oedipus*. The opening phrase of the work displays a *messa di voce* intended to give the word "music" intense expression and meaning.

Suggested listening: Compare performances of soprano Kathleen Battle accompanied by pianist James Levine with tenor David Tayloe and pianist Chris Reed. The latter performance uses the accompaniment created by Benjamin Britten. Listen to countertenor Andreas Scholl perform the song with Tamar Halperin at the harpsichord. All these performers demonstrate how *messa di voce* can be used to express textual meaning.

Additional Application of the Messa di voce *Principle*

1. "O cessate di piagarmi" by Alessandro Scarlatti (1660–1725)

   A native of Palermo, Alessandro Scarlatti trained in Rome and spent most of his career serving the leadership of Naples. Scarlatti composed prolifically, creating more than 30 operas and numerous solo cantatas. Many historians of vocal literature consider Scarlatti's vocal writing particularly "user-friendly" for singers of all levels of expertise. "O cessate di piagarmi" ("O cease to wound me") was written for the opera *Pompeo*. Though it does not feature a single note that allows the display of *messa di voce* skill, the aria opens with a repeated passage that rises in pitch and intensity to express emotion. This aria has multiple verses, making it a useful training ground for Italian diction as well as vocal abilities.

   Suggested listening: Compare performances of mezzo sopranos Cecilia Bartoli (with piano) and Nathalie Stutzmann (with an orchestra of historical instruments). You may also enjoy performances of the young tenor José Carreras accompanied by Magda Pruneda and his 2008 concert where Lorenzo Bavaj is at the piano.

2. "O del mio dolce ardor" by Christoph Willibald von Gluck (1714–1787)

   Composed for the opera *Paride ed Elena* (Paris and Helen), "O del mio dolce ardor" ("O my sweet ardor") embodies the fervor and pathos of the text through a pulsating accompaniment figure. The "A" section of the aria opens with repeated notes that rise by a second and return, emphasizing the word "ardor" meaning "passion" or "devotion." The phrase is a composed *messa di voce* that sets the tone for singing the entire work.

   Suggested listening: Compare performances by soprano Teresa Berganza and bass Dmitri Hvorostovsky with one of soprano Sumi Jo. Notice how the increase in the intensity of expression heightens the drama of each phrase.

Also recommended: "Deep River" African American spiritual, "Into the Night" by Clara Edwards, "Orpheus with His Lute" by William Schuman (especially the last phrase), and "The Lord's Prayer" by Albert Hay Malotte.

Opera, Singspiel, and Operetta

Opera is defined as a theatrical production that is sung throughout. Opera and oratorio repertoire is conceived as vocal works to be accompanied by orchestra. Keyboard reductions of opera and oratorio works are available to be used for rehearsal and performance purposes. The sound ideal and manner of performance for the singer remain the same for both versions. Works intended for performance with orchestra require an advanced level of vocal training and experience.

The German form *Singspiel* (Sung Play) is a hybrid form that includes spoken dialogue with vocal "numbers." Mozart's *Die Zauberflöte* (The Magic Flute) is recognized as one of the first, best examples of a Singspiel.

Operetta or "little opera" contains spoken aspects as well as dance. The operetta works of British creative team William S. Gilbert and Arthur Sullivan, more popularly called "Gilbert & Sullivan" or "G&S," became a genre all its own. You may know of the *Pirates of Penzance, The Mikado, The Gondoliers,* or *Trial by Jury* as popular works in the world of community and professional theater. The American musical theater tradition evolved from these models.

Musical Theater

From the early ballad opera called *Flora* —staged in a Charleston, South Carolina, courtroom in 1735—to contemporary favorites such as *Hamilton*, American musical theater has enjoyed many seasons and styles. For learning fundamental singing skills, selections from musical theater works composed to be sung without amplification, namely, those from the so-called "Golden Age," are ideal. "Some musicologists suggest that the 'Golden Age' of Broadway began in 1925 when four blockbusters by Vincent Youmans, Rudolf Friml, Jerome Kern, and Richard Rodgers and Lorenz Hart opened within a span of seven days" (Hall, 2014, p. 12). In 1968, microphones were used for the musical *Hair* as a means of creating its rock concert atmosphere. Beginning with *Cats* (1981), musical theater works have been conceived with amplification as a standard feature. (See Matthew Edwards's "CCM Versus Music Theater: A Comparison" in *So You Want to Sing CCM (Contemporary Commercial Music): A Guide for Performers* edited by Matthew Hoch.) For Class Voice purposes, songs conceived for performance without microphone or media are the most appropriate.

Note: In contemporary musical theater works, microphones and media ensure that voices are heard without strain. These works offer singers the opportunity to gather various additional skill sets such as belting, character voice singing, "riffing," and female "mix" singing, among others. Many musical theater roles include speaking and dancing assignments. If you wish to expand your skills in those areas, seek the advice of qualified professional teachers and coaches. Class Voice provides you the fundamental skills that will ensure your success in these advanced areas.

Suggested Musical Theater Repertoire for Class Voice

Musical theater songs are associated with a specific role, each with its own expectations regarding character and voice. Use the following suggestions to set your own performance goals. Consult your instructor for the roles and songs that best suit your voice and personality

Sample Study Repertoire for Soprano Voices

- George and Ira Gershwin/DuBose Hayward
  "Summertime" (*Porgy and Bess*)
- Jerry Bock and Sheldon Harnick
  "Far From the Home I Love" (*Fiddler on the Roof*)
- Jerome Kern and Oscar Hammerstein II
  "Bill" (*Showboat*)
  "Can't Help Lovin' Dat Man" (*Showboat*)
- Alan Jay Lerner and Frederick Loewe
  "Waitin' for My Dearie" (*Brigadoon*)
  "I Loved You Once in Silence" (*Camelot*)
  "The Simple Joys of Maidenhood" (*Camelot*)
  "I Could Have Danced All Night" (*My Fair Lady*)
  "Show Me" (*My Fair Lady*)
- Richard Rodgers and Oscar Hammerstein II
  "If I Loved You" (*Carousel*)
  "Many a New Day" (*Oklahoma*)
  "Out of My Dreams" (*Oklahoma*)
  "Climb Ev'ry Mountain" (*The Sound of Music*)
  "Getting to Know You" (*The King and I*)
  "Hello, Young Lovers" (*The King and I*)
- Harvey Schmidt and Tom Jones
  "Much More" (*The Fantasticks*)
- Charles Strouse and Lee Adams
  "Put On a Happy Face" (*Bye Bye Birdie*)
- Kurt Weill and Bertolt Brecht/Trans. Marc Blitzstein
  "Pirate Jenny" (*The Threepenny Opera*)
- Kurt Weill and Ira Gershwin
  "My Ship" (*Lady in the Dark*)
- Meredith Willson
  "Goodnight, My Someone" (*The Music Man*)
  "Till There Was You" (*The Music Man*)

Sample Study Repertoire for Mezzo Soprano/Alto Voices

- Lionel Bart
  "As Long As He Needs Me" (*Oliver!*)
  "Where Is Love?" (*Oliver!*)
- Irving Berlin (music and lyrics)
  "You Can't Get a Man With a Gun" (*Annie Get Your Gun*)
- Jerry Bock and Sheldon Harnick
  "Matchmaker, Matchmaker" (*Fiddler on the Roof*)
- Burton Lane and Alan Jay Lerner
  "What Did I Have That I Don't Have?" (*On a Clear Day You Can See Forever*)
- Cole Porter (Composer/Lyricist)
  "Anything Goes" (*Anything Goes*)
  "Always True to You in My Fashion" (*Kiss Me Kate*)
  "Why Can't You Behave?" (*Kiss Me Kate*)
- Richard Rodgers and Oscar Hammerstein II
  "When I Marry Mr. Snow" (*Carousel*)
  "In My Own Little Corner" (*Cinderella*)
  "I'm Just a Girl Who Cain't Say 'No'" (*Oklahoma*)
  "A Cockeyed Optimist" (*South Pacific*)
  "I'm in Love With a Wonderful Guy" (*South Pacific*)
  "Something Wonderful" (*The King and I*)

"My Favorite Things" (*The Sound of Music*)
"The Sound of Music" (*The Sound of Music*)
- Richard Rodgers and Lorenz Hart
"Bewitched" (*Pal Joey*)
- Stephen Sondheim (Composer/Lyricist)
"Send in the Clowns" (*A Little Night Music*)
- Jule Styne and Betty Comden/Adolph Green
"Long Before I Knew You" (*Bells Are Ringing*)
"The Party's Over" (*Bells Are Ringing*)
- Kurt Weill and Maxwell Anderson
"Stay Well" (*Lost in the Stars*)

Sample Study Repertoire for Tenor Voices

- John Kander and Fred Erb
"Willkommen" (*Cabaret*)
- Jerry Bock and Sheldon Harnick
"Miracle of Miracles" (*Fiddler on the Roof*)
- Burton Lane and E. Y. Harburg
"Old Devil Moon" (*Finnian's Rainbow*)
- Alan Jay Lerner and Frederick Loewe
"Almost Like Being in Love" (*Brigadoon*)
"On the Street Where You Live" (*My Fair Lady*)
"I Talk to the Trees" (*Paint Your Wagon*)
- Frank Loesser and Abe Burrows/Jo Swerling
"Sit Down, You're Rockin' the Boat" (*Guys and Dolls*)
- Richard Rodgers and Oscar Hammerstein II
"You Are Beautiful" (*Flower Drum Song*)
"Everythin's Up to Date in Kansas City" (*Oklahoma*)
"Younger than Springtime" (*South Pacific*)
"You've Got To Be Carefully Taught" (*South Pacific*)
"I Have Dreamed" (*The King and I*)
- Richard Rodgers and Lorenz Hart
"I Could Write a Book" (*Pal Joey*)
- Jule Styne and Betty Comden/Adolph Green
"I Met a Girl" (*Bells Are Ringing*)
"Make Someone Happy" (*DoReMi*)

Sample Study Repertoire for Baritone/Bass Voices

- Irving Berlin (Composer/Lyricist)
"The Girl That I Marry" (*Annie Get Your Gun*)
- George and Ira Gershwin/DuBose Hayward
"I Got Plenty O' Nuttin'" (*Porgy and Bess*)
- Jerry Bock and Sheldon Harnick
"If I Were a Rich Man" (*Fiddler on the Roof*)
- Jerome Kern and Oscar Hammerstein II
"Ol' Man River" (*Showboat*)
- Burton Lane and Alan Jay Lerner
"On a Clear Day" (*On a Clear Day You Can See Forever*)
- Alan Jay Lerner and Frederick Loewe
"How to Handle a Woman" (*Camelot*)
"If Ever I Would Leave You" (*Camelot*)
"I've Grown Accustomed to Her Face" (*My Fair Lady*)
"They Call the Wind Maria (*Paint Your Wagon*)

- Frank Loesser and Abe Burrows/Jo Swerling
  "Luck Be a Lady" (*Guys and Dolls*)
  "More I Cannot Wish You" (*Guys and Dolls*)
- Richard Rodgers and Oscar Hammerstein II
  "A Fellow Needs a Girl" (*Allegro*)
  "If I Loved You" (*Carousel*)
  "Lonely Room" (*Oklahoma*)
  "Oh, What a Beautiful Mornin'" (*Oklahoma*)
  "Some Enchanted Evening" (*South Pacific*)
  "This Nearly Was Mine" (*South Pacific*)
- Harvey Schmidt and Tom Jones
  "Try to Remember" (*The Fantasticks*)
- Kurt Weill and Maxwell Anderson
  "September Song" (*Knickerbocker Holiday*)
- Kurt Weill and Bertolt Brecht/Trans. Marc Blitzstein
  "Mack the Knife" (*The Threepenny Opera*)
- Meredith Willson
  "Ya Got Trouble in River City" (*The Music Man*)

Suggested listening: Compare performances by Frank Sinatra and Bryn Terfel as well as Barbra Streisand and Renée Fleming. Note what is meant by the expression "classically-trained" singing of Broadway repertoire.

Spirituals and African American Art Songs

Spirituals and African American art songs are excellent repertoire for students of singing. "Spirituals, of course, represent an important historic element in the vocal literature of the African American" (Simmons & Wagner, 2004, p. xii). With the publication of *Jubilee Songs of the United States of America* (1916), Harry T. Burleigh (1866–1949) pioneered the concept that spirituals are worthy companions of traditional recital repertoire. African American art song composers contributed a wealth of excellent compositions as well. The following is an introductory list of sources for you to investigate.

- *Album of Negro Spirituals* (1985) arranged by Harry T. Burleigh (Alfred)
- *A New Anthology of Art Songs by African American Composers* (2004) selected by Margaret R. Simmons and Jeanine Wagner (SIU Press)
- *Anthology of Art Songs by Black American Composers* (1984) compiled by Willis Patterson (Marks Music)
- *Art Songs and Spirituals* (2015) Florence Price and Vivian Taylor (Hildegard)
- *In His Hands* (2010) arranged by Margaret Bonds (Theodore Presser)
- *My Favorite Spirituals: 30 Songs for Voice and Piano* (2001) arranged and interpreted by Roland Hayes (Dover)
- *The Deep River Collection* (2000) by Moses Hogan (Hal Leonard)
- *The Mark Hayes Vocal Solo Collection: 10 Spirituals for Solo Voice* (1998) arranged by Mark Hayes (Alfred)
- *30 Spirituals for Voice and Piano* (2007) arranged by Hall Johnson (G. Schirmer)

Include in your exploration works by H. Leslie Adams, David Baker, Nansi Carroll, Adolphus Hailstock, Undine Moore,

Coleridge-Taylor Perkinson, Hale Smith, William Grant Still, and George Walker, among others. There are abundant recordings of spirituals and African American art songs for you to enjoy. Look especially for performances by legendary artists such as Marian Anderson and Mahalia Jackson as well as Kathleen Battle, Simon Estes, Robert McFerrin, Jessye Norman, Paul Robeson, and Sister Rosetta Tharpe. Choral arrangements can be found on recordings by the Mormon Tabernacle Choir, the Moses Hogan Chorale, and Robert Shaw Festival Singers, to mention only a few.

Putting It All Together

Class Voice is the place to become an educated singer. Your Class Voice experience should enhance your understanding of vocal literature and interpretation. The sound of a voice is only part of the art form. The melding of text and music into an expressive whole is the goal.

Let us investigate a poem's symbolism and meaning and the contributions music makes to the expression of them.

Interpreting Text and Music

As you approach a new song or aria, read the text as a literary work. If there are words you do not understand, look them up in a dictionary. Consider how the poet uses symbols in the text. Look for words in the poem that require your specific attention because of their meaning. Identify the words that rhyme or have alliterative qualities. Are there words that repeat frequently? How will you use the repetitions in your interpretation? Are there words that offer expressive possibilities? If so, circle them in the poem and transfer the marks to your score.

What does the music add to the poetic expression of the words? Is the music tuneful or angular? What is the key or mood and are there modulations? What about the form? Are there verses or is the song or aria "through-composed," meaning that it introduces new material throughout. What is the structure of the work? Is there an introduction? If not, how will you establish the tempo and lyricism from the first note? If there is an introduction, what role does it play in preparing your singing? Are there interludes? Is there a coda or postlude? How will you use the musical moments when you are not singing to build the overall shape of your performance? Does the music follow the inflection of the poetic text? How has the composer interpreted the poem? Do you agree with the composer's interpretation?

Here is an example of a poem set by two composers who have very different interpretative concepts for the same poem.

The title of the aria is "Sento nel core" and it has been set by Alessandro Scarlatti and by Stefano Donaudy. You are familiar with the life and work of Alessandro Scarlatti, who wrote "O cessate di piagarmi" in the early 18th century. Let us contrast his setting of "Sento nel core" with that of Stefano Donaudy (1879–1925), a Sicilian and born of a French father and an Italian mother. Stefano Donaudy and his brother Alberto were educated at the music conservatory in Palermo. Stefano Donaudy is best known for his *36 Arie in Stile Antiche* (*36 Arias in the Old Style*) for which Alberto contributed many texts.

Following this paragraph you will find an anonymous text entitled "Sento nel core" ("I feel in my heart"). Clearly, Donaudy could have known about the Scarlatti interpretation of the text. Though both settings are in a minor key, the Scarlatti setting has a welcoming, almost jovial attitude toward the sensations of love that are disturbing his peace. Note the dance-like musical shapes. By contrast, the setting by Donaudy expresses a desperate, hopeless sentiment. Listen to performances of both settings and consider the breadth of interpretative possibilities.

> Sento nel core certo dolore,
> *I feel in my heart (a) certain/ kind of distress/pain*
>
> Che la mia pace turbando va,
> *That (the) my peace disturbing goes (makes),*
>
> Splende una face che l'alma accende,
> *Shines a torch which the soul fires up/inflames,*
>
> Se non è amore, amor sarà.
> *If not (it) is love, love it will be.*

Poetic equivalent: I feel an odd distress in my heart that disturbs my peace. There shines a torch that kindles fire in my soul. If it (the feeling) is not yet love, it will become love.

Listen to performances of both settings. To assist in your comparisons, select singers of the same voice part. Contemplate the broad range of interpretative possibilities inherent in one small, anonymous poetic text.

Performance Strategies for Class Presentations

Two performance milestones in Class Voice shape the teaching and learning throughout the course. Strategies for preparation and presentation are given in the following sections. Align the timing and content of the presentations to fit the course calendar and curriculum.

Midterm and Final Projects and Performances

In an academic setting, learning objectives are measured by assessments. At the midpoint of the semester, your progress will be assessed with a pass/fail project. It will serve as a "dress rehearsal" for your final graded presentation. The midterm and final presentation will have written and performance components. Depending upon the format of your voice class, the presentations could be live performances or prerecorded ones. For both presentations, you will receive an evaluation and useful, constructive feedback. Sample assessment forms are given later in the text.

Midterm Presentation

Select one of the songs that interests you. Using the steps defined in this textbook, analyze the text and music. Research the poet and composer. If assigned, prepare a phonetic (IPA) transcription of the song or aria. Check to be sure that rhyming words have been identified by the same IPA symbol. Memorize the song and rehearse it with your instructor, a collaborative pianist, or an accompaniment app. During the presentation, share with the class the most pertinent information you have gathered about the song you will perform. Trust your instructor to supplement any details you might have missed. Read the poem aloud with the text inflection and emphasis you intend to present in your singing. Perform the song and receive the applause and feedback.

Final Presentation

At the end of the term, celebrate your work with a final presentation. With the instructor's approval, prepare a presentation that includes biographical, historical, and musical information regarding the song or aria. Analyze the poem and its musical setting. Synthesize the pertinent details into a cogent "program note." A program note consists of a few sentences containing the facts you deem essential for your listener to grasp the song's essence. Create a written document including all the information you have gathered through your research. Include a list of reference materials you consulted. If you quote a source, be sure to cite it. The final presentation is a graded event. Plan carefully what you will say and how you will sing. Your written materials and performance will be assessed by your instructor. Save your written work for future reference.

Program Notes and Research

When you sing, you are the vessel through whom the thoughts of a poet/lyricist and composer flow. You represent them and present their work to the audience. Your listeners have only one brief opportunity to experience this multilayered artistic endeavor. Program notes are intended to prepare your listeners to understand what to notice at first hearing. The information you provide should be essential and focused. Through research, you will discover many facts that inform your performance and give you confidence. In their seminal work, *The Art of the Song Recital*, the authors note: "Far from being a disagreeable task, this work often becomes so enjoyable and compelling that devoted and diligent exploration sometimes develops into a positive mania for collecting related memorabilia" (Emmons & Sontag, 1979, p. 171). Gathering information is easy, but distilling it into a few sentences is not. Delete extraneous facts that may be fascinating to you but not necessary for the listener. Select the elements that heighten the listener's experience and enjoyment. If you have an insight that governs your view of the composition, poet, or composer, find a way to include it. Avoid salacious or speculative matters. Concentrate on the evidence that propels your performance. Ask your instructor for assistance in preparing your notes.

Performance Etiquette

There is a saying, "Delivery is everything!" Prepare the delivery of your presentation with care. Plan what you will wear. Your attire should not restrict your performance in any way. Wear shoes that assist you in balancing on the balls of your feet. (Avoid flip-flop sandals, extremely high heels, or tight-fitting shoes or boots that constrict your legs.) Select a garment that allows for the expansion of your abdominal muscles for breathing and encourages a tall, buoyant posture. Jewelry, scarves, or neckties should not shift or squeeze. A full-length mirror is your friend. Take a 360° view. Does what you are wearing "move" easily with you? Does what you are wearing help you feel "like a singer"?

Before walking to the stage, take a deep, cleansing breath. Sense your pulse and stride across the stage tastefully. Once at the piano, center your posture and bow slowly from the waist. Say to yourself "thank you" three times and come up smiling. (Do not close your eyes!) Why say "thank you" three times? Because adrenaline speeds the heart rate, you need to slow your movements accordingly. The repetition of "thank you" elongates your bow and helps you avoid dizziness.

Don't forget that your bow is a grateful acknowledgment of the listeners who have gathered to hear you. This step of gratitude gives you, the performer, a positive mental attitude.

Remember that your collaborative pianist is a teammate who holds essential keys to your success. After taking a moment to focus on your performance, ensure that your collaborative pianist is ready. Address your audience and share your music. At the conclusion of your performance, acknowledge the applause as you did at the beginning. Allow the listeners to express their satisfaction to your collaborative pianist. Flash the audience one last smile and depart as you came.

If your presentation includes spoken text, take time to transition from speaking to singing. Breathe for speaking as you do for singing. Center your speaking voice and keep "melody" in your speech. It may be helpful to have a water bottle on hand so that you can hydrate between the two tasks.

Plan and practice your performance, including your preparation, arrival, and demeanor. Consider how you enter the stage and depart from it. Leave nothing to chance. Visualize the audience and their potential reception of your music making. Decide where you will cast your eyes during your singing. Plan but do not "choreograph" your performance. The excitement of live performance will add spontaneity and freshness to your singing. Receive the warm, encouraging expressions on the faces of your audience members. Concentrate on sharing the meaning of your sung texts with them. Process the constructive feedback you receive from your classmates and instructor. Let your Class Voice performance experience prepare you for future presentations of all kinds. The following are sample evaluation forms. Adjust them to fit your course objectives and goals.

Criteria for Evaluation

CLASS PRESENTATION ASSESSMENT FORM
Midterm Project and Performance

NAME _____

| MUSICAL PREPARATION | 1 | 2 | 3 | 4 | 5 |

Rhythmic Accuracy
Pitch Accuracy/Tuning
Memorization

| PHONETIC READING/IPA | 1 | 2 | 3 | 4 | 5 |

IPA Transcription (optional)
Spoken Delivery of Text

| POETIC EQUIVALENT | 1 | 2 | 3 | 4 | 5 |

Synopsis of Poetic Thought

| PROGRAM NOTES | 1 | 2 | 3 | 4 | 5 |

Oral presentation of information regarding poet, composer, and composition

(To receive full credit for written and oral, you must cite your sources.)

| PERFORMANCE ETIQUETTE | 1 | 2 | 3 | 4 | 5 |

Acknowledgment of Applause
Acknowledgment of Accompanist
Stage Presence and Poise

OVERALL PRESENTATION SCORE   TOTAL =

Grading Scale

- A = 25–24   B– = 18
- A– = 23–22   C+ = 17
- B+ = 21   C = 16–15
- B = 20–19   C– = 14

<u>Instructor Feedback:</u>

CLASS VOICE ASSESSMENT FORM
Final Project and Performance

NAME _____

| MUSICAL PREPARATION | 1 | 2 | 3 | 4 | 5 |

Rhythmic Accuracy
Pitch Accuracy/Tuning
Memorization

| PHONETIC READING/IPA | 1 | 2 | 3 | 4 | 5 |

IPA Transcription (optional)
Spoken Delivery of Text

| POETIC EQUIVALENT | 1 | 2 | 3 | 4 | 5 |

Synopsis of Poetic Thought

| PROGRAM NOTES | 1 | 2 | 3 | 4 | 5 |

Written and Oral Presentation of Information
Poetic Context
Composer: Life and Works
Performance Work

(To receive full credit for written and oral, you must cite your sources.)

| PERFORMANCE ETIQUETTE | 1 | 2 | 3 | 4 | 5 |

Acknowledgment of Applause
Acknowledgment of Accompanist
Stage Presence and Poise

OVERALL PRESENTATION SCORE   TOTAL =

Grading Scale
- A = 25–24   B– = 18
- A– = 23–22   C+ = 17
- B+ = 21   C = 16–15
- B = 20–19   C– = 14

<u>Instructor Feedback:</u>

"An die Musik" ("To Music")— An International Calling Card for Singers

Dietrich Fischer-Dieskau reported that one of the autograph copies of Franz Schubert's original composition "An die Musik" ("To Music") was enclosed in an envelope inscribed "manuscript très précieux" (very precious manuscript) (Fischer-Dieskau, 1984, p. 83). The manuscript consisted of the song that has become a symbol of the lasting friendship of its poet Franz von Schober (1796–1882) and its composer Franz Schubert (1797–1828). Schubert's musical setting of Schober's words is a musical dialogue between the piano's bass line and the singer's melody. The composer's music strides forward to embrace the poet's words. "The poem by Schober is a lyric that thanks the art of music for its comfort and transcendent power" (Stein & Spillman, 1996, p. 149).

Over the centuries, the song has become the "motto" of singers and singing teachers around the globe. Every significant gathering of the National Association of Teachers of Singing and the International Congress of Voice Teachers, its partner organization, opens and concludes with group singing of Schubert's "An die Musik" in German. Many refer to the song as the "Schubert's Hymn to Music."

Listen to performances of qualified singers and study the musical setting of the text. Because there are many German and English words with common Anglo-Saxon roots, you will be able to discern much of the meaning of the German. Notice the German words and their English equivalents: *grauen* (gray), *Lebens* (life's), *Herz* (heart), *Lieb* (love), *Welt* (world), *bessre/bessrer* (better), *Akkord* (harmony/chord/triad), *danke* (thank), and, of course, *Musik* (music).

As a finale to your first experience in Class Voice, sing along with the melody on a lip trill or chewing hum. The song is easily accessible and available in many keys. Its pathos is universally understood.

An die Musik (To Music)
Poet: Franz von Schober
Composer: Franz Schubert

Du holde Kunst, in wieviel grauen Stunden,
You dear art, in how many gray hours,

Wo mich des Lebens wilder Kreis umstrickt,
Where me the life's wild circle tangled up,

Hast du mein Herz zu warmer Lieb entzünden,
Have you my heart to warmer love kindled,

Hast mich in eine bessre Welt entrückt!
Have me into a better world brought back!

Oft hat ein Seufzer, deiner Harf' entflossen,
Often a sigh from your harp flowed forth,

Ein süßer, heiliger Akkord von dir
A sweet, holy chord from you

Den Himmel bessrer Zeiten mir erschlossen,
The heaven's better times to me opened,

Du holde Kunst, ich danke dir dafür!
You dear art, I thank you for it!

Poetic equivalent: You, my dear art, in how many bleak situations in which I was entangled in life's wild stress, have you kindled a warmer love in my heart, have returned me to a better world! Often your harp has released a sigh, a sweet, holy triad of tone that has revealed to me the better times that Heaven sends. You, my dear art, I thank for it!

Conclusion

Class Voice introduces you to the fundamental skills for lifelong singing. Prepare and preserve your vocal instrument by singing warm-ups and cool-downs before and after singing. Shape the way you learn music so that the songs and skills you have mastered will be useful to you always. Vocal exercises build good habits that become useful strategies for singing vocal works. As you have seen, the proper choice of repertoire for study can help you solve vocal problems in a lyric way. There is abundant vocal repertoire appropriate to your gifts and skills. Repertoire for singing should be chosen with care to avoid vocal strain or injury. Wise choices ensure lifetime success in singing.

Discussion Questions

1. Name three vocal problems to be found in music.
2. How can repertoire "teach" vocal skills?
3. What vocal genre intrigues you the most? Folk song? Musical theater? Spirituals? Italian arias? British songs? American songs? German Lieder? French *mélodie*? Why?
4. How will program notes help you, the performer, minimize performance anxiety? How will they enhance the experience of your listener?
5. What elements of stage etiquette will you use in other performance settings?

Recommended Online Resources

The following sections provide useful online materials for lesson planning and repertoire acquisition.

Resources for Lesson Planning

Singer's Repertoire: http://www.archive.org/stream/singersrepertoir027233mbp

Song of America: http://www.songofamerica.net

National Association of Teachers of Singing: http://nats.org

New York Singing Teachers Association: http://nyst.org

Resources for Repertoire Acquisition

Check out music from your appropriate library (college or public). Browse your local music store and ask about used music scores. Browse your local "Friends of the Library book sale" for sheet music, vocal collections, and recordings. Be aware that some sites request a donation or a subscription.

Classical Vocal Reprints: http://www.classicalvocalrep.com

Art Song Central: http://artsongcentral.com

Free Scores: http://free-scores.com

IMSLP Petrucci Music Library: http://www.imslp.org

Indiana University (Cook Music Library): http://www.dlib.indiana.edu/variations/score/

Resources for Music Purchase

Be aware that some sites may require a subscription.

http://www.alfredmusiccompany.com

http://www.amazon.com

http://www.halleonard.com

http://www.jwpepper.com

http://www.musicnotes.com

http://www.sheetmusicplus.com

http://www.8notes.com ($20 subscription to download)

http://www.totalsheetmusic.com

Resources for Further Reading

Dayme, M. (2005). *The performer's voice: Realizing your vocal potential.* W. W. Norton.

Friedlander, C. (2018). *Complete vocal fitness: A singer's guide to physical training, anatomy, and biomechanics.* Rowman & Littlefield.

Hall, K. (2014). *So you want to sing music theater: A guide for professionals.* Rowman & Littlefield.

Hoch, M. (Ed.). (2018). *So you want to sing CCM (Contemporary Commercial Music): A guide for performers.* Rowman & Littlefield.

Leborgne, W., & Rosenberg, M. (2014). *The vocal athlete.* Plural Publishing.

Parker, A. (2007). *Anatomy of melody: Exploring the single line of song.* GIA Publications.

Thomas, A. (2007). *Way over in Beulah Lan': Understanding and performing Negro spirituals.* Heritage Music Press.

References

Emmons, S., & Sontag, S. (1979). *The art of the song recital* (p. 171). Schirmer Books.

Fischer-Dieskau, D. (1984). *Schubert's songs: A biographical study* (p. 83)(K. Whitton, Trans.). Limelight Editions.

Hall, K. (2014). *So you want to sing music theater: A guide for performers* (p. 12). Rowman & Littlefield.

Hoch, M. (2018). *So you want to sing CCM (contemporary commercial music): A guide for performers* (p. 126). Rowman & Littlefield.

Rorem, N. (1983). *Setting the tone: Essays and a diary* (p. 301). Coward-McCann.

Simmons, M., & Wagner, J. (2004). *A new anthology of art songs by African American composers* (p. xii). Southern Illinois University Press.

Stein, D., & Spillman, R. (1996). *Poetry into song: Performance and analysis of Lieder* (p. 149). Oxford University Press.

Wharton, E. (1997). *French ways and their meaning* (p. 39). Berkshire House Publishers.

Zeldin, T. (1996). *The French* (p. 348). Kodansha International.

9
The Singing Life

Considerations for the Adolescent Singing Voice

Vincent Oakes

Let the information that follows help you consider your own early training as a singer, your current journey in developing your voice, and your preparation for a career as a choral conductor. Allow it to broaden your perspective as a music educator or as an informed listener. The author of this section represents the viewpoint of a boy choir conductor.

Working with the adolescent singer's voice affords opportunities for wonderful musical growth and enrichment for developing musicians while simultaneously providing challenges for the choral director. Over the last century, working with this age singer has garnered a great deal of varied attention, as teachers and conductors have tried to encourage continued successful choral participation from the child singer into young adulthood while the vocal instrument itself is undergoing periods of change marked by fluctuations in achieving basic vocal concepts.

After sharing chapters on baton technique, interpretation in the conducting gesture, and other musical matters in his 1919 textbook *Essentials in Conducting*, Karl W. Gehrkens includes the chapter "The Boy Choir and Its Problems." In it, the author attempts to generally address the complexities of including the young male singer—identifying the "compass, registers, possibilities, and limitations" of the boy's voice and lamenting the challenges associated with the onset of puberty (Gehrkens, 1919, p. 118). Perhaps befitting its ominous title, Gehrkens concludes the rudimentary vocal pedagogy section of the chapter with "in justice to the boy's future, he ought probably in most cases to be dismissed from the choir when his voice begins to change" (Gehrkens, 1919, p. 125). Unfortunately, this widespread practice of having young singers not actively participate in ensemble singing at the onset of the adolescent voice change was a common remedy in many schools, community children's choirs, and houses of worship for decades. Existing repertoire and vocal training methods did not adequately accommodate these voices or address their evolving needs. As a result, the choral art likely lost many musicians who did not return to singing following their dismissal from the choir. These singers lost an important opportunity to develop their vocal growth in partnership with their total musicianship and aural skills.

Thankfully, a great deal of musical scholarship and scientific research over the last half century have informed our understanding of the vocal mechanism, influenced the creation of repertoire suited for this age group, and impacted the pedagogy of voice teachers and choral directors. This has led to opportunities for the positive inclusion of the adolescent voice in ensemble singing. In the 1950's, Duncan McKenzie promoted the concept of keeping adolescents participating in church and school choirs through his "alto-tenor" plan, emphasizing a flexibility of voice classification that keeps singers actively participating in the most comfortable part of their available vocal range (McKenzie, 1956). This commitment to keep singers making music through adolescence was followed with more thorough scholarship and practical insight from several notable pedagogues. Irving Cooper and Don L. Collins introduced the Cambiata Concept (from *cambiata nota*, or "changing note"), promoting a practical method for embracing the challenges for music students experiencing vocal mutation to successfully experience progress and achievement in the classroom setting. A focus on the physiological considerations of the changing adolescent voice and the development of a resulting classification system for emerging voices by John Cooksey resulted in his practical Contemporary, Eclectic Theory and his indispensable text *Working with Adolescent Voices*, which has proven helpful in the process of assigning parts and sharing the responsibility for understanding and navigating the voice change process between student and teacher (Cooksey, 1977).

Modern pedagogues Kenneth Phillips, Henry Leck, and Patrick Freer have continued to shape our understanding of the adolescent voice beyond the relatively simplistic strata of unchanged or changed voices. They are helping conductors view the process on a spectrum of somewhat predictable, though still individualistic, development and expansion and going beyond a typical fixed range that ungraciously makes its way down the staff. Lynne Gackle and Bridget Sweet have provided a wealth of research specifically associated with the development of the female changing voice, going beyond range identification and giving added attention to the development of timbre, tone production, and vocal identity. Sweet's newest offering, *Thinking Outside the Box: Adolescent Voice Change in Music Education* explores the voice change process in the larger context of overall adolescent development, its representation in popular culture, and the importance of properly equipped empowerment and encouragement for both teacher and singer.

Singing Fundamentals for the Adolescent Voice

In its simplest form, good singing is good singing. A consistent tone that is grounded in properly aligned posture and started with a healthy onset of phonation, maintains a steady breath support, and utilizes available vocal resonance is the desired goal for singers of any age. It is upon this foundation that the elements of diction, musicality, and expression can be built and expanded upon through advanced musicianship, aural skills, and ensemble participation. Building this foundation takes on added importance and complexity during the voice change process. The young singer is developing awareness (or, if not done in a supportive manner, insecurity) about their vocal ability during adolescence that is often shaped by what they are able to do vocally and what they perceive about the sound they are able to produce. If discouraged by their ability to fully participate or contribute to the ensemble and if not capably guided through this phase of their vocal development, the singer can develop a self-defeating sense of doubt. They may also acquire unhealthy or potentially damaging singing habits or leave singing altogether if they no longer view singing as something at which they are capable or successful or for which their contributions are not valued.

At this stage of vocal development, the successful voice teacher or choir director acts as a guide for the young singer on a journey whose directions change frequently toward a destination that is not always entirely known. In this pursuit, Phillips affirms, "Teaching music to adolescents requires great intuition and patience," (Phillips, 1996, p. 75) and Sweet encapsulates this beautifully, reassuring singers and teachers:

> The voice change is a long and complex process. . . . There is no magic switch that is flipped as students' progress from middle school to high school that suddenly enables the voice in all ways, eliminates breathiness, and abruptly allows for pristine precision in singing. Voice change is a physiological process that lasts many years and involves the psyche and emotions, which tend to remain the most vivid aspects of voice change long after the physiological growth is finished. (Sweet, 2020, p. 13)

To the end that "good singing is good singing," the applicability of this refrain takes on added importance while the singer's instrument is undergoing periods of inconsistent change during adolescence. As the physiology of the vocal mechanism grows and changes, so should the approach and efforts of the singer adjust slightly to keep producing the desired tone built upon fundamentally healthy singing habits. The singer with a still developing instrument begins to access an expanded range, navigate different vocal registers, and experiment with timbre and tone colors. Having an awareness of the intricacies of the expanding voice can help the developing singer explore these newer developments more confidently.

One of the challenges with this aspect of vocal training with adolescents is that the voice teacher or choral director is catching the young singer for a fixed period along a much longer continuum on which they have been literally since the beginning of their life. From singing simple melodies on the preschool playground or learning their letters through the "ABC" song, the joy of singing is often unbridled and unlimited in its youngest, simplest forms. Unlike picking up a new sport for the first time in middle school where each practice brings about the acquisition of a new skill or the learning of a new concept, the challenge of going through the voice change process can complicate an activity that the singer has been practicing for their entire life, adding levels of frustration or self-doubt. It is helpful to assist the singer with understanding more fully that difficulties with navigating the voice change process are both typical and unpredictable. These are typical in that such challenges are experienced by everyone as the vocal mechanism grows and changes. They are unpredictable in that the onset, duration, level, and intensity of both audible and perceived changes vary greatly from one person to the next.

This task is made more difficult because the voice is entirely contained within the body and, unlike encouraging a pianist to try a different fingering to navigate a tricky passage or suggesting a flutist adjust their head joint to play more in tune, the voice teacher must instruct almost exclusively using metaphor and suggestions based on what they can suggest or model without being able to visibly manipulate the instrument itself. To stretch the unknown destination/changing directions metaphor even further, we acknowledge that the vehicle the singer is traveling in changes constantly and continuous slight adjustments to each "new" vehicle should be made to successfully remain on this journey. The rules of the road never change, so a full understanding and constant pursuit of fundamentals—posture, breath, phonation onset and duration, resonance, and so forth—should remain.

Analogies that demonstrate a commitment to fundamental concepts despite specific changing circumstances are often helpful. Walking with two shoes of different sizes, playing tennis while changing racquets after each serve, stepping up to the plate with bats of varying lengths each inning, and attempting to draw a picture while constantly picking up pencils of different lengths or thicknesses in an art class are all examples of actions that require the repeated practice of a developed skill but also benefit from flexibility and adjustment when slight changes in equipment occur. Such is the case with the adolescent voice change. Minute changes in the thickness and length of the vocal folds during adolescence might result in difficulty with the onset of phonation and the ability to sustain a consistent sound due to a slight and temporary lack of coordination of the vocal folds. A confidently delivered initial exhalation on pitch combined with a steady, supportive airstream can assist the young singer, even though they might first encounter some difficulty.

As a tennis player might struggle when first using a different size racquet, slight adjustments to their swing built on the fundamentals of a well-developed stroke and footwork can eventually result in success. Similarly, a singer cannot simply change their vocal mechanism, so keeping an attitude of flexibility and a commitment to sound vocal principles despite slight changes to the instrument is essential. Even with a good basic sense of the mechanics and technique involved, constant self-assessment and adjustment, along with the attentive ear and supportive encouragement of the teacher, can guide the singer toward success. Inherent in this pursuit is the permission for the young singer to experiment with their sound with an approach that emphasizes the importance of *process*—the freedom to adjust their tone production as needed to allow for healthy singing habits supportive of the changing voice—over *product*—where a singer might instead aim for perfecting repertoire or producing what they assume is the conductor's preferred tone. These two pursuits are not mutually exclusive, but permission for a young singer to pursue their best sound over attempting to produce a preconceived one can be empowering.

The analogy of bicycle gears is good for helping young students picture the sequential nature of their expanding voice. Likely, a child's first bicycle was a single-speed bike that contains just one gear while they are first learning to balance, pedal, accelerate, and brake. As the child grows, they might begin riding a 10-speed bike that has multiple gears for going different speeds and traversing new terrain. Those first few days of transition from the single-speed bike to the 10-speed bike are likely not without difficulty. Switching between gears might be rough and even jarring at first, leading to a ride that is anything but smooth. Knowing which gear to use when going uphill or navigating the different speeds for a variety of terrains takes time and practice. After learning how to adjust their riding technique, master gear combinations, and capably navigate other aspects of the 10-speed bicycle, the cyclist graduates to a 21-speed bike, where they temporarily return to the prior state of instability until confidence can be found through consistent experimentation and practice. Such it is with the adolescent voice. Producing a well-supported vocal tone is a fundamental skill that constantly undergoes slight modifications as the vocal mechanism grows and changes. As the vocal folds lengthen and thicken and as the muscles, ligaments, and cartilage of the vocal process also change (as well as other supportive structures for singing, including the bones and muscles supporting good posture, breath support, and resonance), the singer should be allowed and encouraged to make slight adjustments to continue producing the best and healthiest results, built on fundamentally sound habits of vocal production. Even though the cyclist might experience some discomfort or instability when adding new gears, they do not become a poor cyclist when simply switching to a new bike. Similarly, a singer will hopefully not feel discouraged or incapable just because their changing instrument causes temporary inconsistency.

This understanding is especially important as the adolescent voice change is a time when the singer can access new pitches, navigate registration shifts, or make more choices with tone color and timbre. Because of continued progress in music theory and musicianship, they may also be able to access a wider variety and difficulty of repertoire. A feeling of "one step forward, two steps back" may occur in some singers who feel that their changing instrument is inhibiting their growth as a musician and artist. Allowing opportunities for these singers to feel valued and to experience success despite temporary challenges in accessing the entirety of their voice is helpful and important to their continued growth as musicians.

Phonation Onset and Duration

A common challenge for the developing adolescent singer is producing or successfully maintaining confident vocal phonation—the production of sound via the coordinated vibration of the vocal folds. Vocal sound emerges as air passes through these rapidly vibrating folds, and that sound is manipulated by minuscule changes in the folds. As the anatomy of the vocal folds and their support structures (cricoid and thyroid cartilages, arytenoids, muscles in the larynx, etc.) grow in the young singer, there is often an initial lack of coordination between the folds, which can make producing the initial and/or sustained production of a confident tone quite challenging. As a result, hesitancy or timidity often creeps in, and the young singer who is already reticent to produce a singing tone due to their changing instrument might also abandon principles of breath support, posture, focused exhalation, or other elements associated with good singing.

To address this challenge, teachers are encouraged to explore avenues that allow singers to focus on the initial and continuous production of sound, finding the right combination of both effort and ease, to find a tone that is easily produced and sustained. This can be explored by practicing nonpitched exercises or singing limited range exercises specifically designed to allow the singer to experience the feeling of demonstrating good phonation without the demands of producing repertoire which might lie in an uncomfortable part of their range or contain notes that are not easily produced. Like a golfer who practices their swing to make sure the grip, stance, and posture are comfortably aligned prior to approaching the ball, an adolescent singer can benefit from experiencing the feeling of healthy phonation prior to applying their sound to the choral literature.

Nonpitched Exercises for the Adolescent Voice

Understandably, teachers and conductors are attentive to the range of pitches that are accessible to the adolescent singer through the voice change process. For the purposes of selecting repertoire and assigning parts, knowing which pitches are accessible and confidently produced is essential. This insistence on identifying and classifying the adolescent voice can also be a frustrating exercise to the young singer who is having trouble with producing certain pitches, sustaining a consistent tone, or successfully audiating—hearing the pitch before it is produced—before attempting to sing a fixed pitch. For this reason, it is often helpful to start with nonpitched exercises, which reinforce the principles of breath support, the onset of phonation, and the successful maintenance of a healthy singing tone.

Many teachers encourage starting vocal exploration in the speaking range, presumably because this is immediately or easily accessible to a student of any level of ability or experience (or inexperience). Some care should be taken since the emerging speaking voice might be one that does not utilize the principles of a healthy singing tone, itself impacted by the same changes to the vocal mechanism and supporting structures. By encouraging the use of a spoken sound that most closely resembles the qualities of a desired sung sound—unrestricted, open, and well supported—the singer will be able to transition toward a more desired singing tone more effectively. Encouraging the student to speak as though they are greeting a grandparent during the holidays, speaking during a formal meeting with their principal, or dramatically mimicking someone who is trying to sound exceptionally sagacious can help place this tone in a brighter, more forward space.

At this point, when a student can produce a speaking sound with the placement and resonance desired in singing, an approximation of comfortable pitch based on the fundamental speaking frequency can be made. Exaggerated yawns and imitating the sounds of sirens or a hooting owl helps begin this process and are useful for bringing a focused, lighter quality into the medium and low range. Exercises starting from this placement that are given duration (spoken tones held for several seconds) and direction (the melodic contour of "Happy New Year!" on January 1 or "Surprise!" at the start of a surprise birthday party) begin to move toward sung pitch. Moreover, exclamations such as these naturally induce the breath support and onset of phonation desired in singing.

Exercises that transition from a well-spoken tone to "landing" on a given pitch can help move this process of connecting ear to voice for the timid singer who is having difficulty entering accurately on a given note. Example 1 (Figure 9–1) includes an unpitched, inexact starting place in the speaking voice ("X") and slides down to a given musical pitch in an effort to "land" on the correct note using the same support given the starting speaking sound. Similarly, example 2 (Figure 9–2) uses the sound of a Star Wars stormtrooper blaster to prime the pump of air speed and resonance before attempting to land on a given pitch.

Even if the student struggles with matching the destination pitch, they can be told if they landed above or below the desired note, like a baseball player who tries to estimate if they missed their swing high or low when failing to contact a pitch.

As is the case with singers of any age or experience level, breath support is essential. With the developing singer, breath support is imperative to providing the changing voice with stability, like a consistent pedaling motion on the 10-speed bike. Young singers often tend to interrupt their air support when encountering difficulty in phonation, causing them to create an inconsistent sound that suffers from an unreliable tone, undesired timbre, or pitch issues. Building up the stamina of their breath support to support their sound is a much more desirable outcome for singers moving through trouble spots rather than pushing through with unnecessary pressure or tightness. Unpitched exercises such as example 3 (Figure 9–3) build up this breath stamina prior to the production of the pitch, with the last "sh" moving directly into the pitched [u] vowel.

After experiencing some success with speaking and other nonpitched exercises, the emerging singer can then experiment with exercises that gradually build up their ability to successfully navigate the most challenging aspects of working with the changing voice—accurate and healthy onset of sung pitch, maintaining duration of a supported sung sound, and eventually expanding the range, which leads to comfort in transitioning between registers.

Figure 9–1. Example 1.

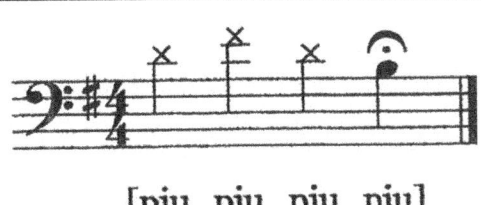

Figure 9–2. Example 2. "X" approximates a stormtrooper blaster.

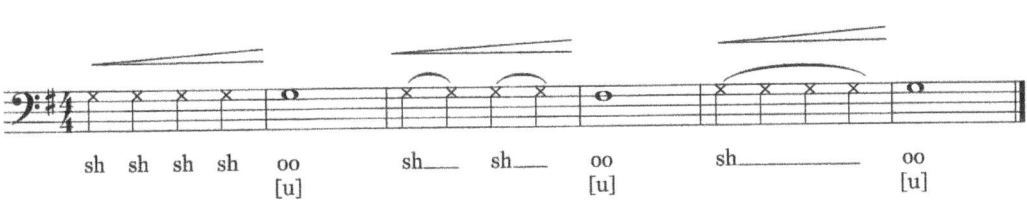

Figure 9–3. Example 3.

Limited Range Exercises for the Adolescent Voice

Limited range exercises afford the adolescent singer opportunities to experience the feeling and benefits of a healthy tone apart from the demands of repertoire. By experiencing success with the basic tenets of sound production and recalling what they did to produce it, the singer can reproduce these conditions on literature that is presented to them in the future. For example, a singer can repeat a short three-note pattern up and down the scale stepwise (Do-Re-Mi-Re-Do) or using skips (Do-Mi-Sol-Mi-Do) while focusing on different aspects of the exercise—that is, having a full sound on the initial note, producing a free and open sound on top, releasing the final note with full support to the end, and so forth, improving each until they can produce all elements of the pattern confidently. The singer can then incorporate different musical elements into this pattern to further refine their technique, that is, performing it staccato then legato, singing it at different dynamic levels, repeating it on different vowel sounds, and so forth. Repeating these steps on a different pattern (e.g., Sol-Mi-Do-Mi-Sol) can help the singer build more confidence throughout their range, across trouble spots in their range, and in different musical contexts such as the difference in approaching a note from either the top or the bottom. By focusing first on effective tonal production and the quality of the sound, the singer can build good habits that they will be able to utilize on any repertoire in the future.

Aural Development of the Adolescent Singer

Often lost in the discussion regarding the adolescent voice is the development of the adolescent musical ear. Given the strong connection between one's ability to audiate and accurately produce sung pitches, the development of the musical ear in tandem with the growth of the voice remains incredibly important. While this might seem an obvious parallel, it is worth noting that adolescent singers who have trouble accurately producing pitches might not suffer from simply being able to match pitch. They could face issues with matching pitches specifically related to the instability in their singing voice. For example, a singer who is going through the voice change and experiences a dramatic period of growth over the summer vacation might come back to school in the fall with a very different vocal instrument and could have considerable trouble matching pitches in their "new" voice.

A common aural issue with developing singers is octave displacement, where a singer accurately produces a given note an octave too high or too low. This issue can have several causes, such as a changing voice singer who regularly had an adult male voice modeling pitches when they were in elementary school and was used to reproducing pitches higher than they heard in the teacher's natural singing voice. It might take some time for this singer to be confident in matching the natural singing voice in the tenor/baritone range. Conversely, an adolescent singer might match pitch an octave too low because the pitch at the correct octave feels inaccessible or uncomfortable but singing it one octave too low still has consonance and allows them to participate, even if they are unaware of the displacement. The aural and singing connection is a developing skill that benefits from practice and repetition. This can often be remedied by removing the focus on the octave from the repertoire entirely. Demonstrating a variety of singular pitches or small patterns, then asking the singers to recreate them one octave higher or one octave lower (resulting in a comfortable place in the singer's range) at the teacher's direction causes the singer to recognize and address the issue, make aural and singing adjustments, and practice this small but important aspect of vocal production.

Even if a singer possesses good aural skills, the challenges of the developing voice can still present as difficulty with matching pitch. For example, the singer might be able to create the same pitch using a variety of methods and varying mixtures of registration choices (head voice, natural voice, chest voice), but the singer must now navigate choices about *how* to sing a specific note for it to be accurately produced. As the voice continues to develop, this perfect solution can change from one rehearsal to the next, and the most confident pitches one week can come out as breathy silence the next simply due to a new lack of coordination in the vocal folds (which will eventually become coordinated again through future growth and practice). Working through this healthily can provide a strong basis for the valuable skills of register navigation and singing across the *passaggio* in the developed voice.

Balance and Physicality for the Developing Singer

One item requiring constant attention from singers of all ages is the balance between "doing" and "allowing" elements of vocal production. The singer must actively perform some tasks—that is, consciously initiate the diaphragm, raise the soft palate, or modify vowels—to allow elements of a healthy choral singing—full breath support, resonance, and choral blend, respectively—to naturally occur. Active engagement of these tasks in support of the free and flexible operation of the vocal mechanism is a constant pursuit in achieving a tone that contains the oft desired qualities of ease, freedom, and warmth.

For the young developing singer, this pursuit takes on added significance as the loss of control or ability associated with the changing voice is often met with added strain, stress, or tension brought on by overcorrection to work through these challenges. This often manifests itself by singers raising their chins and stretching their necks as they attempt to reach higher notes, unnecessarily adding muscle strain around the vocal mechanism. Conversely, when attempting lower notes, they might lower their chin and compress the area around their vocal folds, decreasing flexibility and unnaturally compacting the vocal process. These singers might also adapt their posture in a restrictive position to demonstrate uniformity of effort or overblow in their singing while attempting to keep sound moving through all corners of their expanding range. An approach that emphasizes *better* work over *more* work and supportively *allows* proper elements of vocal production to occur rather than *making* them is key. This often requires disassociating the physicality found in overcorrection from the process of singing and placing it elsewhere in the body so that the voice is free to function.

Having the singers gently and continuously move their head 30° to 40° in each direction, looking first toward their left shoulder, then their right shoulder, then back again, while singing a challenging excerpt encourages flexibility and freedom while maintaining a constant stream of air. If the singer stops their left to right motion, it will likely be at a place where they previously ceased or minimized their breath support, perhaps due to a tricky spot in the passage. By associating the continuous motion of the head with the need for consistent flow of breath through the voice, the singer can experience externally the importance of this very internal concept.

The issue of an elevated or lowered chin can be addressed by having the singer make an "L" shape with their hand and placing their thumb on their chest above their sternum and the tip of their index finger on their chin. If, while singing, the chin raises from the index finger (likely while trying to access higher pitches) or falls below the finger (low pitches), the student is gently reminded of the importance of keeping a balanced chin position to allow the voice to operate freely. Doing this while singing a passage that sounds strained can serve as a self-initiated reminder to remain balanced, and a conductor can use this as a nonverbal communicative gesture in a rehearsal or performance if they hear tension on the tone.

Finally, the presence of tension in the developing voice is a constant concern as the engagement of physicality with the developing physiology of an adolescent are seemingly at odds with each other in singing. Seemingly boundless energy combined with the stress and confusion of the changing instrument can lead to overexertion and vocal fatigue. Allowing the young singer to have other ways of releasing tension and incorporate their physicality during rehearsal can prove very helpful, while also reinforcing musical concepts through movement. Having students imagine they are moving their hands through a large basin of water on a long or legato passage encourages them to not lock up their posture and to keep air purposefully moving through their tone. Pretending to bounce a basketball with their hands at waist level on a quick or staccato passage puts the physicality in their hands and reminds the singers to stay grounded by supporting the separation of notes with their breath and not through overuse of the voice. Pretending that the singer is pulling on a rope tug-of-war style in a long crescendo also moves the physicality away from the voice and reminds them of the importance of consistency in long dynamic changes.

Additional Considerations

A host of other considerations can contribute to the developing singer's comfort and confidence as a contributing member of an ensemble while working through the voice change process. Some of these factors can be easily influenced by the teacher or director, while others might require more nuanced conversation and support.

While vocal models can show the pitches and rhythms of a particular part or provide examples of certain musical concepts, care should be taken to make sure the vocal model doesn't inadvertently demonstrate or reinforce undesirable traits that could be repeated by the singer. For instance, an adult soprano singing the pitch F#3 to demonstrate a part or concept for a young baritone might not be able to model the desired tone, as that pitch likely lies relatively low in the soprano's range. The young singer, attempting to repeat the teacher's example, might try to replicate both the pitch and the timbre of the model. Conversely, a bass singer modeling an A4 for a young singer might do so in their falsetto, which—while it may be the desired pitch—might cause the young singer to model their sound after the vocal model's falsetto, which is not quality of sound a young treble singer should try to replicate. Reminding singers that they should sing in their comfortable octave and placing emphasis on demonstrating the desired tone could prove much more desirable and less confusing for the young singer. Additionally, enlisting the assistance of someone who can model the healthy tone in the singer's correct octave would be most helpful.

The labels of voice parts for young developing singers can also sometimes prove problematic. Adult tenor and bass voice parts carry with them an impression of maturity and refinement that are out of the reach of adolescent singers. A simple internet search of the term "tenor singer" quickly returns videos of operatic tenors and performances of "Nessun Dorma" from Puccini's *Turandot*. Searching the term "bass singer" provides examples of a basso profundo producing deep tones on a C2 or lower. While young singers may receive inspiration and good models of musicianship from these singers, modeling their timbre to demonstrate maturity or achievement is undesirable and, often, unhealthy. Recent choral repertoire trends are addressing this, with some publishers avoiding the traditional labels of soprano, alto, tenor, and bass altogether in repertoire designated for these ages, instead replacing them with Parts I, II, III, or similar. Flexible voicings with alternate pitches and octave options also aid the director with making choices for the young singer which best serve their available range and development.

While there are innumerable joys to be had, there are also many challenges inherent in the role of an adolescent singer as they make their way through their choral experience. While learning the tenets of aural skills, musicianship, music theory, and much more during this time of vocal exploration, combining these elements in performance can occasionally provide specific challenges for the developing musician. For instance, the three examples in example 4 (Figure 9–4) all include the same sounding D4 pitch—on the treble staff, the bass staff, and the "dropped octave" treble clef (sometimes called the tenor clef, but not to be confused with the tenor clef indicating C4 by the placement of a C-clef on the fourth line of the staff), where the sounding pitch should be one octave below where it is displayed on the treble staff.

Though it would be rare to see all three representations of the pitch in one score, it is not uncommon to have multiple clefs in the tenor part for one piece. For instance, a unison melody where all singers perform in their appropriate octave might appear in treble clef, and a following verse including four-part harmony might include the tenor part on a bass staff shared with the bass singers. A section of typical Soprano, Alto, Tenor, Bass (SATB) harmony on two staves (treble staff for sopranos and altos, bass staff for tenors and basses) might be exploded into four separate staves where the tenor part appears on the "dropped octave" treble staff, while all other parts retain their original staff placement. Using all the context clues they can attain, a young singer who associates a

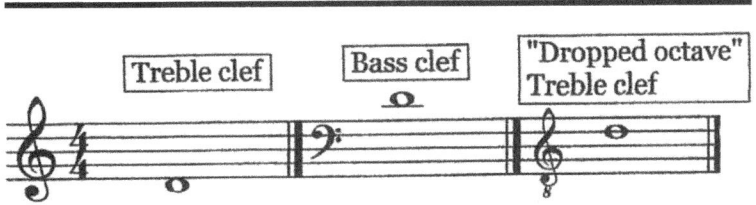

Figure 9–4. Example 4.

note's placement on a given staff as "high" or "low" can become confused when the same pitch appears in multiple places on the printed page. While the conductor or veteran singer might easily navigate this based on years of practice and experience, a young singer might struggle if a pitch "looks" high or low in the score. Taking the time to isolate this concept and review it apart from the repertoire can help ease this concern and build confidence. With supportive guidance, a young tenor can even go from confusion to pride, knowing that they can sing pitches on three different staves while others only have one!

Conclusion

Working with the developing adolescent voice provides its own specific challenges, encompassing physiological, musical, and pedagogical considerations where the only *consistent* attribute is the *inconsistency* associated with working through this progression with individual singers. This process often requires generous amounts of time, patience, and experimentation, but equipping a young singer with the tools to confidently move through this phase and to enjoy a lifetime of enjoyment and mastery in the singing art is a special reward.

Discussion Questions

1. Through what explanations or analogies can a teacher/conductor help a young singer understand more about the voice change process they are experiencing as a developing singer?
2. Why is it important to encourage singers to continue singing, learning, and growing through the voice change, despite the challenges associated with it?
3. How can a teacher assist singers with engaging the onset and supportive continuation of air in the singing process, especially as it relates to the changing voice?
4. What exercises might the conductor, teacher, or singer employ to relieve additional tension or stress in the young singer?
5. What additional challenges beyond the changing physiology do developing adolescent singers face while growing as a musician? What steps should a teacher/conductor take in helping singers address these challenges?

Resources for Further Reading

Abitbol, J. (2019). *The female voice*. Plural Publishing.

Ballantyne, C., & Brunssen, K. (2018). The adolescent years. In K. Brunssen, *The evolving singing voice: Changes across the lifespan* (pp. 61–138). Plural Publishing.

Barham, T. (2001). *Strategies for teaching junior high and middle school male singers*. Santa Barbara Music Publishing.

Barham, T., & Nelson, D. (1999). *The boy's changing voice: New solutions for today's choral teacher*. Belwin-Mills.

Bartle, J. (1993). *Lifeline for children's choir directors*. Gordon V. Thompson Music.

Brinson, B. (1996). The changing voice. In *Choral music: Methods and materials* (pp. 209–242). Wadsworth Group.

Collin, D. (1981). *Cambiata concept*. Cambiata Press.

Collins, D. (1999). *Teaching choral music* (2nd ed.). Prentice-Hall.

Cooksey, J. (1999). *Working with adolescent voices*. Concordia Publishing House.

Cooper, I., & Kuersteiner, K. (1970). *Teaching junior high school music* (2nd ed.). Allyn & Bacon.

Davids, J., & LaTour, S. (2012). Changing voices. In *Vocal technique: A guide for conductors, teachers, and singers* (pp. 223–244). Waveland Press.

Denison, C., & Denison, M. (2019). Uncovering meaning and identity through voice change. *Choral Journal, 59*(11), 28–37.

Freer, P. (2005). *Success for adolescent singers* [DVD]. Choral Excellence Press.

Freer, P. (2009). *Getting started with middle school choirs*. Rowman and Littlefield Education.

Freer, P. (2010). Foundation of the boys' expanding voice: A response to Henry Leck. *Choral Journal, 50*(7), 29–35.

Gackle, L. (2011). *Finding Ophelia's voice, opening Ophelia's heart: Nurturing the adolescent female voice*. Heritage Music Press.

Garretson, R, (1998) Changing voices. In *Conducting choral music* (8th ed., pp. 137–154). Prentice-Hall.

Leck, H. (2009). The boy's changing expanding voice. In *Creating artistry through choral excellence* (Ch. 7). Hal Leonard.

Leck, H. (2009). The boy's changing expanding voice: Take the high road. *Choral Journal, 49*(10), 49–60.

Miller, R. (2004). Registration. In *Solutions for singers: Tools for performers and teachers* (pp.129–168). Oxford University Press.

Oakes, V. (2013). The young singer. In B. Smith & R. T. Sataloff (Eds.), *Choral pedagogy* (3rd ed., pp. 189–203). Plural Publishing.

Palant, J. (2014). The adolescent male voice: Categorization to maturation. In *Brothers, sing on! Conducting the tenor-bass choir* (pp. 90–98). Hal Leonard.

Spurgeon, D. (Ed.). (2012). *Conducting women's choir: Strategies for success*. GIA Publications.

Sweet, B. (2015). The adolescent female changing voice: A phenomenological investigation. *Journal of Research in Music Education, 63*(1), 70–88.

Sweet, B. (2018). Voice change and singing experiences of adolescent females. *Journal of Research in Music Education, 66*(2), 133–149.

Titze, I. (1999). Voice classification and life-span changes. In *Principles of voice production* (pp. 183–194). Prentice-Hall.

Ware, C. (1998). Teaching singing/life-span voice teaching. In *Basics of vocal pedagogy: The foundations and process of singing* (pp. 249–274)). McGraw-Hill.

Wolfe, N. (2016). Adolescent identity formation and the singing voice. *Choral Journal, 57*(3), 49–52.

References

Cooksey, J. (1977). The development of a contemporary, eclectic theory for the training and cultivation of the junior high school male changing voice. *Choral Journal, 18* (pp. 2–5).

Gehrkens, K. (1919). *Essentials in conducting* (pp. 118–125). Theodore Presser Company.

MacKenzie, D. (1956). *Training the boy's changing voice*. Rutgers University Press.

Phillips, K. (1996). *Teaching kids to sing* (p. 75). Wadsworth Group.

Sweet, B. (2020). *Thinking outside the box: Adolescent voice change in music education* (p. 13). Oxford University Press.

Singing and Women

Brenda Smith

To sing successfully from "cradle to grave," all human beings must face and accept the reality that aging involves incremental change. We know that women's bodies are structurally and hormonally quite different from men's bodies. Women encounter unique physical, emotional, and societal challenges that have profound consequences for their voices. "The female voice is the life she listens to—a vibrant part of herself and what she would like to be" (Abitbol, 2019, p. x). Following the principle that "what happens to your life, happens to your voice," let us take a moment to consider voice use in the seasons of a woman's life.

As babies and children, boys' and girls' voices are generally indistinguishable in timbre and pitch. The critical period of the *cambiata* or "changing" voice (also known as "voice mutation"), is a decisive, memorable turn on the road of lifelong voice use. It is a period of vocal uncertainty that makes any young person vulnerable to many influences. "The voice becomes a problem when the sound of the voice and the way it is produced interfere with communication" (Boone, 2016, p. 158). Vocal changes can be subtle or startling to anyone. Consider your responses to the following questions:

- *When you were a young girl seeking your vocal identity, did you imitate the voice of a trusted role model, someone whose voice was very unlike your own?*
- *In competitive situations, do you tend to force the volume of your speaking or singing voice?*
- *Do you allow peer pressure to influence your natural sound or vocal quality?*
- *Do you ever lower the pitch of your speaking voice so that you might sound less aggressive or more mature?*

Finding Your Voice

The sound and quality of your voice is a part of your overall personal image. "Finding your voice" is a complicated task. The late Christine K. Jahnke (1963–2020), top speech coach for many powerful women, noted that since women remain a vocal minority in corporate boardrooms, on TV talk shows, and in the halls of Congress, they pay the price of being voiceless (Jahnke, 2011, p. 15). Many famous professional women sought Jahnke's expert coaching to prevent or remediate vocal weaknesses. Jahnke taught clients the same basic skills (i.e., relaxation, posture, breathing, resonance) you learn as a trained singer. The exercises she suggested included mental preparation and confidence building. Her clients rehearsed and recorded rehearsals of their speeches, lectures, and presentations to hone skills and evaluate results. One outcome was the realization that many women speakers speak at an unnatural, ineffective pitch level. *Have you a tendency to deliver unpleasant information in a lower tone? And maybe, on one pitch?* Learn to trust the authority of your own words and to deliver those words with pleasing pitch variability. It may take time and practice, but it will pay positive benefits. Voice teachers often describe this skill as "keeping melody in your speech."

Once again, consider your responses to the following questions:

- *Do you aspire to "have it all"? Do you expect to have meaningful relationships, combine motherhood and career opportunities? Do you strive for success and personal satisfaction in every sphere?*
- *Have you considered the role of your voice in achieving such goals?*

Such human interactions involve extensive voice use, be it for storytelling, negotiation, entertaining, or teaching. Women are generally known as caregivers who soothe, amuse, encourage, and comfort. Think of the women's voices that have accompanied your life experiences. Do you recall cajoling, playful sounds? Stern admonitions? Gentle and careful instructions? Voices that painstakingly nurture others can thrive, but those voices need watchful care.

Women and Choral Singing

Fear of the unknown may keep a soprano from exploring their chest register. Shyness might cause a woman to self-identify as an alto, avoiding the exposure and potential embarrassment perceived to exist when singing high notes. Either of these practices could jeopardize your vocal range and artistic growth. Take a moment to consider the following:

- *Are you truly a choral soprano or do you simply enjoy singing the melody?*
- *Are you truly a choral mezzo soprano/alto or were you assigned to sing alto because you hear harmony parts easily?*

Many older singers recount having sung a particular choral part for decades, rightly or wrongly, based solely on their placement in a junior or senior high school ensemble. You need a qualified voice teacher, vocal coach, or choral conductor to explore and evaluate your voice with you. Singing the choral part that best suits your voice enhances personal satisfaction and prevents potential vocal harm. Do not forget that vocal parts can be rewritten to suit individual abilities.

There are females, young and old, who enjoy singing tenor parts with their male colleagues. Women who sing tenor parts regularly have found themselves at risk for vocal injury. A female voice in a section of male tenors can be detrimental to the blend and tuning of the whole ensemble. In later life, we all reap the consequences of youthful experiences. Seek careful guidance, so that you are equipped for a lifetime of satisfying, productive voice use.

Healthy Voice Use

To sing and speak well throughout your life, use your voice healthfully at every age. Whether you are a singer or a teacher, stay alert to subtle vocal transitions in range, stamina, and tone quality. Try not to "label" or classify a voice, be it yours or anyone else's. Adapt your vocal tasks to fit the conditions of your life. You may need to adjust your expectations. The long-term goal should be maximum vocal and psychological comfort.

Maintaining Your Voice

What nonmusical endeavors could have an impact on your singing life? Childbearing, parenting, and career building may pose times of vocal strain and stress. It could be difficult for you to maintain a regular regimen of vocal exercise and physical conditioning. When facing family or professional demands, try not to abandon singing. Singing is an excellent outlet for socialization and stress relief at any age. It exacts a readiness of body and mind that builds personal confidence and vocal stamina. Regular, consistent vocal hygiene sustains the range and tone quality of every voice.

During midlife, many women are puzzled by the progress of their voices. Every singer reaches the pinnacle of singing ability at a different rate, but the female menopause makes the approach especially unpredictable. There may come a time to step out of the spotlight, but there is never a time to stop singing altogether.

If you take a leave from singing, expect your vocal strength and acumen to diminish. After a lengthy pause from disciplined singing, you may find an increase in your vibrato rate—a flaw that is disheartening and difficult to correct quickly. Even if you are not participating in regular singing activities, try to include a brief daily warm-up routine in your daily schedule. Such a warm-up can be done almost anywhere, such as in the shower, during a morning walk, or on route to school or work. Don't forget to cool-down your voice after speaking or singing. Warm-ups and cool-downs reset your voice and help you maintain healthy voice use.

Vocal Aging: To Sing or Not to Sing

"Be flexible" is the motto of the able, aging singer. At times, you may become displeased with your voice. Remember two bits of vocal wisdom: First, no one hears their own voice as others hear it. Secondly, the feedback of others is essential. The advice of friends and family could be helpful, but it is rarely as reliable as the observations of a qualified voice expert. It could be that you perceive your singing or speaking voice as "screechy" or "shrill," while your listeners hear a light, lyrical, lovely vocal sound. An honest, professional assessment will yield a clear course of action regarding appropriate performance and repertoire choices. Don't forget that choral singing helps you maintain vocal integrity and skill.

Though commercial media suggest that the effects of aging can be retarded, disguised, or even erased, most women recognize the folly of elaborate product claims. You cannot reverse vocal aging, but you can learn to accept its challenges gracefully. As you age, modify your vocal expectations and maintain consistent physical and vocal conditioning. Research proves that singers who heed this advice can sing and perform well into old age.

Vocal Limitations and Strategies

Why do older voices lose range, tone quality, and intensity? It is because of physical deterioration such as loss of muscle bulk and elasticity, lessened neurologic functions, decreased respiratory function and blood flow, and ossification of cartilage (Baroody & Smith, 2013, p. 91). Many older women identify vocal agility as an obstacle. Stamina and range are vocal issues that frustrate older singers. Qualified physicians and speech-language pathologists can predict potential vocal deficits associated with medications, life circumstances, or surgical procedures.

As you age, perpetuate your musical and vocal fundamental skills. Be artful in your use of breath marks and let alternative phrasing lessen strain. Ask your teacher or conductor if a part can be transposed or edited to eliminate concerns regarding range limitations. Remember: You do not need to sing every note, just like athletes need not play every inning. Stay in the game, even if you need to adjust your position on the team.

In the 21st century, senior citizens are living longer and wishing to participate actively in hobbies, sports, and skills of all kinds. Posts on social media demonstrate that older women around the world are capable of lifelong singing. According to an article in the *New York Times* on Sunday, December 1, 2019, the singer-songwriter Judy Collins (b. 1939) was still performing 120 shows a year at the age of 80 (Hess, 2019). Judy Collins reported working daily on her voice to keep its gentle timbre and flexibility. In her later years, she believed herself to be a better singer than ever. Let these women serve as your role models. They are living examples of wise voice use and preservation.

Conclusion

Your singing life evolves as you do. Youthful singing activities pave the way for singing skills in later life. Pay careful attention to the way you use your voice. Wise choices regarding repertoire and performance activities ensure your success. Vocal transitions, gradual or dramatic, will occur by degrees throughout life. From time to time, you may notice a lack of access to specific notes or skills stemming from various causes such as physical ailments, stressful events, or emotional changes. Though it is impossible to anticipate all changes, expert information is available from trusted professionals as well as print and online media. Exercise regularly, maintain physical conditioning, and continue consistent vocal training. Your voice can and should be heard. If you accept incremental change and address it strategically, you can sing from "cradle to grave" with joy and satisfaction.

Discussion Questions

1. What does it mean to "keep melody in your speech"?
2. What are the factors that influence the proper classification of young voices?
3. What nonmusical activities have an impact on the longevity of a woman's voice?
4. What negative effects can a woman expect after a period of vocal inactivity?
5. What are the factors that make lifelong singing possible for women?

References

Abitbol, J. (2019). *The female voice* (p. x). Plural Publishing.

Baroody, M., & Smith, B. (2013). The aging voice. In B. Smith & R. T. Sataloff (Eds.), *Choral pedagogy* (3rd ed., p. 91). Plural Publishing.

Boone, D. (2016). *Is your voice telling on you? How to find and use your "natural" voice* (3rd ed., p. 158). Plural Publishing.

Hess, A. (2019, December 1). Judy Collins still has a lot to say. *The New York Times*, Arts & Leisure, p. 9.

Jahnke, C. (2011). *The well-spoken woman: Your guide to looking and sounding your best* (p. 15). Prometheus Books.

Singing Life of Men

Ronald Burrichter

Ask the average person who attends choral concerts what choral voicing they prefer to hear, and the response will probably be a strong preference for the sound of a male chorus, even though they rarely hear one. Why this preference? The rich depth of bass and baritone voices blended with the lyric spin and height of tenor voices singing chords that rarely span more than two octaves allows for an acoustic "ring" of sound unlike any other voicing combination. The overtones generated in the "ring" of a barbershop chord can be heard so clearly by the average listener that a high level of excitement is generated through the audience. The same can be said for the lush and vibrant sound generated by a collegiate glee club singing songs of their alma mater or Randall Thompson's "Testament of Freedom." The power to stir emotions at the deepest level can clearly be felt when hearing "Eternal Father, Strong to Save," also known as "The Navy Hymn," sung by The Sea Chanters. Why, then, do we have so few male choruses and what are the idiosyncratic problems associated with male singing, especially as voices age? Let's explore possible reasons and potential solutions.

American society leans heavily toward athletic activity for young males as a badge of masculinity. T-ball, Pop Warner football, and similar activities demand the involvement of young boys, and few communities have a boys' choir to offer as a comparative and similarly admired activity. As a young boy, you may have been encouraged to be "mommy's little man" and admonished that "big boys don't cry," contributing to the idea that your young voice should sound "masculine" and should sound low in pitch and be powerful. If your voice naturally has a higher vocal timbre, you may have been teased about your light, lyric vocal quality. Either circumstance may have caused you to imitate inappropriate vocal models, such as your father or an older family friend or relative. Any attempt to speak or sing with an artificial or imitative tone can place your voice at risk of injury. The resulting vocal quality may restrict access to your head voice register (as opposed to the falsetto). Your voice may temporarily forfeit its lyric beauty in exchange for a vocal quality laden with vocal fry or a growling sound. The voice change that takes place in puberty tends to further dramatize the polarity between naturally deeper voices and higher voices with more lyric quality. As you move into adulthood, the muscle memory pattern of manipulation may impede the development of your vocal range and identity. The assistance of a well-informed vocal teacher can help you find the natural, lyric quality that you will carry through adulthood.

Can this tendency be reversed? This author has found it helpful to begin by studying the natural color differences found in male voices and the need to embrace the free and natural production of sound that will facilitate those colors. Helping you find the head voice (at any post-puberty age) is frequently aided by using the speaking voice demonstrated by another male voice that you can model. To ensure clarity, avoid using falsetto (a vocal harmonic) in exploring the upper range. Simple phrases spoken in the head voice by a respected leader that you then echo back can help you establish the head voice concept. The words of the phrase can then be applied to a descending five-tone scale and echoed back. Be certain that your neck is not stretched to aid in producing the high pitch. Remember to create breath energy for tonal production without abdominal locking or "pushing the sound out." Focus on your need to keep the chest open and proud with your abdominal region active in the breath management process. This will counter the tendency to pull up the chest (heaving the chest) for inhalation and the collapse of the chest for exhalation, habits perhaps acquired in athletic endeavors. If the ideas of breath management and abdominal breathing seem difficult, try lying on your back flat on the floor and placing the hands lightly on the abdomen. Notice how your body naturally brings air in and expels the oxygen depleted air out. This rise and fall of the abdominal wall and the corresponding expansion of the back into the floor as the lower ribs expand may help you understand the breath process for singing. Using energized and managed airflow, you may be surprised to discover that you can sing higher notes and longer phrases with more comfort than you thought possible. There is never a need to drive the sound or to yell. Try delivering a phrase in a "Shakespearian actor's voice" or with a "newscaster production" with the same energized breath. The "ring" of the male actor's or newscaster's voice can be a helpful guide to you. He senses the difference between voice use that is pressed and voice use that is resonant. Producing a resonant tone is more expressive, more pleasing to the ear, and more healthy.

The Singing Life of Tenors

"What about the tenors?" you may ask. *"I'm not sure what part I should be singing. Am I a tenor or a bass?"* Listening carefully for the lighter and more treble quality of your tone may help identify that you have a tenor voice. Arguably, the healthy guide to "classifying" your voice is the timbre, the color of the sound, not the notes that you can produce. The task at hand, then, would be to help you experience the transition or "connection" to the head voice. Some of the strategies described previously would be useful. Model an appropriate vocal quality or play a recording of a tenor voice that demonstrates the desired brilliance and lyric quality. With this aid, you can begin to visualize your potential sound. The perception many singers carry that they should stretch the neck to facilitate pitch in a higher range is inaccurate. Your head should rest gently on your neck without tension or tightness. This author has found that the use of the phrase: "We're tenors and we're proud of it" spoken in the head voice can become a type of "mantra" to which you can return to remind yourself about the use and sensations of the head voice.

Men's Falsetto Voices

"What's wrong with falsetto? Lots of singers use it all the time. What's the big deal?" you might wonder. Falsetto is, perhaps, the most misunderstood factor in male singing. The falsetto is, in fact, a vocal harmonic and carries with it the same limitations of any harmonic used on other instruments, namely, a limitation in control of volume and a singularity of vocal color. While the use of falsetto is not unhealthy, it does present significant tuning and tonal color problems that are better avoided. These limitations do not pose a problem for countertenors or singers who use the falsetto exclusively in their style of music ("doo-wop," barbershop, early music, etc.). The highly trained use of the falsetto by the countertenor presents an exciting and

unique listening experience. The "break" in the tone necessary for the average singer to transfer into the falsetto posture of the vocal folds or to move out of it will normally be problematic. In addition, the falsetto sound, by the unique acoustical characteristic within it, becomes very difficult to fit into the choral blend of either the tenor or the alto section. The falsetto voice tends to ride high on the pitch center, thereby inviting tuning difficulties. Sustained use of the falsetto may tend to develop muscle memory patterns that are very difficult to reverse as you wish to use your full vocal spectrum.

The Singing of Life of Baritones and Basses

"What about the baritones and basses? Are there specific concerns and challenges faced by this majority of male singers?" The answer would be, in this author's opinion, a resounding "yes." The baritone voice presents with the warmth and richness of the lower male quality while "mixing" some of the lyric brightness of the tenor sound. This wide potential for vocal colors has been the chosen format for many composers of solo vocal literature. Age and size appropriate melodies and texts are readily available for you to explore, regardless of your age or experience. As a baritone (often referred to as "First Bass" or "Bass I" by composers or conductors), you must traverse the broad vocal range from slightly above the lowest notes of the low basses to slightly below the top notes of the tenors. You must incorporate enough head voice quality to freely produce the upper pitches and use the same lyric quality to access lower notes. This skill demands breath energy and subtle adjustments. Tendencies to reach for notes by stretching of the neck for high pitches and by pressing down with the head and neck for lower ones must be avoided. The same strategies used to train access to the head voice for tenors are useful for you as a baritone as well. It is important to use abdominal muscles with flexible strength, avoiding tightness in the abdominal region and forcing of the breath. Such rigidity causes shrillness and pitch irregularities in your voice. Any downward pressure from the head and neck forces a tone that lacks "ring" and may be "raspy." Maintaining a tall posture and energized low breath, you can enjoy resonant voice production throughout your range. It is useful to remind yourself of the lyric beauty that is a defining feature of your *Fach*.

The mantra, "Sing younger than your years" will apply as you advance into adulthood or if you are an older baritone or bass. The admonition, "Sing mellow! Don't bellow!" applies too. With age and structural changes, older men may find it more difficult to maintain a singer's posture. Breath energy may become more difficult to access. For the tone to remain vibrant, the older male singer must stand as tall as is comfortable and activate his breathing muscles. Here are useful exercises for you to use at any age.

1. Equate the physical sensation of energizing breath with the action taken by your hand and wrist when sharing a warm, welcoming handshake. Avoid tightness or rigidity, no squeezing or stiffness. Engage in such a handshake with a friend. Concentrate on duplicating that energetic but unlocked energy in the abdominal wall as you release a gentle hissing sound of exhalation.
2. Align your body by placing your little finger in your belly button and

your thumb under your sternum. Make as much space as possible between the two points. Next, move your hands to place your thumbs under your rib cage and extend your fingers to your beltline. Gently blow imaginary smoke rings while contracting your fingers toward your thumbs and release. The gentle movement of your abdominal muscles illustrates the flexibility required for an energized breath connection. (See Figure 1–3 in Chapter 1 for a visual representation of this posture.)

3. Gently but with energy, call common greetings such as "Hello!" or "Hi there!" in a range slightly above normal speaking range. Be sure to avoid the use of falsetto. Introduce a five-tone descending vocal glide that confirms the use of the lighter head voice quality. In repetitions of the exercise in descending half steps, incorporate phrases such as "Go to school today" or "How I love to sing" or "I like apple pie." The connection between the spoken experience with healthy singing habits will remind you how to find the lyric center of your speaking and singing voice in the future. The blending of upper voice resonance with the lower range is best done through sighs and gliding patterns. Once access to the lower range is achieved, the exercise patterns can be more varied. Allow the descending glides to ascend using a blended vocal sound. With time and practice, you will be able to sing evenly throughout your vocal range.

As you become older, the tendency to allow your voice to deepen persists. Keeping a buoyant posture may be a challenge. Finding a ringing head voice quality may be more difficult to maintain. The following are strategies that might be of assistance as you age.

1. Whether in a seated or standing posture, seek to widen the distance between your collarbone "nubs." As the chest expands, you will release the abdominal muscles and enjoy an instant wave of relaxation. Let this tip help you easily achieve a buoyant posture. Do not allow posture to be a chore.
2. As you age, remember that the beauty of your voice is found in its majestic richness. You need not press or force your voice. As said earlier in this chapter, "Sing mellow! Don't bellow!"
3. Select a spot on a distant wall or in an imaginary baseball mitt. Toss your sound to the spot or to the center of the mitt. With each repetition, adjust the point of focus farther away. The projection of your voice will be facilitated by an energetic, deep breath.
4. Begin warm-up procedures with speech patterns in a head voice quality, as described earlier in this chapter. Develop simple descending gliding patterns using lip trills, chewing hums, and "raspberries." Sighing, sliding, and gliding exercises that use a lighter, more lyric approach will preserve your voice.

As you become entrenched in an active professional career, you may place singing in the "I haven't got time for that right now" category. Those who do sing actively may find their singing compromised by the tensions and pressures of an all-consuming workplace. Singing can relieve some of the stress and offer beautiful moments of music making. As with any athletic activity, singing requires physical as well as mental conditioning. If you continue to be physically active, the conditioning of your body will contribute to the health and well-being of your voice. Lifelong singing involves flexibility and fitness in mind, body, spirit, and voice.

Conclusion

The stories to be told in song by the male voice, the different colors required by the many differing texts, and the resonant power of the male sound all contribute to the uniqueness of male singing. Whether the lyric tenor is singing a serenade to his beloved in Schubert's "Ständchen," or the powerful baritone is telling us the chilling story of "Erlkönig," or a cowboy is singing to his herd in an old TV western, or a bass is rumbling "Rocked in the Cradle of the Deep," the variety of emotions, colors, and power of the male voice captures our interest. Careful attention to solid vocal technique established through proper breath management, freely produced tone, articulate diction, and elegant posture opens the world of beautiful singing to you—a world that invites you from your youth and will embrace you as a senior citizen.

Discussion Questions

1. Describe the unique qualities of sound found in men's choruses.
2. What characteristics would indicate that a male voice is a tenor? A baritone? A bass?
3. Describe "breath management." How can it be achieved?
4. What is the unique challenge facing the baritone regarding his vocal range?
5. Explain factors that can hinder men singing well into later years. How can these factors be corrected?

Resources for Further Reading

Estes, S. (1999). *Simon Estes: In his own voice.* LMP, L.C.
Miller, R. (1993). *Training tenor voices.* Schirmer Books.
Miller, R. (2008). *Securing baritone, bass-baritone, and bass voices.* Oxford University Press.
Smith, B., & Sataloff, R. (2012). *Choral pedagogy and the older singer.* Plural Publishing.
Smith, B., & Sataloff, R. (2013). *Choral pedagogy* (3rd ed.). Plural Publishing.

Gender Spectrum Voice

Erin Nicole Donahue

Whether ordering food at a drive-through, calling to schedule an appointment, completing a phone interview, or answering a call from a friend, our voices communicate much about who we are, even when we aren't saying a lot. Much of how we are perceived by others is dependent on how we communicate. This may include both nonverbal communication—which includes facial expressions, eye contact, hand gestures, the way we dress, and posture—as well as verbal communication. Verbal communication is arguably the most important feature of communication, as we are able to communicate effectively without visual cues, such as when we talk on the phone. Singing may be considered an extension of speech, as the basic process of phonation or making sound is fundamentally similar whether one is talking on the phone or singing an aria. The technical requirements for those tasks vary immensely but the subsystems of breath, phonation, and resonance are at work in both examples.

For gender diverse individuals—including but not limited to transgender, gender nonconforming, and/or nonbinary persons—it is often particularly impactful and satisfying when voice is congruent with their gender to aid in conveying who they are to communication partners. A person may be considered gender diverse when their gender does not match their assigned sex at birth. Some common terms and definitions related to gender diverse individuals are included in Table 9–1. For readers looking to expand their knowledge and cultural competence, there are many available resources, some of which may be found at the end of this chapter. Readers are encouraged to increase their knowledge independently, to do the work it takes to achieve cultural competency, and to keep abreast of current terminology,

Table 9–1. Common Terms and Definitions Related to Gender Diverse Individuals

Term	Definition
Cisgender	When someone's assigned sex at birth is congruent with their gender
Dysphoria	Emotional distress or a feeling of dissatisfaction, anxiety, and/or restlessness
Gender dysphoria	Emotional distress due to incongruency between assigned sex at birth and gender identity
Gender expression	How someone expresses their gender through the way they dress, act, or communicate
Gender identity	How someone thinks or feels about their gender or how they experience their gender internally
Nonbinary	Gender that is outside of the binary male or female designations
Transgender	Someone whose assigned sex at birth does not match their gender identity

research, and best practices that are refined on an ongoing basis for optimal support, understanding, and representation of gender diverse individuals' experiences and needs. Current and future educators, vocal professionals, and student peers should strive to learn directly from gender diverse individuals such as transgender, nonbinary, nonconforming, agender, and/or genderqueer individuals who offer opportunities for education. It is important to recognize transgender and gender diverse voices as the leading experts related to this topic, as they have lived experience and knowledge that cis individuals do not possess. These individuals should always be acknowledged and compensated for their time and teaching. As the author of this chapter is a cisgender individual who is aware of her inherent privilege, it is important to note that this chapter includes information learned through clinical experience working with gender affirmative voice training in the outpatient voice clinic setting, working with gender diverse singers and students, and learning from trainings, presentations, and publications by researchers and experts. Readers of all backgrounds and levels are strongly encouraged to seek out resources or trainings developed, written, and/or presented by gender diverse individuals.

Working With the Gender Diverse Population

Gender diverse individuals are at increased risk of traumatization as compared to cisgender individuals. This is important to note, as trauma-informed pedagogy or care requires extra time, research, education, and sensitivity on the part of the educator, pedagogue, or practitioner. Gender diverse individuals' voices have often been silenced, quite literally, in the past or throughout their lives. Affirmative voice work can be very empowering for the individual, but it can also trigger intense dysphoria, and thus it is essential that the student or client feels secure and supported throughout the process. Whenever a student is in a potentially vulnerable position, a compassionate and informed approach is required for best practice. It is important that the gender diverse student feels they can speak openly and honestly about their thoughts and feelings related to their voice and psyche throughout the process of any voice work. It is also important that all students know they are not required to disclose any information they wish to keep private, as gender identity and voice can be extremely personal and sensitive matters. The relationship between gender diverse individuals and their voice teacher, choral director, or other voice professional must be strong and firmly rooted in trust in order for the student to feel safe to be willing to experiment with new sounds and techniques that will ultimately aid in discovery and eventual success.

One of the best ways to build trust between student and teacher is upon a solid foundation of respect. For educators working with transgender or gender diverse individuals, it is of utmost importance to endeavor to learn about and respect names and pronouns. The educator must engender a culture of acceptance, openness, flexibility, and support not only for their gender diverse students but for all of their students. One needs to be aware of each of their student's preferred way of being addressed and to ensure they consistently use the correct names and terminology appropriately. It may be advisable for each teacher to meet with their students at the beginning of their work together in order to gain information about that student including their preferred name and their pronouns.

For larger groups, demographic information may be gathered through completion of a questionnaire, although this is less personal in nature. This may be helpful for those looking to gain preliminary information about many individual students within a larger choral or group voice setting. These questionnaires may include general information about all students' preferred names and pronouns as well as past singing voice training and experience, past or current voice part, vocal comfort range, any potential voice-related symptoms or problems, and whether a student is looking to discuss anything specific with the educator regarding their voice. This can gather information from the students about their preferences in the use of their names and pronouns within different settings, such as in private meetings and/or in class. Upon review of the completed questionnaires, the educator would be able to identify any students who may benefit from or who specifically request further opportunity for discussion related to any current vocal considerations, limitations, and ultimate voice goals.

Meeting with a student individually should be open and voluntary for any student if this is not part of the standard curriculum for all students, as individuals may not be comfortable with being singled out. When meeting with a student, it would be beneficial to learn more about the student's current comfort with their voice including pitch range as well as comfort with various terminology used in music and voice work. For example, in a choral setting, a student may be uncomfortable with being labeled a "bass," even if they are comfortable with being placed in this section. The educator must be sensitive to the student's preferences in order to establish a sense of security for that student. The educator may benefit from careful consideration regarding the terminology used in the classroom with all students. More specific ideas related to modifications that may be advantageous are included later in this chapter.

It is important to note that voice is highly individual and personal, and it should never be assumed that an individual would want and/or intend to modify voice. Many gender diverse individuals do not wish to change their voice at all. Speaking and singing voice goals may be varied as well. For example, a transfeminine individual may wish to modify speaking voice to be perceived as more feminine within the context of our societal and cultural perception of what constitutes feminine voice. However, the same individual may wish to maintain their current singing voice part and sing in the bass section. Another transfeminine individual may wish to femininize both speaking and singing voice to some degree, with a goal of maintaining consistent quality and range in their speaking and singing voice. This hypothetical individual may wish to sing in the alto section instead of the bass section. Just as gender identity, personal pronouns, and individual interests are highly individual, preferences surrounding voice are highly individual as well. For music and voice professionals working with transgender and/or nonbinary singers, it is recommended to take the lead of that person and to discuss their goals and preferences when considering what, if any, aspects of voice to address.

Transition and Hormones

An endocrinologist or other specialized physician is typically the provider who manages hormone replacement therapy. It is outside of the scope of this book to include any in-depth details relating to hormones and transition. If one is to work closely with this population, it would be beneficial to learn some of the specifics regarding changes that may occur in response to hormone therapy. To oversimplify what can be a very complex subject, hormone therapy may be utilized to help facilitate changes that aid in achieving physical congruence with an individual's gender.

For transfeminine individuals, estrogens and/or antiandrogens may be prescribed and taken for their feminizing effects. These hormones typically result in effects on the body which may include breast development, skin softening, and change in fat distribution, which are desirable for many transfeminine individuals. For these individuals, it is important to understand that voice will not change as a result of initiation of hormone therapy. If an individual has gone through puberty and associated postpubertal "voice change," it cannot be reversed by hormones. Similarly, the size of the "Adam's apple," or laryngeal prominence of the thyroid cartilage, will not change secondary to hormone therapy in the case of feminizing hormones. For these patients, the primary way to feminize voice is through behavioral modification. Therefore, these individuals may be more likely to pursue voice training regardless of whether they are undergoing hormone replacement therapy, as hormone therapy does not aid them in any pursuit of feminization of voice.

Transmasculine individuals may be prescribed testosterone, which has many masculinizing effects on the body, including increase in body hair and facial hair, and potential changes in muscle mass. Notably, and conversely to feminizing hormones, there can be significant changes to the voice in transmasculine individuals who are taking testosterone. These changes develop at different rates and to varying degrees. However, in general, the majority of these individuals eventually present with a deeper, lower voice that is often perceived by others as masculine. These individuals may be less likely to seek professional voice training for masculinization of speaking voice. However, singing voice can be particularly challenging for this population, as the speed and amount of voice change is highly variable between individuals, and there is no way to confidently predict these factors ahead of time. Therefore, transmasculine singers who choose to take testosterone may wish to work with a trusted teacher or voice practitioner throughout the process of their vocal transition. Some specific issues that sometimes arise for this population may include vocal instability, hoarseness, decreased range, throat discomfort with voice use, and/or vocal fatigue, among others. Many of these issues commonly occur during the period of transition in which the voice is in flux on the way to stabilization. If any symptoms persist or worsen significantly beyond the point of maintenance, the singer may be advised to seek help from an experienced voice professional if possible.

Aspects of Voice and Verbal Communication

There are many separate aspects of verbal communication that may fall within the realm of "voice" that include, but are not limited to, pitch, resonance, articulation, prosody/intonation, and language. For singers, these features of voice are likely familiar, as singing necessitates specific frequencies (pitch) be produced in a particular pattern (intonation/prosody) while maintaining optimal placement (resonance) on text (utilizing articulation and language). For gender diverse individuals, modification of one or more of these aspects of voice may be desired in order to better express their gender or to be congruent with their gender.

Modification of voice may include masculinization and/or feminization of aspects of voice. The specific details of modification vary and are individual to each person based on what resonates with that person as authentic or results in a voice that is congruent with their gender. Voice modification may be undertaken independently or the individual may seek help from a professional such as a speech-language pathologist (SLP) with specialized training and knowledge related to gender diverse voice. An experienced SLP can provide gender affirmative voice training, which is designed on an individual basis for each client. Gender diverse clients of SLPs are provided with tools and exercises to aid in voice modification with a goal of discovering and developing an authentic voice. The initial evaluation may include a case history, assessment of voice, and may or may not also include laryngeal stroboscopy to screen for any laryngeal pathology and to assess baseline laryngeal function. Subsequent voice therapy sessions vary in length and frequency based on individualized factors.

Laryngologists, or specialized physicians who have advanced training in surgery and medical treatment of laryngeal disorders, may offer voice feminization surgery as an option for transfeminine patients. The specifics regarding technique and efficacy of laryngeal surgeries are outside of the scope of this chapter. Generally, these surgeries aim to increase the frequency of phonation. Those who pursue vocal feminization surgery frequently undergo preoperative and postoperative direct voice therapy to maximize surgical and functional outcomes.

The time frame regarding transition of voice is variable and highly individual. Educators and choral conductors working with transgender singers should plan on being flexible with these students, as pending their current comfort, range, and goals, their voices likely will not always be predictable during this transition period. Conversely, the transgender individual may not wish to modify voice. This is important to note, as one size does not fit all when it comes to gender and voice. Information regarding various aspects of voice that may be addressed during gender affirmative voice work is included in more detail in the following sections. This information is not meant as a comprehensive guide to gender affirmative voice work, but rather as an overview to familiarize the reader with some of the aspects of voice and communication an individual may be addressing as they work toward congruency between voice and gender.

Pitch

When one considers what aspect of voice may be an indicator of gender to communication partners, pitch usually tops the list. There is a physiologic basis for differences in pitch in relation to gender. The perceptual aspect of pitch is determined by the frequency of phonation, or the rate of vibration of the vocal folds, which is measured in hertz (Hz). The frequency, or number of Hz, is the number of cycles of vibration per second. The faster the vocal folds vibrate, the higher the Hz or frequency. For example, vocal folds vibrating at 800 Hz would produce sound that is higher than vocal folds vibrating at 200 Hz. Pitch is associated with frequency and is what we typically measure frequency by when speaking in musical terms. For reference, 440 Hz is equivalent to A4 in pitch, whereas A3 is 220 Hz and A5 is 880 Hz.

The larger and heavier the vocal folds are, the lower the frequency of vibration or pitch, as larger vocal folds vibrate at less cycles per second, or slower. Therefore, postpubescent vocal folds of those assigned male at birth will likely produce lower fundamental frequency and lower pitch as compared to a larynx that houses smaller and thinner vocal folds. The smaller, lighter, thinner vocal folds vibrate at a faster rate, resulting in higher average speaking pitch. In regard to both speaking and singing voice, there is a range that is generally considered to be more feminine or more masculine. There is also an overlapping portion of the ranges that tends toward being more ambiguous or gender neutral. Female-speaking pitch typically falls in the range of 165 to 255 Hz (approximately E3–C4), whereas male speaking range falls more around 85 to 155 Hz (approximately F2–Eb3). Within the overlapping gender ambiguous or neutral pitch range, other characteristics of sound are integrated by the listener to help in determining whether the voice is perceived as masculine, feminine, or either/neither. Interestingly, a voice can be inside or significantly outside of the limits of "typical" masculine or feminine pitch range and still be perceived by unfamiliar listeners as a different gender. This highlights the fact that pitch is not the only aspect of voice that a listener's brain takes into account when determining the gender of an unfamiliar or unseen speaker.

Within masculine or feminine pitch range there is much variability as to where a voice may be situated. This varies based on several factors that may include an individual's anatomy and physiology, personality, culture, and background. A great way to make this idea more tangible is to think of three to five different "female" voices. These could be the voices of actors, singers, professional speakers such as news anchors or podcasters, or people one knows personally. When comparing the more detailed characteristics and overall sound of these voices, pitch is likely to vary, sometimes to a significant degree, despite all of the voices being categorized as "female." For transfeminine individuals, it is helpful to explore various pitches that fall within the potential goal range in order to determine what feels and sounds the most authentic and comfortable for that person.

There are many exercises that an individual may utilize in order to explore pitch within the context of gender affirmative voice work. Depending on their goals, comfort, starting point, and/or current ability, this could be very simple or more complex. One specific example that can be a great starting exercise in pitch exploration is to perform gentle stretching and contracting in the form of pitch glides. Pitch glides may begin at a comfortable pitch before gliding up and down, higher and lower through the range, such as in a "siren." The student can perform these pitch glides by starting in a limited range before gradually increasing and decreasing the top and bottom notes until they have stretched through the entire range. The student should be advised to maintain neutral and relaxed posture, breathe as often as needed, and ensure easy sound throughout. Many sounds may be utilized for this exercise. Lip buzzes/trills or tongue trills are excellent sounds in which to perform glides. Other options may include gentle humming on /m/ or /ng/, an extended

/z/, or a vowel such as an /u/. The student may be advised to gently glide through their range on the chosen sound, with a focus on the range they wish to target for speaking and/or singing voice. This simple exercise can be very useful when working on exploring the limits and possibilities of their pitch range.

Resonance

Resonance may not be the first aspect of voice one thinks of when considering the gender of a voice. However, resonance largely shapes the sound that ultimately comes out when speaking or singing. The resonance system filters the voice. The way one shapes the sound through alterations in resonance may result in changing the overall quality or efficiency of the voice. An example of a specific shift in resonance would be an extremely "nasal" voice, where much of the sound is being filtered through the nose. The extreme nasality may help the sound carry, such as in the case of some popular characters on comedic sitcoms, resulting in the listener hearing the "nasal" voice or laugh from across the room. Resonance can also work to change the overall timbre, or color, of the sound. A sound can be brighter or darker, lighter or heavier and have pressed or relaxed and open quality depending on the resonance.

A simple yet effective exercise that may be utilized to explore resonance is humming. The student is asked to perform a gentle hum on an /m/ or on an /ng/ while focusing on the "buzzy" sensation or vibrations that are produced. The student may be encouraged to maintain space inside the mouth while moving the vibrations around backward and forward, up and down, from the nose to the lips, and from the back of the mouth to the front.

The pitch may be varied within the context of the resonance exercise. For example, there may be an increase or decrease in the strength of vibration sensation in the nose or lips while changing pitch, which can be insightful for the student, especially when considering which pitches might be optimal for their voice. Through exploration, repetition, and consequent motor learning, the student may then begin to develop a schema for how to modify resonance. This control over resonance is essential to shape the overall sound output.

Prosody, Intonation, Articulation, and Language

Prosody includes the pitch variability (or intonation), loudness, stress patterns, pauses, and rate of speech. The intonation of speech is similar to the melody of a song. Prosody includes both the "melody" and "rhythm" of speech. There are some specific characteristics of prosody that are often perceived to be more masculine or feminine by listeners. During gender affirmative voice work, the student or client is encouraged to trial different prosodic patterns including slower and faster rate of speech (similar to tempo) with more or less fluidity (legato vs. staccato) and greater or smaller pitch range and variation within a phrase (range).

Typically, prosody that has historically been considered to be more feminine is faster in rate of speech with smoother, connected flow (more legato) and greater pitch variability with a wider range of pitches. Conversely, masculine speech patterns may include less words per minute (slower rate), separated words (more staccato), and less pitch variability with a smaller range of pitches, or more monotone intonation. Generally, feminine speech patterns may convey more emotion through prosodic cues. Therefore, there may be more variability in loudness and pitch and more contrast in stressed versus unstressed syllables.

Articulation is the way speech sounds are formed. There are patterns of articulation or the shape of speech sounds that may be perceived as more or less feminine or masculine. The placement, precision, and pressure of articulation of each phoneme, or distinct unit of sound, depend on many factors including the speaker's native language, age, dialect, gender, and/or culture. This may or may not be addressed as an area of modification within gender affirmative voice work.

Language is a complex topic, and language choice—much like all aspects of verbal communication—depends on a multitude of factors. These determining factors may include the individual's vocabulary, location of residence, dialect, education level, gender, age, environment, and multiple cultural factors. Language may be addressed during gender affirmative voice training if the individual chooses to explore language choices that are traditionally and/or historically associated with a certain gender.

It is important to note that many of an individual's inherent speech patterns or language choices may be related to their personality or disposition and are independent of their gender. Therefore, although one aspect of prosody or language may be deemed "more feminine," it may not resonate as authentic with an individual as it is not congruent with their personality and how they wish to communicate with others. For example, a reserved transfeminine client with a timid and shy disposition may not wish to increase their pitch and loudness variability to an extreme degree, as they may not be comfortable exhibiting significant emotion in their daily verbal communication. Much like the choice of whether to modify voice, all aspects of voice modification are highly individual and may or may not be a target for each person.

Overall, there are many areas of verbal communication that may be potential targets within the context of gender affirmative voice training. The individual goals should be determined by the transgender, nonbinary, or gender nonconforming individual, as education and training is provided by the professional. Professionals, educators, and peers should never assume a specific area should or should not be a target as the individual works toward congruency between their gender, self, and voice. One must never give unsolicited advice or opinions to their students related to their voice and gender, just as one would never give advice or opinions related to a student's appearance and gender. It is also important to note for peers that it is not their place to lend judgement to any individual's voice as it pertains to their gender. As such, comments regarding voice are inappropriate and are often negatively impactful on many levels.

As singers themselves (and as human beings), educators and professionals should always be sensitive to giving any solicited feedback that may be considered negative criticism, even though feedback has been requested, as this can be devastating to a student's confidence and may result in increased dysphoria, which can lead to lack of motivation and the possibility of the individual resigning themselves to any chance of progress toward their goals. Hence educators and professionals must remain steadily compassionate and encouraging when providing any requested feedback or training to the student or client and check in with that individual regularly to monitor for thoughts and feelings that may help or hinder their progress.

The Transgender or Gender Diverse Singer

All of the aforementioned aspects of verbal communication obviously apply to speaking voice. For the gender diverse singer, similar aspects may apply to singing voice as well. The individual may or may not be working with a professional in their pursuit toward vocal congruency with their gender. Whether they are actively working with an SLP or practicing in their own at home without professional guidance on speaking voice modification, singing voice presents with an additional set of challenges.

The transgender singer may note that their goal is for consistency between their speaking and singing voices, or they may feel that their singing voice is separate from their speaking voice and is independent of their gender. Others may feel that voice is completely separate from their gender and not wish to change anything. It is important to discuss the goals of the student before and frequently throughout any vocal work together. Depending on the level of experience, years of training, age of the singer, and voice type, singing voice goals may be extremely difficult or relatively easy to accomplish. The amount of difficulty depends to some degree on how far the goal is from the baseline vocal range and characteristics. Some goals may not be realistic due to physiologic limitations. If a student expresses a goal that the educator or voice professional deems potentially improbable, the educator should be open to delicately discussing possible limitations with the student. Even if the student's goals are unlikely to be achievable, it is prudent to attempt to take baby steps with the student toward their goals. Often, if the student has lofty long-term goals, more manageable short-term goals can be agreed upon between the student and teacher. Throughout the course of their work together, the student may make discoveries that lead to modifications of the long-term goal. Ultimately, the process of working toward a goal and celebrating any successes, big or small, can be extremely rewarding and motivating for both the student and teacher.

Considerations for the Music Educator

For educators working with the transgender population, there are many important individual factors that may be taken into consideration depending on the student. Whether within the context of a choral or solo singing setting, it is important to consider the individual's preference and comfort with specific ranges and/or voice parts. As mentioned earlier in the chapter, nomenclature used in the classroom should ideally mirror the terminology that the individual singer or student uses or prefers, as some singers may be uncomfortable with specific terms that may "label" their voice and potentially contribute to increased dysphoria. The educator must also be sensitive to any gendered language in the classroom. An example of gendered language would be asking a section to sing a specific portion of a piece by saying, "Let's have all men sing from the beginning of the piece." Instead, the director may choose to use terminology that is gender neutral such as "low voices" or "lowest section." Alternately, names of the sections may also be used.

Music educators have the opportunity to be advocates for their gender diverse students. Educators are encouraged to take a look at institutional rules to ensure there are no discriminatory policies in place that may cause undue stress for gender diverse students. Discriminatory policies that are specific to the music classroom may include not allowing a singer to audition for or sing in the part they wish to sing based on their gender. Additionally, educators may wish to consider gender neutral uniforms for all students or to allow students to select the uniform garments they are most comfortable wearing for any given ensemble. Examples of gender neutral attire may include simple concert blacks or black pants with a white shirt. More options are becoming available through established uniform providers, and directors are advised to reach out to their specific uniform company to discuss options for their students in advance of the performance season. Choral directors should think about how to accommodate gender diverse singers in any choral ensembles, including those that are traditionally gendered, such as "men's chorus" or "women's chorus." Some possible options for names for these specific ensembles include "treble choir" or "high-voice choral ensemble."

For choral educators, one-on-one discussion with the student should include determining their current vocal range as well as learning more about their target or goals related to voice. It bears repeating that it is not the job of the educator to provide unsolicited advice or any judgement regarding the student's vocal goals. It is in the best interest of the educator to support the student by offering potential options and solutions to allow for the best fit and most comfort for the student in order to build rapport and foster trust. If the student is not able to consistently sing in one part for all of the choir's repertoire, the student may need to be allowed to sing in various sections depending on the range and requirements of different choral pieces. The educator may need to be prepared to write different voicings of a part in order to allow for the student to consistently sing in a specific section that is more in alignment with their gender. Some additional options also may include allowing the student to sing in a different octave or skip specific notes in a choral work pending the technical requirements of the piece.

Overall, flexibility is key, as the singer's preferred voice part and range may differ from what is physiologically comfortable and/or easy at that time. Working with gender diverse singers allows for opportunities for collaboration regarding when and how to make adjustments to repertoire in order to best match their comfort and preference. It is advisable to consult with the singer individually in order to discuss any modifications that may be necessary or advisable prior to implementing modifications. Collaboration with the student helps the student to feel heard throughout the process and allows the student to voice any of their opinions or thoughts regarding potential options. Some specific modifications may include addressing aspects of pitch range to facilitate comfort and preferred range, which may be accomplished through changing keys of a solo piece or singing a different voicing of a part in a choral work.

All singers should understand the intrinsic connection between voice and self and that one's identity and spirit is completely interconnected to our voice. Singing can be an outlet to release many negative emotions, has the power to help alleviate feelings of stress, and can foster a sense of happiness, achievement, and positivity. It is important that we take the time to learn about an individual's comfort level, terminology, skills, goals, and preferences in order to support them in their journey. The encouragement and assistance provided by a compassionate and respectful educator can help facilitate holistic feelings of success and well-being for that student through the act of singing. This can have immensely positive effects on that individual's psyche which, ultimately, can improve quality of life and happiness.

Conclusion

Music educators and singing teachers are likely to encounter gender diverse individuals or singers over the course of their work. It is imperative that professionals strive to become culturally competent in order to best serve this unique population. This is equally important for peers. Transgender, nonbinary, and/or gender nonconforming individuals may or may not wish to modify some or all aspects of their voices in order to achieve congruency between voice and gender. The music educator's or voice professional's job is not to tell the student or client what to do, but rather to support that individual in their vocal journey. This always includes respecting and supporting the student or client but may also include being flexible and providing options to allow for optimal vocal comfort. If an educator, voice professional, or trusted peer can provide a safe space to allow the transgender individual to freely explore their voice without fear of judgement, discoveries may be made that ideally lead to finding an authentic voice that is not only congruent with their gender but also represents who they are as a person.

Discussion Questions

1. What are gender identity and gender expression?
2. Describe the masculinizing effects of testosterone for transmasculine individuals.
3. What are the typical frequency ranges for feminine and masculine speaking voices?
4. What does the prosody of speech entail?
5. How can a choral educator support a transgender student who is unable to sing the written part in their section?

Resources for Further Reading

Adler, R., Hirsch, S., & Pickering, J. (Eds.). (2018). *Voice and communication therapy for the transgender/gender diverse client: A comprehensive clinical guide* (3rd ed.). Plural Publishing.

Aguirre, R. (2018). Finding the trans voice: A review of the literature on accommodating transgender singers. *National Association for Music Education, 37*(1), 36–41.

Azul, D., Nygren, U., Södersten, M., & Neuschaefer-Rube, C. (2017). Transmasculine people's voice function: A review of the currently available evidence. *Journal of Voice, 31*(2), 261.e9–261.e23.

Jackson Hearns, L., & Kremer, B. (2018). *The singing teacher's guide to transgender voices*. Plural Publishing.

Manternach, B. (2017). Teaching transgender singers. Part 2: The singers' perspectives. *Journal of Singing, 74*(2), 209–214.

Manternach, B., Chipman, M., Rainero, R., & Stave, C. (2017). Teaching transgender singers. Part 1: The voice teachers' perspectives. *Journal of Singing, 74*(1), 83–88.

Palkki, J. (2020). "My voice speaks for itself": The experiences of three transgender students in American secondary school choral programs. *International Journal of Music Education, 38*(1), 126–146.

Sauerland, W. (2018). *Legitimate voices: A multicase study of trans and non-binary singers in the applied voice studio* [Doctoral dissertation, Columbia University]. Retrieved from ProQuest Dissertations and Theses database. (UMI No. 10825714)

Steele, D., & Rice, A. (2018). Every person's voice matters: The lived theology of a teacher of transgender singers. In K. S. Hendricks & J. Boyce-Tillman (Eds.), *Music and spirituality series: Vol. 6. Queering freedom: Music, identity, and spirituality* (pp. 219–242). Peter Lang.

Young, V., Yousef, A., Zhao, N., & Schneider, S. (2021). Vocal and stroboscopic characteristics in transgender patients seeking gender-affirming voice care. *Laryngoscope, 131*(5), 1071–1077.

10

The Science of Healthy Singing

Erin Nicole Donahue

Vocal Health and Wellness

Whether you sing in a choral setting or solo, classical or contemporary, are an educator or student, or are a novice or professional level singer, maintenance of vocal health is of utmost importance for all who sing. There are many physical and psychological benefits of singing that may be enjoyed throughout a singer's life if they take care of their voice. If a singer does not maintain a healthy voice, they are unlikely to have the vocal strength, stamina, flexibility, longevity, and/or agility to sing what they would like for as long as they would like. Maximizing the health of the laryngeal mechanism helps to promote the performance of the voice throughout the years.

There are many proven benefits of vocal hygiene for singers such as reduced vocal fatigue in response to hydration and vocal rest. Phonotrauma, or harmful vocal behavior, is considered to be a primary contributing factor to the formation of many benign vocal fold pathologies, including nodules and polyps. Inhaled irritants are known to be damaging to the larynx, and smoking has been identified as a causative factor for oral and laryngeal carcinoma. Therefore, good vocal hygiene practices should minimize the occurrence of pathology.

Every singer should be aware of habits and practices that may help to optimize vocal health. Many recommendations regarding healthy vocal habits are consistent regardless of the voice type, years of experience, age, and/or gender. Some of the most obvious and frequently quoted recommendations include maintenance of proper hydration and avoidance of behaviors that can be harmful to the laryngeal tissue. Some recommendations, however, may be more relevant than others for each singer based on individual factors. For example, one adolescent singer may habitually speak with inefficient technique causing increased vocal fatigue and therefore may need more focus on adjusting speaking technique through learning how to coordinate respiration and voicing while optimizing resonance. Another singer, however, may not experience any issues with their speaking or singing voice but presents with complaints of chronic throat clearing and coughing that need to be addressed through reflux and behavioral management. This may also vary based on whether the individual is primarily a singer or an educator. For example, a music educator should understand the benefits of optimizing classroom acoustics and use of amplification in the classroom while the student needs to know how to prioritize vocal activities. Each individual is likely to present with a unique set of lifestyle factors, preferences, and challenges when considering ways to optimize vocal health.

When a singer understands the reason behind why they are making a specific choice to optimize their vocal health, they are more likely to contentedly and consistently comply with the decision. Therefore, it is beneficial to have a general understanding of vocal anatomy and physiology in order to understand the rationale for specific vocal hygiene recommendations. To that end, a brief overview of anatomy and physiology of voice production is included in the following section. For further discussion, detailed information is included in Dr. Robert T. Sataloff's "Anatomy and Physiology of the Voice" chapter within this book. See the reading list at the end of Chapter 2 for further readings.

A Brief Overview of Anatomy and Physiology

A working knowledge of vocal anatomy and physiology is helpful when considering the best practices for maintaining optimal vocal health. One does not necessarily need to memorize all of the specific details such as the name of each of the intrinsic laryngeal muscles and what they do (although this is helpful), but it is necessary to have, at a minimum, a general understanding of how the voice is produced. Knowledge of the mechanics of phonation, or sound production, can help in consciously producing voice that is most efficient and thus healthier than inefficient voicing techniques.

There are three subsystems that work together to produce voice: respiration, phonation, and resonance. These three systems must work in a coordinated and cooperative fashion to produce healthy sound. Respiration is the system responsible for breath, phonation for sound, and resonance for filtering and shaping the sound.

Respiration

The respiratory system, which controls breath, is the power source for sound production. Most singers understand that maximizing the mechanics of breathing is advantageous in singing, as breath support and control are essential to healthy and efficient vocal fold vibration when singing. Breathing is an automatic process in that a person continues to breathe whether they are awake or sleeping and whether purposefully focusing on breathing or not. The acts of inhalation and exhalation may be unconscious and passive or purposeful and active.

When one breathes in, or inhales, the diaphragm contracts inferiorly and the intercostals contract away from the thoracic cavity. This action pulls the lungs down and out, resulting in lower pressure inside of the lungs. The air then flows into the lungs, filling the space. As inhalation occurs, the ribcage expands outward as does the abdominal cavity due to the displacement of its contents from the movement of the diaphragm. During quiet, tidal breathing, passive recoil forces are primarily responsible for exhalation. The diaphragm relaxes superiorly, resulting in the air being expelled from the lungs through the trachea, the larynx and vocal folds, and out through the nose or mouth.

Production of speech or singing requires a steady, controlled manner of exhalation in which the muscles of inspiration act to regulate the air. This process is primarily accomplished through contraction of the intercostal muscles within the rib cage to overcome the natural tendency of the lungs to passively recoil in order to maintain sufficient levels of subglottic pressure required for continuous phonation. During phonation, the air passing through the glottis, or the level of the vocal folds in the larynx, results in vocal fold vibration.

The Vocal Folds

The vocal folds are housed within the larynx, or voice box, and vibrate to create voice, or phonation. The vocal folds of adult women are about 11 mm to 15 mm long and 17 mm to 21 mm long in adult men. The vocal folds may also be referred to as vocal cords, although "folds" is a more accurate descriptor of their structure. It is helpful to keep in mind the histology, or microanatomy, of the vocal folds in order to understand how they vibrate to produce sound and why harmful behaviors or substances may result in injury or damage that leads to voice-related symptoms. The vocal folds are made up of several layers that can be organized into a body and cover layer. The body includes the innermost layers and includes a muscular layer and deep layer of the lamina propria, while the cover is made up of intermediate and superficial layers of the lamina propria covered on the outermost layer by the epithelium. Due to the structure of the vocal folds, vibration has specific properties that result in the quality of voice. The vocal folds must be pliable, flexible, and moisturized to vibrate efficiently.

Phonation

Vocal folds open, or abduct, when breathing at rest, allowing for open flow of air through the glottis. During phonation, the vocal folds move into an adducted, or closed, position. As air is pushed out of the lungs during phonation, the pathway is closed off at the laryngeal level by the adducted vocal folds. In order for the air to escape, enough air pressure must build below the glottis to overcome the resistance of the adducted vocal folds. Once the air pressure overcomes the glottic resistance, the vocal folds are blown apart, allowing air to rush through. The vocal folds are then set into a cycle of vibration, due to the Bernoulli effect. The Bernoulli principle states that there is an inverse relationship between velocity and pressure for fluids or gases moving along a constricted space. Therefore, as air rushes through the open glottis at a high velocity, there is a decrease in pressure along the medial edge of the vocal folds, which pulls the vocal folds back together. Once the vocal folds have adducted, the subglottic pressure builds up until the resistance is overcome again, and the cycle continues. This, in short, is the process of phonation.

Pitch is determined by how quickly the vocal folds are vibrating, or the frequency of phonation. The rate of vocal fold vibration or frequency or phonation is measured in hertz (Hz) or the number of cycles of vibration per second. This correlates to the perception of pitch. For example, if the vocal folds are vibrating at a frequency of 440 Hz, or 440 cycles of vibration per second, the pitch that will be produced is A4, or A above middle C. The faster the vocal folds vibrate, the higher the frequency and pitch. The vocal folds of sopranos singing above the staff can vibrate over 1000 Hz, while the vocal folds of a bass can vibrate at a lower rate than 90 Hz, depending on the pitch being sung.

Resonance

Resonance is responsible for filtering the sound produced in the larynx. Singers with formal training are often very familiar with the concept of resonance. Resonance helps to "shape" the sound that we hear. The portion of the acoustic theory of voice production that describes the role of the filter in sound production is called the source-filter theory. The source-filter theory details the relationship between the source of phonation, which produces the sound, and the filter, which shapes the sound into particular vowels or other speech sounds. The structures that make up the resonating system, or vocal tract, include the supraglottic structures that are located above the level of the vocal folds: the pharynx; the oral cavity including the hard palate, soft palate, and tongue; the nasal cavity; and the sinuses. The sound that moves from the larynx up into the various resonators is filtered and specific harmonics are strengthened while others are dampened depending on the shape of the resonating structures. This sound is shaped into various phonemes, or speech sounds, which combine to form words. Vowels are produced with little obstruction and a relatively open vocal tract. The articulators—including the tongue, teeth, lips, and so forth—are utilized to obstruct the sound in various patterns to create individual consonants. For example, the sound stream is obstructed by the upper teeth and lower lip to create /v/, a voiced fricative.

An example of how sound can be modified through changes in resonance include voices that may be considered hypernasal such as character voices of actors in television shows or on the stage, although the actor typically does not speak in that voice naturally. This is accomplished through modifications to resonance. Shifts in vocal timbre may be achieved through modification of structures in the vocal tract to change the resonance, and thus change the way the sound is filtered. Resonance can be optimized in order to maintain vocal health, as there are more and less efficient ways to filter voice and utilizing efficient resonance can be a powerful tool for singers and speakers alike. Singing relies on extensive coordination of the muscles of respiration and phonation as well as manipulation of the variables of resonance to maintain appropriate sound production for the style of singing.

The subsystems of voice: respiration, phonation, and resonance work together to create all of the varied sounds the human voice can produce. Ensuring that adequate breath is utilized to support phonation while maintaining easy, consistent phonation patterns with efficient resonance is the goal for a singer looking to optimize vocal technique. For more information regarding specifics of anatomy and physiology, including names of specific structures such as muscles and cartilages and how they work, see the anatomy and physiology of the voice chapter in this book.

Maximizing Vocal Health

Physiologic processes of voice production during both speaking and singing can be supported in many ways through consistent compliance with vocal health practices. General guidelines for vocal health and hygiene are similar whether a singer is old or young, a baritone or a soprano, or someone with no formal training or postgraduate training. Some of the most important factors that contribute to vocal health optimization include hydration, avoidance of irritants, vocal training, ensuring healthy patterns of phonation through strong vocal technique, minimization of phonotraumatic behaviors, and regular performance of warm-ups and cool-downs.

Hydration

Even those with only rudimentary knowledge of vocal health basics know that it is important to hydrate for optimal vocal health. However, many people do not know the details of why drinking water is so important with regards to voice use and singing. In short, hydration is important in order to maintain lubrication of the tissues in the larynx. Just as it is important to put oil into a car to help it run optimally, it is important for the singer to hydrate their body.

In thinking back to anatomy and physiology of phonation, one will remember that the vocal folds vibrate upward of 100 times/cycles per second (100 cycles of vibration per second = 100 Hz). Sopranos may sing frequencies upward of 1000 Hz and therefore 1000+ cycles of vibration per second when singing their highest pitches. With so many instances of the vocal folds coming into contact with one another, there is the potential for friction. Friction may result in the creation of heat and possibly irritation, inflammation, and redness of the tissues. However, lubrication of the tissue provides some protection against friction. This may best be explained by the example of rubbing your hands together quickly when they are dry versus wet or moistened by lotion. Proper lubrication in the form of naturally occurring thin secretions can aid in protecting the vocal fold mucosa. Although the tissue of the vocal folds is resilient and meant to withstand the shearing forces and impact of vibration, lack of lubrication may result in increased likelihood of friction and, ultimately, redness and swelling of the vocal folds.

Nothing you eat or drink touches the larynx or vocal folds. People are often surprised by this fact. However, upon consideration of the anatomy of the laryngeal area, the vocal folds sit above the trachea which is part of the respiratory system. If any foods or liquids were to pass over or through the vocal folds, they would go into the trachea and potentially into the lungs. This would result in choking, as the material would be going "down the wrong pipe." Therefore, in order for hydration to get to the level of the vocal folds, it can occur systemically or at a surface level.

The process of systemic hydration starts with drinking water, which is then absorbed to hydrate the whole body. Systemic hydration may result in thinner secretions in the larynx, that is, thinner mucus. This helps to create a thin layer of protective coating on the vocal folds to decrease the likelihood of friction or irritation from vocal use. Individuals often present to the voice clinic with complaints of "thick mucus" or dryness sensation in their mouth and throat, which is frequently a result of poor hydration practices. These symptoms generally improve or resolve relatively quickly simply by ensuring hydration needs are met on a daily basis.

One may have questions regarding how much water is enough. It is important to note that individual water requirements vary. The general rule of thumb in the past was that adults should drink approximately 64 ounces, or 8 cups, of water per day. More recently, it has been suggested that an individual may take their weight in pounds and divide by half to get the approximate number of ounces that should be consumed per day. For example, a 160 pound adult may require approximately 80 ounces of water per day for optimal hydration. However, many additional factors may be important to consider such as activity level, temperature or humidity of the environment, medications that cause drying, and possible water restriction due to medical concerns. On the other end of the spectrum, there is also the possibility of overconsumption of water which can, although rarely, result in illness or death. Many simple hydration calculators exist online and are easily accessible as a starting place to determine the optimal amount of water to consume per day. For specific questions, one may always consult with their personal physician to discuss recommendations and/or concerns.

Drinking more water isn't the only way to hydrate. Much of the water in your body can be derived from foods you eat. Adding high water content foods to one's diet is often an easy way to increase systemic hydration when an individual is already drinking an appropriate amount of water but continues to feel dry. The foods with the highest water content include many fruits and vegetables such as cucumbers, lettuce, melons, apples, peaches, and berries.

In this author's personal clinical experience, some asymptomatic young singers may present with signs of dryness at baseline. They may not be experiencing significant issues with hoarseness or throat irritation but do frequently note minimal complaints of thick mucus, dryness sensation, and increased urge to throat clear. For these young singers, ensuring water-rich foods are a part of their diet may be a good way to add hydration when they are already consuming the recommended amount of water daily.

Surface hydration can be another useful tool in promoting hydration of the laryngeal tissues. Surface hydration may be accomplished through adding moisture to the air one breathes. Humidification may be an effective strategy through the use of a humidifier in the singer's bedroom at night or in a room where the singer spends time over the course of the day. There are numerous humidifier options that have many differing specifications including cost, size, and maintenance requirements. The singer is advised to keep the humidifier clean and to only use clean water as recommended in the instructions of their specific humidifier product guide as many, for example, recommend only the use of bottled distilled water to avoid buildup. Personal steam inhalers can also be effective and are small and portable to allow steam inhalation prior to voice use or performance. Some singers prefer to use a nebulized saline solution instead of plain water in their steamer as they perceive greater benefit. Lower-tech options include passive inhalation of steam in a room such as a bathroom with a hot shower running or standing over a bowl of steaming water. Individuals are advised to avoid directly breathing hot steam, as burns of the tissue can occur. Many singers who perceive benefit from regular steaming opt for a personal steamer device, which can help with regulation of the steam inhalation. Some singers may not perceive significantly increased benefit from surface hydration strategies, so it is important to note that one size does not fit all when it comes to hydration strategies. Each singer is advised to trial different methods while ensuring adequate systemic hydration in order to determine which methods and routines derive the maximum perceived benefit.

Avoidance of Laryngeal Irritants

Anything you breathe in passes over your vocal folds in order to go into the trachea and down to the lungs. Any substances or materials that may be deemed "irritants" have the potential to negatively impact vocal fold health. Some examples of possible inhaled irritants include smoke or environmental irritants such as dust and allergens.

Smoke is one of the most concerning irritants, which may come from many sources. Smoking tobacco is the obvious example, such as smoking cigarettes or cigars. Smoking other substances such as marijuana can be similarly detrimental to the tissues of the vocal folds. More recently, vaping has become an alarming trend, particularly among young people. Many vapers, who may or may not be singers, do not fully understand the consequences as they assume it is "safer" than traditional smoking. Although individuals may use different materials in e-cigarettes when vaping, the apparent increased bioavailability of nicotine and exposure to aldehydes, which are considered carcinogenic, are a few of the many causes for concern. Whether smoking or vaping, the vocal folds are in the "line of fire" of any materials that are being inhaled.

Vocal folds that are regularly exposed to heat and irritants, such as in the case of smokers, often present with significant swelling and redness. This swelling and redness can increase over time, resulting in a boggy appearance due to excess fluid retention. This causes the classic "smoker's voice" that is often characterized by low pitch, decreased ability to access higher frequency phonation or reduced range, and a "husky" hoarseness. In severe cases, these individuals complain of significant hoarseness or voice loss and can even note breathing complaints due to the severe vocal fold swelling that can be so large as to partially obstruct the glottic airway. The other potential result of chronic exposure to smoke is a higher likelihood of developing an oropharyngeal or laryngeal (mouth or throat) cancer or lung cancer. This diagnosis can be devastating to anyone, but to a singer it can mean permanent damage to their instrument and functionality. Therefore, it is always advised that everyone, but particularly people who rely on their voices, avoid smoking and/or vaping of any kind.

Other potential irritants to the voice may include environmental irritants such as dust or allergens. Individuals with symptoms of allergies may benefit from evaluation and treatment by a provider such as an allergy and asthma physician or allergist. Environments that are not well-ventilated and contain chemicals also can cause laryngeal and airway irritation. Individuals who are exposed to environmental irritants may be advised to wear a mask or respirator during periods of exposure in order to minimize any chronic irritation. Those who are exposed to irritants may experience symptoms such as scratchy throat, throat pain, hoarseness, sensation of increased mucus, or dryness. These symptoms can result in increased throat clearing and coughing, which can further damage the laryngeal tissue. Therefore, individuals are advised to decrease exposure to materials and substances that may cause laryngeal irritation whenever possible.

Aside from inhaled irritants, there are other possible irritants to the laryngeal mucosa that are prevalent among singers, including acid reflux. Many singers may experience "silent reflux" where they do not perceive symptoms of esophageal reflux such as heartburn but do note complaints of increased sensation of mucus or a lump in the throat, burning throat, and/or increased urge to cough and throat clear. Many symptoms are triggered after lying down, in the morning upon waking, or after meals. These individuals may benefit from referral to a specialist such as a gastroenterologist (GI) in addition to an otolaryngologist (ENT) for evaluation and treatment. Foods that may increase likelihood of reflux or increased acidity of refluxed material include tomato-based products, spicy foods, high fat foods, citrus, alcohol, carbonated beverages, and/or caffeine. Individuals who experience acid reflux should attempt to avoid these foods and beverages. Overall, attempts should be made to avoid, manage, or minimize exposure to any materials that may be irritating to the tissues of the larynx.

Vocal Conditioning

Just as an athlete requires regular physical training to optimize physical performance, singers require regular vocal training to optimize vocal performance. The concept of relating singing to physical activity continues to gain traction, as research has revealed some similarities in physical and vocal performance. After all, a singer is also continuously using muscles and ligaments and cartilages in order to perform, just as an athlete. In continuing with this analogy, a singer would require regular stretching for warm-up and cool-down, exercise for stamina and power building, periodic rest after exertion, and practice to refine technique—just as an athlete working to optimize performance of their sport.

It is generally recognized that a singer should work with a professional voice teacher if they wish to enhance their performance through improving their vocal technique. Formal vocal training has been documented to improve the quality of the singing voice. When compared with individuals who have not received formal training, individuals with formal voice training produce measurable differences in phonatory behavior, contact area of the vocal folds, pitch and loudness control, and glottal adduction during increased vocal intensity. Research has shown that untrained singers are more likely to strain their voices to produce a wide range of frequencies. In addition to differences in sound production, individuals with vocal training have been noted to have better vocal hygiene habits than untrained singers, possibly due to the fact that untrained singers often are thought to have less knowledge of vocal hygiene practices.

A voice teacher can be an invaluable resource to a student, providing feedback and instruction from a trusted, knowledgeable source. The voice teacher assigns or provides the student with guidance regarding selection of appropriate repertoire, provides vocal exercises for singing and conditioning that target specific goals, and provides direction through adjustments in technique in order to optimize performance within the context of the student's repertoire. Even very experienced professional singers benefit from having a trusted teacher to provide feedback from an outside perspective. For novice singers, the experience and knowledge a vocal pedagogue can provide is vital when endeavoring to improve vocal performance. Over time, an enriching relationship can develop that is ideally built on trust in which the teacher knows the student's voice and can help in unlocking potential through ongoing guidance during their regular meetings. A voice teacher can also help in determining whether a student may be having vocal difficulty that is outside of normal limits that may warrant referral to a vocal health specialist or voice clinic.

The quest for optimizing vocal technique in order to improve performance is often a lifelong process. Balancing the subsystems of voice is required along with maximizing efficiency in order to achieve peak performance of any given piece, regardless of the style or genre of music. For many novice singers, aspects of technique that seem simple at first glance, such as the concept of "breath support," often take years to understand and master. Once the student has accomplished their specific technical goal in one piece, the work isn't over, as the same technique must then be built into a newer piece of repertoire. Vocalises or targeted voice exercises help to familiarize the body with sensory-motor feedback and provide opportunities for motor learning that are required to integrate a new technique into practice. For example, ascending scales on a particular vowel help the body to learn to adjust and coordinate muscular activity of the vocal folds, resonators, and articulators as the frequency increases up to the top of the range, ideally resulting in maintenance of consistent vocal quality. It can be very helpful for singers to engage in discussion with their teacher regarding the purpose and goals of the individualized vocalises and warm-ups that have been provided so the student can actively participate in their training process. A few specific examples of aspects of singing that may be targeted with vocal exercises include coordination of breath and sound production, increased vocal power, improvement of agility and/or flexibility, dynamic control, range expansion, consistency of vocal quality through various registers or with various sounds produced, and/or maximization of vocal efficiency.

Warm-Ups and Cool-Downs

An elite athlete, such as a gymnast, would be unlikely to wake up and jump straight out of bed into a back handspring. Similarly, a singer should not assume they should be able to jump straight into a difficult aria without an adequate warm-up. Most singers understand that a warm-up is advisable and have regularly performed warm-ups with their voice teacher or choral group. Research has documented that most singers report regular warm-ups as part of their routine. However, specifics regarding the type or length of warm-ups are varied. Warm-ups can be equated to a preperformance "stretching session" for the vocal athlete. Exercise physiology literature has proven that stretching prior to performance results in improved flexibility and less energy being required to complete a physical task as well as a potential decrease in incidence of injury. Therefore, the singer should regularly utilize warm-ups with a goal of stretching, contracting, and engaging the muscles that will be used during the singing task that is to follow the warm-up. The type and length of warm-ups to be performed should be individualized based on the singer's preferences, goals, and experience. They should, at a minimum, include engagement of breath, alignment of posture, facilitation of efficient sound production, and refinement of resonance.

Cool-downs are often recommended for athletes in order to bring the body back down to baseline after operating in a high energy state. Research regarding vocal cool-downs has indicated that singers generally report a positive perception of the impact on their voices when regularly engaging in a vocal cool-down practice. Specific exercises to be included should be individualized based on the singer, but generally must aim to return the voice to baseline following a period of heavy use. These may include exercises to bring the voice back into a speaking range and refocus resonance in the speaking voice. A voice teacher can help provide both an individualized warm-up and cool-down regimen and instruct the singer in proper technique in order to get the most out of these practices.

Voice Rest and Vocal Pacing

A runner, even a highly skilled and high-performing runner, cannot run nonstop on a daily basis without adequate rest. Rest is required in order to allow muscles time to recover and rebuild. During periods of rest, muscles are allowed the time required to adapt to the stress of challenges presented during practice and performance. Vocal rest can include short periods of voice rest, similar to a vocal "nap," throughout the day as well as longer periods of conservative voice use where extended or demanding phonation is avoided for a period of time to allow for recovery.

Vocal pacing is an important concept for anyone who relies on their voice on a regular basis. This concept is particularly important for the music educator or the avocational singer who also works in a job that requires heavy voice use on a daily basis. There is only so much voice use one can engage in before eliciting negative symptoms such as vocal fatigue, throat discomfort, or hoarseness. In considering how to pace one's voice use, it may be helpful to create a list of all voice use and the approximate amount of that activity during a typical week. This should include both job-related obligations and any recreational voice use. Examples may include answering phones and taking part in meetings at work, speaking with family on the phone, going out with friends socially, singing at a choir rehearsal, personal singing practice, and 1-hr, weekly voice lessons. It is important to consider the intensity of voice use and how stressful the use may be on the voice. For example, high intensity or loud voice use may be required for educators who have cafeteria duty. These individuals may only be speaking in this environment for a short time daily, but the use is more strenuous on the voice due to the environmental and situational demands. Anyone who has experienced hoarseness the next day after being in a very loud environment, such as a rock concert, knows that it doesn't take a very long time for voice to be significantly impacted in a negative way. Once an individual has created their list of voice use, they should work to prioritize the list in order of importance. Voice use that is required for someone to maintain their livelihood or income are typically prioritized at the top of the list. Recreational, more inconsequential voice use is usually lowest, especially if that communication could be adjusted to not require voice such as in the case of texting someone instead of calling on the phone. When someone is experiencing vocal fatigue regularly, they may look at their list in order to determine where they can decrease overall vocal load in order to improve vocal quality and stamina. This may be particularly impactful for vocal professionals such as educators. Adjustments for the sake of vocal pacing including incorporation of short periods of voice rest throughout the day or elimination of less important voice-use tasks can be small changes with relatively big rewards for those who engage in a heavy vocal load on a regular basis.

Avoidance or minimization of behaviors that may be phonotraumatic, or harmful to the vocal folds, is important for voice users. Phonotraumatic behaviors may include high intensity voice use, such as when screaming, yelling, or talking over loud noise; harsh and/or frequent throat clearing or coughing; and excessive voice use. Minimizing high intensity voice use, especially over a prolonged period of time, is helpful in reducing the overall vocal dose, which is key to vocal pacing. Voice users should try to avoid pushing significantly beyond the point of fatigue during periods of heavy voice use, especially if experiencing increased hoarseness or throat pain.

Impact of Acute Illness on the Voice

Acute illness may result in many voice- and throat-related symptoms including hoarseness, vocal fatigue, or throat pain. It is important to distinguish between acute symptoms that are attributable to illness versus chronic issues that may warrant evaluation. It is normal to have acute symptoms for up to approximately 10 to 14 days with illness. If symptoms of illness resolve and voice-related symptoms persist beyond that time, evaluation may be recommended. Despite the "show must go on" mentality of many performers and professional voice users, it is best to rest and conserve the voice when ill. Pushing through and performing or engaging in a heavy vocal load despite illness often results in prolonging symptoms and may cause chronic problems, which take much longer to resolve.

People experiencing chronic throat clearing and/or coughing that is nonproductive in nature may wish to seek evaluation and treatment. A cough may be considered chronic when it has lasted longer than 8 weeks. Frequent coughing or throat clearing has the potential to cause acute irritation to the tissue in the larynx due to the repeated impact of the vocal folds. The causes of chronic throat clearing and coughing may be treated either medically or behaviorally based on whatever etiology is determined to be the cause.

Amplification

Any professional voice users who speak to groups on a regular basis benefit from utilization of amplification. Professional voice users who frequently need amplification include public speakers, trainers, and educators. Ideally, these professionals will have access to microphones that allow a close mouth-to-mic distance and adequate amplification through a speaker system. Some employers have access to amplification devices or are willing to purchase for use during work. Other times, amplification is purchased by the individual for personal and professional use, if this is an accessible option. The difference in using one's voice at a comfortable loudness level and manually projecting all day when speaking to a group can be enormous when considering maintenance of vocal quality over a period of time.

Educators sometimes balk at the idea of using amplification when teaching, especially to a small class or in a small space. The difference, however, in vocal endurance, quality, ease, and comfort can be stark in comparison to unamplified voice use all day, and many converts have touted the benefits to others once they have experienced the difference amplification can make. There have also been documented benefits on the part of the students, including improved comprehension of educational material. Amplification can be an important tool for those working to decrease their vocal effort and load in order to maximize stamina and quality.

Mental Wellness

The mind-body connection is a very real factor in vocal quality and performance for every person who uses verbal communication. The neurologic and physiologic underpinning of the relationship between the voice and emotions or psychological states is complex and beyond the scope of this chapter. It is important, however, to be aware that significant emotions, stress, or anxiety can manifest as voice-related symptoms. An example of voice problems secondary to stress may include increase in muscle tension disorders with resultant hoarseness, voice loss, increased effort to phonate, and/or throat pain. It is imperative that singers and professional voice users work to maintain psychological wellness. Specific practices or habits that may be beneficial include mindfulness meditation, therapy with a licensed psychologist or counselor, yoga, prayer, and/or medical management by a psychiatrist if required.

Voice Disorders and Laryngeal Pathology

A voice disorder is defined as a laryngeal disturbance that impairs verbal communication or when the voice quality is considered to be outside the parameters of normal for an individual's age, gender and/or culture. Voice disorders result from changes in the anatomy or functioning of the laryngeal structures and musculature. Many laryngeal pathologies result in hoarseness, or dysphonia. Dysphonia may have negative implications on an individual's daily functioning, especially for vocal performers or professional voice users.

The subject of vocal disorders and vocal pathology has been written about extensively. Specialists including laryngologists and speech-language pathologists who specialize in working with voice are experts in the field of evaluation and treatment of vocal disorders and pathology. For music educators and singers, a thorough knowledge of voice disorders and pathology is not expected nor required. However, it is important to have a basic understanding of possible problems that may arise and what to do when they occur.

Vocal performers are at high risk for developing voice disorders. Etiologies of laryngeal pathologies that frequently present in vocal performers may include, but are not limited to, excessive muscle tension in the larynx while performing; overcompensation or compensatory strategy use when the laryngeal mechanism is irritated or inflamed or the subsystems of voice are imbalanced due to physical fatigue; inadequate vocal training or technique; performing and pushing through an acute illness; and/or phonotraumatic behaviors including screaming, yelling, or throat clearing. Production of sound with improper technique may contribute to the formation of vocal fold structural lesions. For example, in order to increase the intensity or loudness level of a sound, a singer or speaker must increase both the glottal resistance and the airflow from the lungs. If the individual regularly increases intensity solely through increased glottal resistance without increasing airflow, they may begin to produce sound with too much tension through recruitment of accessory muscles. Increased tension may cause vocal fold strain potentially resulting in pathology. Symptoms of voice disorders and/or pathology may include hoarseness, vocal fatigue, decreased vocal stamina, reduced vocal range or "holes" in the range, breaks in pitch or phonation, throat discomfort or pain, sensation of a "lump in the throat" or increased mucus, frequent throat clearing/coughing, and/or loss of voice. Anything that is outside of normal for an individual may be a potential red flag.

Symptoms occur when damage or injury occurs to the vocal folds, resulting in decreased glottic closure and/or disruptions to vocal fold vibration patterns. Pathologies or abnormalities of the larynx and vocal folds have a variable effect on the patient's voice quality, depending on the extent, severity, and location of the pathology. Problems may occur within different layers of the vocal folds. Some common benign pathology of the vocal folds includes nodules, polyps, or cysts. Vocal fold redness (erythema), swelling (edema), and stiffness also often result in symptoms of hoarseness. Pathology may also occur at other areas of the larynx, such as behind the vocal folds in the vocal process areas or in the interarytenoid space. The location and severity of the pathology often correlates with the severity and type of symptoms. For singers with voice complaints, it is important to note that pain is not directly indicative of problems with the vocal folds themselves, as vocal folds do not have pain receptors. Pain is often caused by muscular strain or tension that occurs as a compensatory mechanism when the vocal folds are not vibrating efficiently. Pain can also occur due to lesions or pathology in other areas of the larynx. Overall, it is impossible to determine what pathology may be occurring based on symptoms alone. One must undergo evaluation including imaging of the vocal folds and larynx, preferably with stroboscopy in order to assess function in addition to structure, in order to know what may be causing the individual's complaints.

The Voice Care Team

Music educators, including choral directors and voice teachers, are often the first to notice problems in a singer's voice. This may present as a student who demonstrates difficulty with their upper range following illness or complains of throat pain with voice use during their lesson. Choral students may come to their directors for advice when they experience problems and aren't sure what to do. For these music educators, it is advisable that they refer their students to medical professionals if warranted. There are voice centers with specialists located throughout the country, and technology now increases options for researching and contacting these clinics and professionals. There are specialists and subspecialists who evaluate and treat voice. It is important to understand who to seek treatment from, as there are specific considerations to take into account for singers versus nonsingers. To that end, a brief explanation of different vocal care specialists is included in the following text.

An otolaryngologist is an ear, nose, and throat (ENT) physician, while a laryngologist is a fellowship-trained ENT with specialization in medical and surgical treatment of disorders of the larynx. A speech-language pathologist (SLP) is a therapist who is trained in evaluation and treatment of disorders of articulation, language, voice, and swallowing. It is important to note that not all SLPs have the knowledge or experience to work with voice patients. While there is currently no recognized specialty certification for SLPs who specialize in working with voice, there are SLPs who have advanced training and experience working with voice and voice disorders. These specialized SLPs may or may not, however, have experience and knowledge of working with singing voice. Since there is no current certification for these professionals, they may have various titles, such as "singing voice rehabilitation specialist."

The voice teacher is an important part of the voice-care team and is often the only or first resource that is readily available to the student. Therefore, the educator would benefit from having relationships with and/or knowledge of vocal health professionals to reach out to as resources for help in the case of a student who is experiencing voice issues. The voice teacher or choral music educator may be advised to make connections in their community with vocal health professionals in order to refer students as needed. Timely evaluation and treatment of voice problems is vital to effective resolution of voice-related problems. Voice problems or symptoms can be very concerning for vocal performers, but it is important to keep in mind that early intervention with evaluation and treatment as warranted can help optimize outcomes for these singers.

Conclusion

Maximization of vocal health and wellness is important in order to optimize vocal quality and performance. A basic understanding of vocal anatomy and physiology is important to have when considering how to increase vocal efficiency and better understand the rationale behind many recommended vocal hygiene practices. Some important practices to support maintenance of vocal health include hydration, avoidance of laryngeal irritants, vocal conditioning and training, utilization of regular warm-ups and cool-downs, vocal pacing, voice rest as needed, minimization of phonotraumatic behaviors, and use of amplification. The voice teacher or choral educator is an important part of the voice care team and is often the first person to notice potential problems. Timely and appropriate referral is necessary for efficient and effective treatment of any voice disorder or pathology in order to get the singer back into performance.

Discussion Questions

1. Name the three subsystems involved in voice production.
2. Describe two ways to hydrate.
3. What is a voice disorder?
4. Name three potential vocal symptoms.
5. Name and describe two members of the vocal care team.

Resources for Further Reading

Donahue, E., LeBorgne, W., Brehm, S., & Weinrich, B. (2014). Reported vocal habits of first-year undergraduate musical theatre majors in a pre-professional training program: A ten-year retrospective study. *Journal of Voice, 28*(3), 316–323.

Hoffman Ruddy, B., Lehman, J., Crandell, C., Ingram, D., & Sapienza, C. (2001). Laryngostroboscopic, acoustic, and environmental characteristics of high-risk vocal performers. *Journal of Voice, 15*(4), 543–552.

Khlystov, A., & Samburova, V. (2016). Flavoring compounds dominate toxic aldehyde production during e-cigarette vaping. *Environmental Science and Technology, 50,* 13080–13085.

LeBorgne, W., & Rosenberg, M. (2021). *The vocal athlete* (2nd ed.). Plural Publishing.

Pomaville, F., Tekerlek, K., & Radford, A. (2020). The effectiveness of vocal hygiene education for decreasing at-risk vocal behaviors in vocal performers. *Journal of Voice, 34*(5), 709–719.

Ragan, K. (2018). The efficacy of vocal cool-down exercises. *Journal of Singing, 74*(5), 521–526.

Sataloff, R. (2017). *Treatment of voice disorders* (2nd ed.). Plural Publishing.

Sataloff, R. (2017). *Vocal health and pedagogy: Science, assessment, and treatment* (3rd ed.). Plural Publishing.

Stemple, J., Roy, N., & Klaben, B. (2020). *Clinical voice pathology: Theory and management* (6th ed.). Plural Publishing.

Tanner, K., et al. (2010). Nebulized isotonic saline versus water following a laryngeal desiccation challenge in classically trained sopranos. *Journal of Speech, Language, and Hearing Research, 53*(6), 1555–1566.

Thibeault, S., & Hartley, N. (2014). Systemic hydration: Relating science to clinical practice in vocal health. *Journal of Voice, 28*(5), 652.e1–652.e20.

Titze, I. (2000). *Principles of voice production.* National Center for Voice and Speech.

Yiu, E., & Chan, R. (2003). Effect of hydration and vocal rest on the vocal fatigue in amateur karaoke singers. *Journal of Voice, 17*(2), 216–227.

Zeine, L., & Waltar, K. (2002). The voice and its care: Survey findings from actor's perspectives. *Journal of Voice, 16*(2), 229–243.

Conclusion

The Benefits of Skillful Lifelong Singing

Brenda Smith and Ronald Burrichter

Singing Alone and With Others

Whether you are singing alone or with others, you are involved in teamwork. As you have learned, a song combines words with music and poets with composers. Singing, too, has a way of uniting spirits. In most situations, a solo singer performs with a collaborative pianist or an ensemble. Singing helps human beings get to know one another in new ways.

Though vocal repertoire derives from many cultures and languages, the subject of most songs is basically the same, namely, love. As singers, we explore love in its many guises. Our song lyrics examine the love human beings feel for one another or for a supreme one. With song, we praise and exult the wonder and mystery of nature. Often, we sing about our desire for love and our sorrow at the loss of it. Through song, a composer or singer wraps a poet's study of love in musical garments. We singers are the vessels through whom these amorous insights reach listeners. We sing in service of those who combined the words and music to create our songs. We sing alone and with others to bring moments of beauty to the lives of others.

The Intrinsic Value of Singing

There is more to learning to sing than meets the eye. Though you may not consider yourself a solo singer, you observed in Class Voice how singing enhances personal well-being for those who sing and those who listen. Class Voice offered you new perspectives as you identified your own vocal gifts and appreciated those of others. During each class, you were encouraged to relax and stand tall. Both habits are healthy and productive in daily life. Voice training for speaking and singing will serve you well as a professional voice user. "To breathe is to sing and to sing is to breathe" is the motto of many singers. Breathing is vital to life. So, you see, learning to sing has intrinsic value for everyone.

Singing is a simple, priceless gift. Good singing requires the mastery of many skills, some of which are fundamental; others are more advanced. You have amassed a useful toolkit of basic vocal skills and wisdom. To preserve your training and talent, try to use the tools regularly. Your voice demands close attention and protection. It is likely that you increased your vocal range and found new reasons to express yourself in song. Beyond the scope of this textbook, there are many other styles of singing that await your study.

Singing in the 21st Century

The use of electronic devices in live and virtual performance is rapidly altering the vista for vocal music in our time and in the future. Digital music is here to stay. Singers are learning to anticipate latency in real time, to sing with headphones, and to edit and upload recorded segments to a virtual location. From the American Songbook and cabaret songs to contemporary musical theater, Contemporary Commercial Music or CCM, blues, Rhythm & Blues or R&B, and vocal jazz, there are many singing styles and techniques. Find what works best for you, for your voice, and for your spirit. To duplicate the singing sounds of certain styles, you will need amplification to be heard over a band, orchestra, or synthesized accompaniment. Seek advice from a qualified professional to learn the proper way to use amplification and to negotiate any vocal challenges presented by the repertoire you choose to sing. Remember that healthy singing does not come by chance. It is a lifelong learning process.

21st Century Vocal Pedagogy

Singers in the early 20th century lived in a world with very limited voice science. Best practices for singing were based on theories and subjective reporting.

> There was little awareness of health issues affecting performing artists until approximately 1980, but since then the medical specialty of performing arts medicine has begun to evolve, associated with a growing recognition by health care practitioners of the frequency and seriousness of occupational injuries in the arts. (Brandfonbrener, 1998, p. 19)

Research in voice science and vocal pedagogy has advanced rapidly. Today, there are experts who are proficient in the clinical and practical aspects of voice and voice care. Though the teaching of singing remains an art form, it is now grounded in scientific and medical evidence. As you advance in your training, seek to study with an evidence-based voice teacher.

You can stay abreast of exciting research and singing strategies by consulting websites, attending conferences, and participating in the activities of professional organizations. The following is a list of selected resources:

National Association of Teachers of Singing (NATS)

The Voice Foundation (TVF)

American Choral Directors Association (ACDA)

Chorus America

Pan-American Vocology Association (PAVA)

Music Teachers National Association (MTNA)

National Association for Music Education (NAfME)

New York Singing Teachers Association (NYSTA)

Many mysteries about singing are yet to be solved, but there is scientifically proven evidence upon which you can rely. Do not be fooled by rumors and trends. Rely on trusted voice scientists as well as qualified medical and voice professionals for vocal knowledge and advice.

Maintaining Fundamental Skills for Singing

To protect your voice from fatigue and injury, apply the skills you have learned in this course.

- Preserve the basics of singing: relaxation, posture, breathing, and resonance.
- Warm-up and cool-down your voice before and after voice use.
- Continue to train your musicianship skills.
- Practice singing regularly. Consider it a pleasant rendezvous with your voice.
- Challenge yourself to learn new music.
- Exercise regularly and stay physically fit.
- Take time to rest and sleep.
- Remember the principles of vocal health and hygiene.
- Do not take risks. Do not push or force your voice.
- Resist competing with others.
- When singing with others, contribute only what is elegant and easy for your voice.
- Expect vocal changes and seek professional help, if needed.
- Respect expert advice and follow it.

Cautions and Strategies

Your voice is your closest friend, always with you and ready to respond. It gives "voice" to your most intimate thoughts and emotions. In his poem entitled "The Voice You Hear When You Read Silently," Thomas Lux characterizes the relationship between your mind and your voice in the following way:

> It's the writer's words,
>
> Of course, in a literary sense
>
> His or her *voice*, but the sound
>
> Of that voice is the sound of your voice.
>
> (Lux, 1997, p. 15)

Here are a few words of caution: The voice has an uncanny way of acknowledging truths you may not have consciously faced. Remember that whatever transpires in your life, be it happy or sad, has an impact on the functioning of your vocal instrument. To keep your voice fresh and healthy, try to remain alert to vocal changes and adjust how you use your voice. Don't forget that your voice is finite. Sing what feels "right" for you and your voice; that is, what is age and size appropriate for your time in life. Listen to good vocal role models. Knowing that others hear your voice more clearly than you do, accept praise when it comes and be receptive to competent, constructive criticism.

As you age, do not allow your vibrato to invade your vocal quality. Excessive vibrato will constrain your ability to sing with others. Physical conditioning and regular vocal practice are good strategies for preventing unnecessary motion in your tone. Also, keep your voice "lyric" with a light, lilting spin. Try not to darken your tone quality artificially or let it drop in pitch.

Vocal growth is rarely linear. Be patient. Recognize and celebrate vocal breakthroughs. Singing with others during difficult times can be very therapeutic. Choral singing offers you a fellowship of like-minded musicians in a safe environment. It is a place where you can relax and sing freely. With your voice, you announced your presence on earth. Let its presence in your life be a constant source of creativity, comfort, and companionship.

Conclusion

Galway Kinnell, in his poem entitled "The Choir," wrote, "Everyone who truly sings is beautiful" (Kinnell, 1980, p. 10). There is always something to sing about, a familiar song to savor, and a new song to learn. Search for the "ultimate" song, the one that expresses your innermost joys or sorrow. The journey will be endless, but along the way you will encounter unspeakable beauty and enrichment. May the fundamental skills of Class Voice form a firm foundation for your exploration of singing alone and with others throughout your life.

Discussion Questions

1. What are the personal benefits of lifelong singing?
2. What vocal habits strengthen speaking and singing skills?
3. How will singing voice training assist you with other professional tasks?
4. Discuss how a solo singing teacher could be of value to a choral ensemble.
5. Discuss strategies for maintaining good vocal skills as you age.

Resources for Further Reading

Helding, L. (2020). *The musician's mind, teaching, learning, and performance in the age of brain science.* Rowman & Littlefield.

Ragan, K. (2020). *A systematic approach to evidence-based vocal pedagogy: The art of studio application.* Plural Publishing.

References

Brandfonbrener, A. (1998). The etiologies of medical problems in performing artists. In R. Sataloff, A. Brandfonbrener, & R. Lederman (Eds.), *Performing arts medicine* (2nd ed., pp. 19–45). Singular Publishing.

Kinnell, G. (1980). *Mortal acts, mortal words.* (p. 10). Houghton Mifflin.

Lux, T. (1997). *New and selected poems 1975–1995* (p. 15). Houghton Mifflin.

Glossary

This glossary was adapted from a glossary developed from the experience of authors Brenda Smith and Robert T. Sataloff and also from a review of glossaries developed by Johan Sundberg (personal communication, June, 1995), Ingo Titze (1994; *Principles of Voice Production* [pp. 330–338], Prentice-Hall Inc.), and other sources. It is used by permission of Plural Publishing. It is difficult to credit appropriately contributions to glossaries or dictionaries of general terms, as each new glossary builds on prior works. The authors are indebted to colleagues whose previous efforts have contributed to the compilation of this glossary.

This glossary contains definitions not only of terms in this text but also of terminology encountered commonly in related literature. Readers are encouraged to consult other sources, and these additional definitions are included for the convenience of those who do so.

abduct: To move apart, separate.

abduction quotient: The ratio of the glottal half-width at the vocal processes to the amplitude of vibration of the vocal fold.

absolute voice rest: Total silence of the phonatory system.

Adam's apple: Prominence of the thyroid cartilage in males.

adduct: To bring together, approximate.

affricate: Combination of plosive and fricative.

alto: (See contralto)

antagonist (muscle): An opposing muscle.

anterior: Toward the front.

appoggio: Translated as "support"; in the terminology of vocal technique, it refers to the point of appoggio, whether it be of the abdominal or the thoracic region where the maximum muscular tension is experienced in singing (appoggio at the diaphragm, appoggio at the chest).

articulation: Shaping of vocal tract by the positioning of its mobile walls such as the lips, the lower jaw, the tongue body and tip, the velum, the epiglottis, the pharyngeal sidewalls, and the larynx.

arytenoid cartilages: Paired, ladle-shaped cartilages to which the vocal folds are attached.

aspiration: (1) In speech, the sound made by turbulent airflow preceding or following vocal fold vibration, as in "ha" [hɑ]. (2) In medicine, refers to breathing into the lungs substances that do not belong there such as food, water, or stomach contents following reflux. Aspiration may lead to infections such as pneumonia, commonly referred to as *aspiration pneumonia*.

baritone: The most common male vocal range; higher than bass and lower than tenor. Singer's formant is around 2600 Hz.

bass: (See basso)

bass baritone: In between a bass and a baritone. Not as heavy as basso profundo, but typically with greater flexibility. Must be able to sing at least as high as F4.

basso: The lowest male voice; singer's formant is around 2300 Hz to 2400 Hz.

basso profundo: Deep bass; the lowest and heaviest of the bass voices. Can sing at least as low as D2 with full voice. Singer's formant is around 2200 Hz to 2300 Hz.

bel canto: Literally means "beautiful singing"; refers to a method and philosophical approach to singing voice production.

Bernoulli's principle: If the energy in a confined fluid stream is constant, an increase in particle velocity must be accompanied by a decrease in pressure against the wall.

bleating: Fast vibrato, like the bleating of a sheep.

body: With regard to the vocal fold, the vocalis muscle.

bravura: Brilliant, elaborate, showy execution of musical or dramatic material.

breathy phonation: Phonation characterized by a lack of vocal fold closure, which causes air leakage (excessive airflow) during the quasiclosed phase, producing turbulence that is heard as noise mixed in the voice.

cartilage of Wrisberg: Cartilage attached in the mobile portion of each aryepiglottic fold.

castrato: A male singer castrated at around age 7 or 8 to retain alto or soprano vocal range.

chest voice: Heavy registration with excessive resonance in the lower formants.

coloratura: In common usage, refers to the highest of the female voices, with range well above C6; may use more whistle tone than other female voices. In fact, coloratura refers to a style of florid, agile, complex singing that may apply to any voice classification. For example, the bass melisma in Handel's *Messiah* requires coloratura technique.

complex sound: A combination of sinusoidal waveforms superimposed on each other. May be complex periodic sound (such as musical instruments) or complex aperiodic sound (such as random street noise).

complex tone: Tone composed of a series of simultaneously sounding partials.

component frequency: Mathematically, a sinusoid; perceptually, a pure tone. Also called a partial.

concert pitch: Also known as international concert pitch.

contraction: A decrease in length.

contralto: The lowest of the female voices; able to sing F3 below middle C as well as the entire treble staff. The singer's formant is at around 2800 Hz to 2900 Hz.

corner vowels: [ɑ], [i], and [u]; vowels at the corners of a vowel triangle; they necessitate extreme placements of the tongue.

countertenor: A male voice that is primarily falsetto, singing in the contralto range.

cover: (1) In medicine, with regard to the vocal fold, the epithelium, and superficial layer of lamina propria. (2) In music, an alteration in technique that changes the resonance characteristics of a sung sound, generally darkening the sound.

creaky voice: The perceptual result of subharmonic or chaotic patterns in the glottal waveform. According to I. R. Titze, if a subharmonic is below about 70 Hz, creaky voice may be perceived as pulse register (vocal fry).

crescendo: To get louder gradually.

cricoid cartilage: A solid ring of cartilage located below and behind the thyroid cartilage.

cricothyroid muscle: An intrinsic laryngeal muscle that is used primarily to control pitch (paired).

crossover frequency: The fundamental frequency for which there is an equal probability for perception of two adjacent registers.

damp: To diminish or attenuate an oscillation.

dB: (See decibel)

decibel: One-tenth of a bel. The decibel is a unit of comparison between a reference and another point. It has no absolute value. Although decibels are used to measure sound, they are also used (with different references) to measure heat, light, and other physical phenomena. For sound pressure, the reference is 0.0002 microbar (millionths of one barometric pressure). In the past, this has also been referred to as 0.0002 dyne/cm^2 and by other terms.

decrescendo: (See diminuendo)

diaphragm: A large, dome-shaped muscle at the bottom of the rib cage that separates the lungs from the viscera. It is the primary muscle of inspiration and may be coactivated during singing.

diminuendo: Gradually reducing in loudness or force.

divisi: Literally "divided," used in choral scores to indicate that a section is to be divided into two or more parts; generally intended for the rendering of fuller harmony.

dramatic soprano: A soprano with powerful, rich voice suitable for dramatic, heavily orchestrated operatic roles; sings at least to C6.

dramatic tenor: A tenor with heavy voice, often with a suggestion of baritone quality; suitable for dramatic roles that are heavily orchestrated. Also referred to as *Heldentenor*, a term used typically for tenors who sing Wagnerian operatic roles.

dynamics: (1) In physics, a branch of mechanics that deals with the study of forces that accelerate objects. (2) In music, it refers to changes in the loudness of musical performance.

edema: Excessive accumulation of fluid in tissues, or "swelling."

electroglottography (EGG): Recording of electrical conductance of vocal fold contact area versus time; EGG waveforms frequently have been used for the purpose of plotting voice source analysis.

electromyography (EMG): Recording of the electric potentials in a muscle, which are generated by the neural system and which control its degree of contraction; if rectified and smoothed, the EMG is closely related to the muscular force exerted by the muscle.

elongation: An increase in length.

embouchure: The shape of the lips, tongue, and related structures adopted while producing a musical tone, particularly while playing a wind instrument.

epiglottis: Cartilage that covers the larynx during the act of swallowing.

epithelium: The covering, or most superficial layer, of body surfaces.

extrinsic muscles of the larynx: The strap muscles in the neck, responsible for adjusting laryngeal height and for stabilizing the larynx.

Fach (German): Literally, subject or box. It is used to indicate voice classification. For example, lyric soprano and dramatic soprano are each a different Fach.

false vocal folds: Folds of tissue located slightly higher than and parallel to the vocal folds in the larynx.

falsetto: High, light register, applied primarily to men's voices singing in the soprano or alto range. Can also be applied to women's voices.

flow: The volume of fluid passing through a given cross section of a tube or duct per second; also called volume velocity (measured in liters per second).

flow glottography (FLOGG): Recording of the transglottal airflow versus time, that is, of the sound of the voice source. Generally obtained from inverse filtering, FLOGG is the acoustical representation of the voice source.

flow phonation: The optimal balance between vocal fold adductory forces and subglottic pressure, producing efficient sound production at the level of the vocal folds.

F_0: Fundamental frequency.

force: A push or pull; the physical quantity imparted to an object to change its momentum.

formant: Vocal tract resonance; the formant frequencies are tuned by the vocal tract shape and determine much of the vocal quality.

formant tuning: A boosting of vocal intensity when F_0 or one if its harmonics coincides exactly with a formant frequency.

frequency tremor: A periodic (regular) pitch modulation of the voice (an element of vibrato).

fricative: A speech sound, generally a consonant, produced by a constriction of the vocal tract, particularly by directing the airstream against a hard surface, producing noisy air turbulence. Examples include s [z] produced with the teeth, s [s] produced with the lower lip and upper incisors, and th [θ] produced with the tongue tip and upper incisors.

functional residual capacity (FRC): Lung volume at which the elastic inspiratory forces equal the elastic expiratory forces; in spontaneous quiet breathing, exhalation stops at FRC.

functional voice disorder: An abnormality in voice sound and function in the absence of an organic anatomic or physiologic abnormality.

fundamental: Lowest partial of a spectrum, the frequency of which normally corresponds to the pitch perceived.

fundamental frequency (F_0): The lowest frequency in a periodic waveform; also called the first harmonic frequency.

glissando: A "slide" including all possible pitches between the initial and final pitch sounded. Similar to portamento and slur.

globus: Sensation of a lump in the throat.

glottal chink: Opening in the glottis during vocal fold adduction, most commonly posteriorly. It may be a normal variant in some cases.

glottal resistance: Ratio between transglottal airflow and subglottal pressure; mainly reflects the degree of glottal adduction.

glottal stop (or click): A transient sound caused by the sudden onset or offset of phonation.

glottis: The space between the vocal folds.

glottis vocalis: The portion of the glottis in the region of the membranous portions of the vocal folds.

harmonic: A frequency that is an integer multiple of a given fundamental. Harmonics of a fundamental are equally spaced in frequency; partial in a spectrum in which the frequency of each partial equals n times the fundamental frequency, n being the number of the harmonic.

harsh glottal attack: Initiating phonation of a word or sound with a glottal plosive.

Heldentenor: (See dramatic tenor)

hyoid bone: A horseshoe-shaped bone known as the "tongue bone." It is attached to the muscles of the tongue and related structures and to the larynx and related structures.

hyperfunction: Excessive muscular effort, for example, pressed voice or muscular tension dysphonia.

hypernasal: Excessive nasal resonance.

hypofunction: Low muscular effort, for example, soft breathy voice.

hyponasal: Deficient nasal resonance.

infraglottic: Below the level of the glottis. This region includes the trachea, thorax, and related structures.

infraglottic vocal tract: Below the level of the vocal folds. This region includes the airways and muscles of support. (Infraglottic is synonymous with subglottic.)

infrahyoid muscle group: A collection of extrinsic muscles including the sternohyoid, sternothyroid, omohyoid, and thyroid muscles.

intensity: A measure of power per unit area. With respect to sound, it generally correlates with perceived loudness.

interarytenoid muscle: An intrinsic laryngeal muscle that connects the two arytenoid cartilages.

intercostal muscles: Muscles between the ribs.

interval: The difference between two pitches, expressed in terms of musical scale.

intrinsic laryngeal muscles: Muscles in the larynx responsible for abduction, adduction, and longitudinal tension of the vocal folds.

intrinsic pitch of vowels: Refers to the fact that in normal speech, certain vowels tend to be produced with a significantly higher or lower pitch than other vowels.

jitter: Irregularity in the period of time of vocal fold vibrations; cycle-to-cycle variation in fundamental frequency; often perceived as hoarseness.

lamina propria: With reference to the larynx, the tissue layers below the epithelium. In adult humans, the lamina propria consists of superficial, intermediate, and deep layers.

laryngeal ventricle: Cavity formed by the gap between the true and false vocal folds.

laryngitis: Inflammation of laryngeal tissues.

laryngologist: A physician specializing in disorders of the larynx and voice. In some areas of Europe, the laryngologist is primarily responsible for surgery, while diagnosis is performed by phoniatricians.

laryngopharyngeal reflux (LPR): A form of gastroesophageal reflux disease in which gastric juice affects the larynx and adjacent structures; commonly associated with hoarseness, frequent throat clearing, granulomas, and other laryngeal problems, even in the absence of heartburn.

larynx: The body organ in the neck that includes the vocal folds; also called the "voice box."

laser: An acronym for "light amplification by stimulated emission of radiation." A surgical tool using light energy to vaporize or cauterize tissue.

lateral cricoarytenoid muscle: Intrinsic laryngeal muscle that adducts the vocal folds through forward rocking and rotation of the arytenoids (paired).

lift: A transition point along a pitch scale where vocal production becomes easier.

loft: A suggested term for the highest (loftiest) register; usually referred to as falsetto voice.

Lombard effect: Modification of vocal loudness in response to auditory input, for example, the tendency to speak louder in the presence of background noise.

longitudinal: Along the length of a structure.

longitudinal tension: With reference to the larynx, stretching the vocal folds.

loudness: The amount of sound perceived by a listener; a perceptual quantity that can only be assessed with an auditory system. Loudness corresponds to intensity and to the amplitude of a sound wave.

lung volume: Volume contained in the subglottic air system; after a maximum inhalation following a maximum exhalation, the lung volume equals the vital capacity.

lyric soprano: A soprano with flexible, light vocal quality, but one who does not sing as high as a coloratura soprano.

lyric tenor: A tenor with a light, high flexible voice.

marcato: Each note accented; a manner of performance frequently associated with music of the Baroque period.

marking: Using the voice gently (typically during rehearsals) to avoid injury or fatigue.

martellato: A technique for singing melismatic passages in music in which certain notes are accentuated within the context of legato singing, generally found in works of the Baroque period.

messa di voce: A traditional exercise in Italian singing tradition consisting of a prolonged crescendo and diminuendo on a sustained tone.

mezza voce: Literally means "half voice." In practice, means singing softly, but with proper support.

mezzo-soprano: A range of the female voice, higher than contralto but lower than soprano.

middle (or mixed): A mixture of qualities from various voice registers, cultivated to allow consistent quality throughout the frequency range.

middle C: C4 on the piano keyboard, with an international concert pitch frequency of 261.6 Hz.

modal: Used frequently in speech, refers to the voice quality used generally by healthy speakers, as opposed to a low, gravelly vocal fry or high falsetto. Modal register describes the laryngeal function in the range of fundamental frequencies most commonly used by untrained speakers (from about 75 Hz to about 450 Hz in men; 130 Hz to 520 Hz in women).

modulation: Periodic variation of a signal property; for example, as vibrato corresponds to a regular variation of fundamental frequency, it can be regarded as a modulation of that signal property.

mucosa: The covering of the surfaces of the respiratory tract, including the oral cavity and nasal cavities as well as the pharynx, larynx, and lower airways. Mucosa also exists elsewhere, such as on the lining of the vagina.

muscle tension dysphonia: Also called muscular tension dysphonia. A form of voice abuse characterized by excessive muscular effort and usually by pressed phonation. A form of voice misuse.

mutational dysphonia: A voice disorder. Most typically, it is characterized by persistent falsetto voice after puberty in a male. More generally, it is used to refer to voice with characteristics of the opposite gender.

myoelastic-aerodynamic theory of phonation: The currently accepted mechanism of vocal fold physiology. Compressed air exerts pressure on the undersurface of the closed vocal folds. The pressure overcomes adductory forces, causing the vocal folds to open. The elasticity of the displaced tissues (along with the Bernoulli effect) causes the vocal folds to snap shut, resulting in sound. "Myoelastic" refers to the muscle (myo) and its properties. "Aerodynamic" refers to activities related to airflow.

nasal tract: Air cavity system of the nose.

nervous system: Organs of the body including the brain, spinal cord, and nerves. Responsible for motion, sensation, thought, and control of various other bodily functions.

neurotologist: Otolaryngologist specializing in disorders of the ear and ear-brain interface (including the skull base), particularly hearing loss, dizziness, tinnitus, and facial nerve dysfunction.

nodules: Benign growths on the surface of the vocal folds; usually paired and fairly symmetric. They are generally caused by chronic, forceful vocal fold contact (voice abuse).

objective assessment: Demonstrable, reproducible, usually quantifiable evaluation, generally relying on instrumentation or other assessment techniques that do not involve primarily opinion, as opposed to subjective assessment.

open quotient: The ratio of the time the glottis is open to the length of the entire vibratory cycle.

organic voice disorder: Disorder for which a specific anatomic or physiologic cause can be identified, as opposed to psychogenic or functional voice disorders.

oscillation: Back-and-forth repeated movement.

oscillator: With regard to the larynx, the vibrator that is responsible for the sound source, specifically the vocal folds.

otolaryngologist: Ear, nose, and throat physician.

overtones: Partials above the fundamental in a spectrum.

partial: Sinusoid that is part of a complex tone; in voiced sounds, the partials are harmonic, implying that the frequency of the nth partial equals n times the fundamental frequency.

passaggio (Italian): The shift or break between vocal registers.

period: In physics, the time interval between repeating events; shortest pattern repeated in a regular undulation. A graph showing the period is called a waveform.

pharynx: The region above the larynx, below the velum, and posterior to the oral cavity.

phonation: Sound generation by means of vocal fold vibrations.

phonetics: The study of speech sounds.

phonosurgery: Originally, surgery designed to alter vocal quality or pitch. Now commonly used to also refer to all delicate microsurgical procedures of the vocal folds.

pitch: Perceived tone quality corresponding to its fundamental frequency.

plosive: A consonant produced by creating complete blockage of airflow, followed by the buildup of air pressure, which is then suddenly released, producing a consonant sound.

posterior: Toward the back.

posterior cricoarytenoid muscle: An intrinsic laryngeal muscle that is the primary abductor of the vocal folds (paired).

power source: The expiratory system including the muscles of the abdomen, back, thorax, and the lungs. The power source is responsible for producing a vector of force that results in efficient creation and control of subglottal pressure.

pressed phonation: A type of phonation characterized by low airflow, high adductory force, and high subglottal pressure; not an efficient form of voice production. Pressed voice is often associated with voice abuse and is common in patients with lesions, such as nodules.

pulmonary system: The breathing apparatus including the lungs and related airways.

pulse register: The extreme low end of the phonatory range. Also known as vocal fry or Strohbass, characterized by a pattern of short glottal waves alternating with larger and longer ones and with a long closed phase.

recurrent laryngeal nerves: The paired branches of the vagus nerve which supply all the intrinsic muscles of the larynx except for the cricothyroid muscles. The recurrent laryngeal nerves also carry sensory fibers (feeling) to the mucosa below the level of the vocal folds.

reflux laryngitis: Inflammation of the larynx due to irritation from gastric juice.

registers: A weakly defined term for vocal qualities; often, register refers to a series of adjacent tones on the scale that sound similar and seem to be generated by the same type of vocal fold vibrations and vocal tract adjustments. Examples of register are vocal fry, modal, and falsetto, but numerous other terms are also used.

relative voice rest: Restricted, cautious voice use.

resonance: Peak occurring at certain frequencies (resonance frequencies) in the vibration amplitude in a system that possesses compliance, inertia, and reflection; resonance occurs when the input and the reflected energy vibrate in phase. The resonances in the vocal tract are called formants.

resonator: With regard to the voice, refers primarily to the supraglottic vocal tract, which is responsible for timbre and projection.

sensory: Having to do with the feeling or detection of other nonmotor input. For example, nerves responsible for touch, proprioception (position in space), hearing, and so on.

singer's formant: A high-spectrum peak occurring between about 2.3 kHz and 3.5 kHz in voiced sounds in Western operatic and concert singing. This acoustic phenomenon is associated with "ring" in a voice and with the voice's ability to project over background noise, such as a choir or an orchestra. A similar phenomenon may be seen in speaking voices, especially in actors. It is known as the speaker's formant.

singing teacher: Professional who teaches singing technique (as opposed to *voice coach*).

singing voice specialist: A singing teacher with additional training and specialization in working with injured voices, in conjunction with a medical voice team.

skeleton: The bony or cartilaginous framework to which muscle and other soft tissues are connected.

soft glottal attack: Gentle glottal approximation often obtained using an imaginary [h].

spectrum: Ensemble of simultaneously sounding sinusoidal partials constituting a complex tone; a display of relative magnitudes or phases of the component frequencies of a waveform.

spectrum analysis: Analysis of a signal showing its partials.

speech-language pathologist: A trained, medically affiliated professional who may be skilled in remediation of problems of the speaking voice, swallowing, articulation, language development, and other conditions.

spinto: Literally means "pushed"; usually applied to tenors or sopranos with a lighter voice than dramatic singers but with aspects of particular dramatic excitement in their vocal quality, Enrico Caruso being a notable example.

staccato: Each note accented and separated.

stroboscopy: A technique that uses interrupted light to simulate slow motion. (See also strobovideolaryngoscopy)

strobovideolaryngoscopy: Evaluation of vocal folds utilizing simulated slow motion for detailed evaluation of vocal fold motion.

Strohbass (German): Literally "straw bass"; another term for *pulse register* or *vocal fry*.

subglottal pressure: Air pressure in the airway immediately below the level of the vocal folds. The unit most commonly used is centimeters of water; that is, the distance in centimeters that a given pressure would raise a column of water in a tube.

subglottic: The region immediately below the level of the vocal folds.

subjective assessment: Evaluation that depends on perception and opinion, rather than independently reproducible, quantifiable measures—as opposed to objective assessment.

superior laryngeal nerves: Paired branches of the vagus nerve that supply the cricothyroid muscle and supply sensation from the level of the vocal folds superiorly.

support: Commonly used to refer to the power source of the voice; includes the mechanism responsible for creating a vector force that results in efficient subglottic pressure; includes the muscles of the abdomen and back as well as the thorax and lungs; primarily the expiratory system.

supraglottic: Vocal tract above the level of the vocal folds. This region includes the resonance system of the vocal tract, including the pharynx, oral cavity, nose, and related structures.

suprahyoid muscle group: One of the two extrinsic muscle groups. Includes the stylohyoid muscle, the anterior and posterior bellies of the digastric muscle, the geniohyoid, the hyoglossus, and the mylohyoid muscles.

temporomandibular joint: The jaw joint; a synovial joint between the mandibular condyle and skull anterior to the ear canal.

tenor: The highest of the male voices, except countertenors; must be able to sing to C5. Singer's formant is around 2800 Hz.

thoracic: Pertaining to the chest.

thorax: The part of the body between the neck and abdomen.

thyroarytenoid muscle: An intrinsic laryngeal muscle that comprises the bulk of the vocal fold (paired). The medial belly constitutes the body of the vocal fold.

thyroid cartilage: The largest laryngeal cartilage. It is open posteriorly and made up of two plates (thyroid laminae) joined anteriorly at the midline. In males, there is an anterior, superior prominence known as the "Adam's apple."

tidal volume: The amount of air breathed in and out during respiration (measured in liters).

timbre: The quality of a sound. Associated with complexity, or the number, nature, and interaction of overtones.

tracheobronchial tree: The air passages of the lungs and trachea (commonly referred to as the windpipe).

tremolo: An aesthetically displeasing, excessively wide vibrato.

trill: A vocal or instrumental ornament involving an oscillation of pitch within a discrete range.

trillo: The repetition of a given pitch with frequent interruptions; a vocal ornament of the late Medieval and early Renaissance.

tympanic membrane: The eardrum.

velar: Relating to the velum or palate.

velum: A general term that means "veil" or "covering." With regard to the vocal tract, it refers to the region of the soft palate and adjacent nasopharynx that closes together under normal circumstances during swallowing and phonation of certain sounds.

ventricular folds: The "false vocal folds," situated above the true vocal folds.

vibrato: In classical singing, vibrato is a periodic modulation of the frequency of phonation. Its regularity increases with training. The rate of vibrato (number of modulations per second) is usually in the range of five to six per second. Vibrato rates over 7 s to 8 s are aesthetically displeasing to most people and sound "nervous." The extent of vibrato (amount of variation above and below the center frequency) is usually one or two semitones. Vibrato extending less than 50.5 semitone is rarely noted in singers, although it is encountered in wind instrument playing. Vibrato rates greater than two semitones are usually aesthetically unacceptable and are typical of elderly singers in poor artistic vocal condition, in whom the excessively wide vibrato extent is often combined with excessively slow rate.

viscera: The internal organs of the body, particularly the contents of the abdomen.

visceral pleura: The innermost of two membranes surrounding the lungs.

vital capacity: The maximum volume of air that can be exchanged by the lungs with the outside; it includes the expiratory reserve volume, tidal volume, and inspiratory reserve volume (measured in liters).

vocal cord: An old term for vocal fold.

vocal folds: A paired system of tissue layers in the larynx that can oscillate to produce sound.

vocal fry: A register with perceived temporal gaps; also known as *pulse register* and *Strohbass*.

vocal ligament: Intermediate and deep layers of the lamina propria. Also forms the superior end of the conus elasticus.

vocal tract: Resonator system comprised of the larynx, the pharynx, and the mouth cavity.

vocalis muscle: The medial belly of the thyroarytenoid muscle.

voce coperta: "Covered registration."

voce di petto: Chest voice.

voce di testa: Head voice.

voce mista: Mixed voice.

voice abuse: Use of the voice in specific activities that are deleterious to vocal health, such as screaming.

voice coach: (1) In singing, a professional who works with singers, teaching repertoire, language pronunciation, and other artistic components of performance (as opposed to a singing teacher, who teaches singing technique); (2) The term voice coach is also used by acting-voice teachers who specialize in vocal, bodily, and interpretive techniques to enhance dramatic performance.

voice misuse: Habitual phonation using phonatory techniques that are not optimal and then result in vocal strain. For example, speaking with inadequate support, excessive neck muscle tension, and suboptimal resonance. Muscular tension dysphonia is a form of voice misuse.

voice source: Sound generated by the pulsating transglottal airflow; the sound is generated when the vocal fold vibrations chop the airstream into a pulsating airflow.

volume: "Amount of sound"; best measured in terms of acoustic power or intensity.

wavelength: The initial distance between any point on one vibratory cycle and a corresponding point of the next vibratory cycle.

whisper: Sound created by turbulent glottal airflow in the absence of vocal fold vibration.

whistle voice: The highest of all registers (in pitch); it is observed only in females, extending the pitch range beyond F6.

wobble: A slow, irregular vibrato; aesthetically unsatisfactory. Sometimes referred to as a *tremolo*, having a rate of less than four oscillations per second and an extent of greater than ± two semitones.

Bibliography: Resources for Research and Learning

Websites for Accessing Songs/Arias/IPA Transcriptions

http://www.recmusic.org/lieder

http://www.artsongcentral.com

http://www.leyerlepublications.com/?v=song_texts

http://www.halleonard.com

http://www.stmpublishers.com

Resources for Score Preparation

Cartier, F., & Todaro, M. (1971). *The phonetic alphabet* (2nd ed.). Wm. C. Brown Publishers.

Author. (2003). *Handbook of the International Phonetic Association: A guide to the use of the International Phonetic Alphabet*. Cambridge University Press.

https://www.internationalphoneticassociation.org

http://www.arts.gla.ac.uk/IPA/ipachart/html

http://www.dictiondomain.com/

http://www.ipasource.com

http://www.cherimontgomery.com

http://www.blugs.com/IPAPalette/

http://www.personlongman.com/dictionaries/LPD/

Books Containing Texts and Translations

Coffin, B. (1982). *Phonetic readings of songs and arias* (2nd ed.). Scarecrow Press.

Miller, P. (1973). *The ring of words: An anthology of song texts*. W. W. Norton.

Retzlaff, J., & Montgomery, C. (2015). *Exploring art songs lyrics*. Oxford University Press.

Opera Libretti

Castel, N. (1999). *French opera libretti* (3 vols.). Leyerle Publications.

Castel, N. (2000a). *Italian bel canto opera libretti* (3 vols.). Leyerle Publications.

Castel, N. (2000b). *Italian verismo opera libretti* (2 vols.). Leyerle Publications.

English Diction Textbooks

Cox, R. (1990). *Singing in English: A manual of English diction for singers and choral directors.* Schirmer Books.

LaBouff, K. (2008). *Singing and communicating in English: A singer's guide to English diction.* Oxford University Press.

Marshall, M. (1943). *The singer's manual of English diction.* Schirmer.

Uris, D. (1971). *To sing in English.* Boosey & Hawkes.

French Diction Textbooks

Davis, E. (2004). *Sing French: Diction for singers.* Eclairé Press.

Grubb, T. (1990). *Singing in French: A manual of French diction and French vocal repertoire.* Schirmer Books.

German Diction Textbooks

Johnston, A. (2011). *English and German diction: A comparative approach.* Scarecrow.

Odom, W. (1997). *German for singers: A textbook of diction and phonetics* (2nd ed.). Schirmer.

Paton, J. G. (1999). *Gateway to German diction.* Alfred Publishing.

Italian Diction Textbooks

Colorni, E. (1995). *Singer's Italian.* Schirmer Books.

Paton, J. G. (2004). *Gateway to Italian diction.* Alfred Publishing.

Multilanguage Diction Textbooks

Adams, D. (2008). *A handbook of diction for singers: Italian, German, French* (2nd ed.). Oxford University Press.

Moriarty, J. (1975). *Diction: Italian, Latin, French, German.* E. C. Schirmer.

Sheil, R. (2004). *A singer's manual of foreign language dictions* (6th ed.). YBK Publishers.

Smith, B. (2020). *Diction in context: Singing in English, Italian, German, and French.* Plural Publishing.

Wall, J. (1989). *International Phonetic Alphabet for singers: A manual for English and foreign language diction.* Pst. Inc.

Wall, J. (1990). *Diction for singers: A concise reference for English, Italian, Latin, German, French and Spanish.* Pst. Inc.

Books on Interpretation of Songs and Arias

English

Barzun, J. (1985). *Simple & direct: A rhetoric for writers* (Rev. ed.). University of Chicago Press.

Bostridge, I. (1988). *A singer's notebook.* Faber & Faber.

Bryson, B. (1990). *The mother tongue: English and how it got that way.* Perennial.

Butterfield, J. (Ed.). (2015). *Modern English usage* (4th ed.). Oxford University Press.

Carmen, J., Gaeddert, W., Myers, G., & Resch, R. (2001). *Art song in the United States, 1759–1999* (3rd ed.). Scarecrow Press.

Clifton, K. (2008). *Recent American art song.* Scarecrow Press.

Fogiel, M. (1996). *REA's handbook of English grammar, style and writing.* Research and Education Association.

Forward, G., & Howard, E. (2001). *American diction for singers: Standard American diction for singers and speakers.* Alfred Publishing.

Friedberg, R. (1981). *American art song and American poetry* (3 vols.). Scarecrow Press.

Harrison, N. (2016). *The wordsmith's guide to English song: Poetry, music & imagination* (Vol. 1). Compton Publishing.

Heyman, B. (1992). *Samuel Barber: The composer and his music.* Oxford University Press.

Hold, T. (2002). *Parry to Finzi: Twenty English song-composers*. The Boydell Press.

Jorgens, E. (1982). *The well-tun'd word: Musical interpretation of English poetry 1597–1651*. University of Minnesota Press.

McCrum, R., Cran, W., & MacNeil, R. (1986). *The story of English* (Rev. ed.). Viking.

Pilkington, M. (1989). *Campion, Dowland, and the Lutenist songwriters*. Indiana University Press.

Pilkington, M. (1989). *Gurney, Ireland, Quilter, and Warlock*. Indiana University Press.

Villamil, V. (1993). *A singer's guide to the American art song: 1870–1980*. Scarecrow Press.

The following are two websites that give you in-depth information about the American Art Song:

The American Art Song:
http://www.americanartsong.org

Song of America:
http://www.songofamerica.net

Websites of Contemporary American Composers

Judith Cloud: http://www.judithcloud.com

Ricky Ian Gordon: http://www.rickyiangordon.com

Jake Heggie: http://www.jakeheggie.com

Lori Laitman: http://www.artsongs.com

Libby Larsen: http://www.libbylarsen.com

Ned Rorem: http://www.nedrorem.com

French

Bathori, J. (1998). *On the interpretation of the melodies of Claude Debussy*. Pendragon Press.

Bernac, P. (1977). *Francis Poulenc: The man and his songs*. Norton.

Bernac, P. (1978). *The interpretation of the French song*. Norton.

Cobb, M. (1982). *The poetic Debussy: A collection of his song texts and selected letters* (R. Miller, Trans.). Northeastern University Press.

Davies, L. (1967). *The Gallic muse*. A. S. Barnes.

Gartside, R. (1992). *Interpreting the songs of Maurice Ravel*. Leyerle Publications.

Gartside, R. (1996). *Interpreting the songs of Gabriel Fauré*. Leyerle Publications.

Hahn, R. (1990). *On singers and singing* (L. Simoneau, Trans.). Amadeus Press.

Johnson, G., & Stokes, R. (2000). *A French art song companion*. Oxford University Press.

Johnson, G., & Stokes, R. (2009). *Gabriel Fauré: The songs and their poets*. Ashgate Publishing.

LeVan, T. (1991). *Masters of the French art song: Translations of the complete songs of Chausson, Debussy, Duparc, Fauré and Ravel*. Scarecrow.

Leyerle, A., & Leyerle, W. (1983). *French diction songs: From the 17th to the 20th centuries*. Leyerle Publications.

Meister, B. (1980). *Nineteenth-century French song: Fauré, Chausson, Duparc and Debussy*. Indiana University Press.

Nectoux, J. (1991). *Gabriel Fauré: A musical life* (R. Nichols, Trans.). Cambridge University Press.

Nichols, R. (1987). *Ravel remembered*. W. W. Norton.

Northcote, S. (1949). *The songs of Henri Duparc*. Dennis Dobson.

Noske, F. (1970). *French song from Berlioz to Duparc*. Dover.

Orenstein, A. (1975). *Ravel: Man and musician*. Columbia University Press.

Panzéra, C. (1964). *Mélodies Françaises: Fifty lessons in style and interpretation*. Schott.

Poulenc, F. (1989). *Diary of my songs* (W. Radford, Trans.). Victor Gollancz.

Resick, G. (2018). *French vocal literature: Repertoire in context*. Rowman & Littlefield.

Rohinsky, M. (1987). *The singer's Debussy*. Pelion Press.

Vuillermoz, E. (1960). *Gabriel Fauré*. Chilton Book Co.

Walsh, S. (2018). *Debussy: A painter in sound*. Knopf.

Wenk, A. (1976). *Claude Debussy and the poets*. University of California Press.

German

Bell, A. C. (1954). *The songs of Schubert*. Alston Books.

Bostridge, I. (2015). *Schubert's winter journey: Anatomy of an obsession*. Alfred A. Knopf.

Brody, E., & Fowkes, R. (1971). *The German Lied and its poetry*. New York University Press.

Chernaik, J. (2018). *Schumann: The faces and the masks*. Knopf.

Cooper, J. M. (2007). *Mendelssohn, Goethe, and the Walpurgis Nacht: The heathen muse in European culture, 1700–1850*. University of Rochester Press.

Fischer-Dieskau, D. (1977). *Schubert: A biographical study of his songs*. Alfred A. Knopf.

Fischer-Dieskau, D. (1984). *The Fischer-Dieskau Book of Lieder*. Limelight Editions.

Fischer-Dieskau, D. (1988). *Robert Schumann: Words and music, the vocal compositions*. Amadeus Press.

Glass, B. (1996). *Brahms' complete song texts*. Leyerle Publications.

Glass, B. (2000). *Hugo Wolf's complete song texts*. Leyerle Publications.

Glass, B. (2002). *Schumann's complete song texts*. Leyerle Publications.

Glass, B. (2004). *Strauss's complete song texts*. Leyerle Publications.

Gorrell, L. (1993). *The nineteenth-century German Lied*. Amadeus Press.

Harrison, M. (1972). *The Lieder of Brahms*. Praeger.

Jefferson, A. (1971). *The Lieder of Richard Strauss*. Praeger.

Jensen, E. F. (2001). *Schumann*. Oxford University Press.

Loges, N. (2017). *Brahms and his poets: A handbook*. The Boydell Press.

Loges, N., & Hamilton, K. (Eds.). (2014). *Brahms in the home and the concert hall: Between private and public performances*. Cambridge University Press.

Miller, R. (2005). *Singing Schumann: An interpretive guide for performers*. Oxford University Press.

Moore, G. (1975). *The Schubert song cycles*. Hamish Hamilton.

Moore, G. (1981). *Poet's love: The songs and cycles of Schumann*. Taplinger.

Parsons, J. (Ed.). (2004). *The Cambridge companion to the Lied*. Cambridge University Press.

Reich, N. (2001). *Clara Schumann: The artist and the woman* (Rev. ed.). Cornell University Press.

Reinhard, T. (1988). *The singer's Schumann*. Pelion Press.

Sams, E. (1973). *Brahms songs*. University of Washington Press.

Sams, E. (1992). *The songs of Hugo Wolf* (Rev. ed.). Methuen.

Sams, E. (1993). *The songs of Robert Schumann* (3rd ed.). Methuen.

Snyder, L. (1995). *German poetry in song*. Fallen Leaf Press.

Stein, D., & Spillman, R. (1996). *Poetry into song: Performance and analysis of Lieder*. Oxford University Press.

Swafford, J. (1998). *Johannes Brahms: A biography*. Knopf.

Youens, S. (1991). *Retracing a winter's journey: Schubert's Winterreise*. Cornell University Press.

Youens, S. (1992a). *Hugo Wolf: The vocal music*. Princeton University Press.

Youens, S. (1992b). *Schubert: Die schöne Müllerin*. Cambridge University Press.

Youens, S. (1996). *Schubert's poets and the making of Lieder*. Cambridge University Press.

Italian

Gerhart, M. (2003). *Italian song texts from the 17th through the 20th centuries* (2 vols.). Leyerle Publications.

Lakeway, R., & White, R. (1989). *Italian art song*. Indiana University Press.

LeVan, T. (1991). *Masters of the Italian song*. Scarecrow Press.

Resources for Vocal Repertoire and Style

Coffin, B. (Ed.). (1962). *Singer's repertoire* (2nd ed.). Scarecrow Press.

Doscher, B. (2002). *From studio to stage: Repertoire for the voice*. The Scarecrow Press.

Elliott, M. (2006). *Singing in style: A guide to vocal performance practices*. Yale University Press.

Emmon, S., & Watkins, W. (2006). *Researching the song*. Oxford University Press.

Emmons, S., & Sonntag, S. (2001). *The art of the song recital* (Rev. ed.). Schirmer Books.

Espina, N. (1977). *Repertoire for the solo voice*. Scarecrow Press.

Goleeke, T. (2002). *Literature for voice: An index to songs in collections and source book for teachers of singing* (Vols. I and II). Scarecrow Press.

Hall, J. (1953). *The art song*. University of Oklahoma Press.

Holoman, D. K. (1988). *Writing about music*. University of California Press.

Ivey, D. (1970). *Song: Anatomy, imagery, and styles*. Free Press.

Kagen, S. (1968). *Music for the voice* (Rev. ed.). Indiana University Press.

Katz, M. (2009). *The complete collaborator: The pianist as partner*. Oxford University Press.

Kimball, C. (2013). *Art song: Linking poetry to song*. Hal Leonard Corp.

Kimball, C. (2015). *Song: A guide to art song style and literature* (2nd ed.). Hal Leonard Corp.

Kramer, L. (1984). *Music and poetry: The nineteenth century and after*. University of California Press.

Lehmann, L. (1972). *More than singing: The interpretation of songs*. Praeger.

Lowenberg, C. (1991). *Musicians wrestle everywhere: Emily Dickinson and music*. Fallen Leaf Press.

Mabry, S. (2002). *Exploring twentieth-century vocal music: A practical guide to innovations in performance and repertoire*. Oxford University Press.

MacClintock, C. (1973). *The solo song, 1580–1730*. W. W. Norton & Co.

Meister, B. (1980). *An introduction to the art song*. Taplinger Publishing.

Meister, B. (1992). *Art song: The marriage of music and poetry*. Hollowbrook Publishing.

Miller, R. (1996). *On the art of singing*. Oxford University Press.

Moore, G. (1975). *Singer and accompanist: The performance of fifty songs*. Greenwood Press.

Rosen, C. (1995). *The romantic generation*. Harvard University Press.

Schiøtz, A. (1970). *The singer and his art*. Harper & Row.

Seaton, D. (1987). *The art song: A research and information guide*. Garland Publishing.

Stein, D., & Spillman, R. (1996). *Poetry into song: Performance and analysis of Lieder*. Oxford University Press

Stein, J. (1971). *Poem and music in the German Lied from Gluck to Hugo Wolf*. Harvard University Press.

Stevens, D. (1970). *A history of song* (Rev. ed.). W. W. Norton & Co.

Resources for the Study of Poetry

Appelbaum, S. (1969). *Introduction to French poetry: A dual-language book*. Dover Publications.

Hirsch, E. (1999). *How to read a poem and fall in love with poetry*. Harvest Books.

Hollander, J. (1996). *Committed to memory: 100 best poems to memorize*. Riverhead Books.

Oliver, M. (1994). *A poetry handbook: A prose guide to understanding and writing poetry*. Houghton Mifflin.

Pinsky, R. (1998). *The handbook of heartbreak*. William Morrow.

Biographical and Historical Materials

Armstrong, J. (2006). *Love, life, Goethe: Lessons of the imagination from the great German poet*. Farrar, Straus & Giroux.

Baudelaire, C. (1982). *Les fleurs du mal* (R. Howard, Trans.). David R. Godine.

Bell, M. (Ed.). (2016). *The essential Goethe*. Princeton University Press.

Benjamin, W. (1973). *Charles Baudelaire*. Verso Classics.

Bodley, L. B. (2009). *Goethe and Zelter: Musical dialogues*. Ashgate Publishing.

Boyle, N. (1992). *Goethe: The poet and the age: The poetry of desire, 1749–1790* (Vol. 1). Oxford University Press.

Boyle, N. (2000). *Goethe: The poet and the age: Revolution and renunciation, 1790–1803*. Oxford University Press.

Celenza, C. (2017). *Petrarch: Everywhere a wanderer*. Reaktion Books.

Gautier, T. (2011). *Selected lyrics* (N. R. Shapiro, Trans.). Yale University Press.

Heine, H. (n. d.). *Werke in drei bänden, band I: Gedichte*. Winkler Verlag.

Housman, A. E. (2010). *A Shropshire lad and other poems*. Penguin Books.

Hugo, V. (2001). *Selected poems of Victor Hugo: A bilingual edition* (E. H. & A. M. Blackmore, Trans.). University of Chicago Press.

Hunter, D. (2012). *Understanding French verse: A guide for singers*. Oxford University Press.

Perraudin, M. (1989). *Heinrich Heine. Poetry in context: A study of the Buch der Lieder*. St. Martin's Press.

Petrarch, F., (1985). Selections from *Canzoniere and other work* (M. Musa, Trans.). Oxford.

Rees, W. (1990). *The Penguin book of French poetry, 1820–1950*. Penguin Books.

Reeves, N. (1994). *Heinrich Heine: Poetry and politics*. Libris.

Safranski, R. (2017). *Goethe: Life as a work of art* (D. Dollenmayer, Trans.). Liveright.

Sammons, J. (1979). *Heinrich Heine: A modern biography*. Princeton University Press.

Sternfeld, F. W. (1979). *Goethe and music: A list of parodies and Goethe's relationship to music*. DaCapo Press.

Tudor, J. M. (2011). *Sound and sense: Music and musical metaphor in the thought and writing of Goethe and his age*. Peter Lang International Academic Publishers.

Verlaine, P. (1999). *One hundred and one poems by Paul Verlaine: A bilingual edition* (N. R. Shapiro, Trans.). University of Chicago Press.

Verlaine, P. (2003). *The cursed poets* (C. Madar, Trans.). Green Integer.

Williams, C. (1943). *The figure of Beatrice*. Apocryphile Press.

Zweig, S. (2018). *Paul Verlaine*. CreateSpace Independent Publishing Platform.

Books on Singing Related Concepts

Callaghan, J. (2014). *Singing & science: Body, brain & voice*. Compton Publishing.

Dimon, T. (2018). *Anatomy of the voice: An illustrated guide for singers, vocal coaches, and speech therapists*. North Atlantic Books.

Feindel, J. (2009). *The thought propels the sound*. Plural Publishing.

Friedlander, C. (2018). *Complete vocal fitness: A singer's guide to physical training, anatomy, and biomechanics*. Rowman & Littlefield.

Gorman, D. (2019). *The body moveable*. Learning Methods Publications.

Harrison, N., & Watson, A. (2020). *A singer's guide to the larynx*. Compton Publishing.

Heirich, J. R. (2005). *Voice and the Alexander Technique: Active explorations for speaking and singing* (2nd ed.). Mornum Time Press.

Laban, R. (1974). *The language of movement: A guidebook to chorneutics*. Plays Inc.

Leborgne, W., & Rosenberg, M. (2013). *The vocal athlete*. Plural Publishing.

Leigh-Post, K. (2014). *Mind-body awareness for singers: Unleashing optimal performance*. Plural Publishing.

Levitin, D. (2006). *This is your brain on music*. Dutton/Penguin.

Levitin, D. (2008). *The world in six songs: How the musical brain created human nature*. Plume/Penguin.

Lyle, H. (2014). *Vocal yoga: The joy of breathing, singing, and sounding*. Bluecat Music & Publishing.

McClosky, D. B. (2011). *Your voice at its best* (5th ed.). Waveland Press.

Melton, J., & Tom, K. (2012). *One voice: Integrating singing and theatre voice techniques* (2nd ed.). Waveland Press.

Moselle, V. (2019). *Breathwork: A 3-week breathing program to gain clarity, calm, and better health*. Althea Press.

Olsson, A. (2020). *Conscious breathing: Discover the power of your breath*. DiggyPOD Press.

Walker, G. (2007). *An ocean of air: Why the wind blows and other mysteries of the atmosphere*. Harvest/Harcourt.

Resources for Choral Singing and Repertoire

Ashley, M. (2014). *Contemporary choral work with boys*. Compton Publishing.

Horn, D. (2013). *Imperfect harmony: Finding happiness singing with others*. Algonquin Books of Chapel Hill.

LaBarr, C., & Wykoff, J. (2019). *The melodic voice: Conversations with Alice Parker*. GIA Publications.

Nelson, S., & Blades, E. (2018). *Singing with your whole self: A singer's guide to Feldenkrais Awareness through movement* (2nd ed.). Rowman & Littlefield.

Nesheim, P., & Noble, W. (1995). *Building beautiful voices*. Roger Dean.

Page, S. E. (1995). *Hearts and hands and voices: Growing in faith through choral music*. Fred Bock Music.

Parker, A. (2006). *The anatomy of melody: Exploring the single line of song*. GIA Publications.

Parker, A. (2014). *The answering voice: The beginnings of counterpoint*. GIA Publications.

Winnie, B. (Ed.). (2020). *The choral conductor's companion: 100 rehearsal techniques, imaginative ideas, quotes, and facts*. Meredith Music Publications.

Resources for Lifelong Singing

The following is a selected list of books regarding the singing life.

Anderson, M. (1956). *My Lord, what a morning: An autobiography*. University of Illinois Press.

Bergner, D. (2016). *Sing for your life: A story of race, music, and family*. Little, Brown, and Company.

Estes, S., & Swanson, M. (1999). *Simon Estes in his own voice: An autobiography*. LMP, L. C.

Fischer-Dieskau, D. (1989). *Reverberations: The memoirs of Dietrich Fischer-Dieskau* (R. Hein, Trans.). Fromm International Publishing.

Fleming, R. (2004). *The inner voice: The making of a singer*. Viking.

Hines, J. (1987). *Great singers on great singing*. Limelight Editions.

Larmore, J. (2015). *Una voce: The drama in opera, both onstage and off*. Lulu Publishing.

Norman, J. (2014). *Stand up straight and sing! A memoir*. Houghton Mifflin Harcourt.

Voigt, D. (2015). *Call me Debbie: True confessions of a down-to-earth diva*. Harper Collins.

The following publications may assist you in developing greater context for the study and performance of specific genres. The *So You Want to Sing* . . . series is sponsored by the National Association of Teachers of Singing and edited by Matthew Hoch.

The title of the books in the series are as follows:

Clark, D., & Biffle, B. (2017). *So you want to sing barbershop: A guide for performers*. Rowman & Littlefield.

Edwards, M. (2014). *So you want to sing rock 'n' roll: A guide for professionals*. Rowman & Littlefield.

Elliott, M. (2019). *So you want to sing early music: A guide for performers*. Rowman & Littlefield.

Garner, K. (2016). *So you want to sing country: A guide for performers*. Rowman & Littlefield.

Hall, K. (2014). *So you want to sing music theater: A guide for professionals*. Rowman & Littlefield.

Hoch, M. (2017). *So you want to sing sacred music: A guide for performers.* Rowman & Littlefield.

Hoch, M. (2018). *So you want to sing CCM (contemporary commercial music): A guide for performers.* Rowman & Littlefield.

Hoch, M. (2019). *So you want to sing world music: A guide for performers.* Rowman & Littlefield.

Hoch, M. (2020). *So you want to sing with awareness: A guide for performers.* Rowman & Littlefield.

Hoch, M., & Lister, L. (2019). *So you want to sing music by women: A guide for performers.* Rowman & Littlefield.

Hochmiller, S. (2019). *So you want to sing chamber music: A guide for performers.* Rowman & Littlefield.

Jones, R. (2019). *So you want to sing spirituals: A guide for performers.* Rowman & Littlefield.

Lister, L. (2018). *So you want to sing light opera: A guide for performers.* Rowman & Littlefield.

Mindel, V. (2017). *So you want to sing folk music: A guide for performers.* Rowman & Littlefield.

Robinson-Martin, T. (2016). *So you want to sing gospel: A guide for performers.* Rowman & Littlefield.

Sabella, D., & Matsuki, S. (2020). *So you want to sing cabaret: A guide for performers.* Rowman & Littlefield.

Shapiro, J. (2015). *So you want to sing jazz: A guide for professionals.* Rowman & Littlefield.

Sharon, D. (2017). *So you want to sing a cappella: A guide for performers.* Rowman & Littlefield.

Smith, B. (2018). *So you want to sing for a lifetime: A guide for performers.* Rowman & Littlefield.

Yamin, E. (2018). *So you want to sing the blues: A guide for performers.* Rowman & Littlefield.

Index

Note: Page numbers in **bold** reference non-text material.

A

A cappella, 64
Abitbol, Jean, 5, 101
Absolute pitch, 43
Acoustical pyramid, 70
Acute illness, 181
"Adam's apple," 25, 162
Adolescent singers
   additional considerations for, 146–148
   aural development of, 144–145
   balance and physicality in, 145–146
   limited range exercises for, 144
   nonpitched exercises for, 142–143, **143**
   octave displacement in, 144
   overview of, 137–138
   phonation onset and duration in, 141–142
   tension in, 146
   voice of, 138–141
African American art songs, 126–127
Agility, in singing, 115–116
Ainsley, Mark, 113
Air, breathing and, 14–15
Air pressure, 34
Album of Negro Spirituals, 126
Alexander Technique, 99, 101
"All Through the Night," 109
"Alma del core," 114
Alto
   in choir, 68–69
   history of, 63–64
   repertoire for, 124–125
Alveolar ridge, 52
"Amarilli, mia bella," 114
Ameling, Elly, 109
American Appalachian English, 53
American songs, 106
Amplification, 181
"An die Musik," 133
Anthology of Art Songs by Black American Composers, 126
Anxiety
   description of, 7–8
   performance, 99–100
Appoggio, 17
Arias
   definition of, 58
   Italian, 106
   learning to sing, 84
Arne, Thomas, 115–116
Arnold Book of Songs, 112
Art of the Song Recital, The, 129
Art songs, 107–108, 111–113, 126–127
Art Songs and Spirituals, 126
Articulation, 165–166
Articulators, 174
Aryepiglottic fold, **25**
Aryepiglottic muscle, **25**
Arytenoid cartilage, **24**, **25**, **27**
Arytenoideus muscle, **26**
Assessment form, for class presentations, 131–132
Audiation, 18

Auditory feedback, 29
Aural development, of adolescent singers, 144–145
Aural skills, 42–43

B

Bailey, Norman, 114
Baker, Janet, 114
Bar, 38
Baritones
   description of, 69–70
   men as, 156–158
   vocal repertoire for, 125–126
Bartoli, Cecilia, 114, 116, 122
Bass
   in choir, 69–70
   history of, 63–64
   men as, 156–158
   vocal fold vibration in, 174
   vocal repertoire for, 125–126
Battle, Kathleen, 122
Bavaj, Lorenzo, 122
Beats, 39–40
"Beautiful Dreamer," 120
Bel canto, 47, 58–61, 64, 105, 120
Berganza, Teresa, 122
Bernoulli effect, 173
Bernoulli force, 31–32
Bernstein, Leonard, 106
Bilabial consonants, 52
Bishop, Elizabeth, 58
Blake, William, 106
Body alignment, 8
Bonney, Barbara, 110
Boulanger, Nadia, 106
Bow, 130
Brahms, Johannes, 106–107, 109, 111–112
Breath "bridges," 71
Breath management, 17
Breath marks, 71
Breath support, 179
Breathing
   air and, 14–15
   automaticity of, 172
   choral, 65
   constricted, 14
   deep, 14

   exhalation, 14–15
   importance of, 105
   inhalation, 14–15
   mental coordination, 6
   mouth, 15–16
   nasal, 15–16
   reverse, 16–17
   for singing, 14–15
   for solo singing, 15
   tidal, 172
Breathing pose, **18**
Breathy phonation, 34
Breathy tone, 19
British English, 53
British songs, 106
Britten, Benjamin, 106, 111, 117–118, 122
Burleigh, Harry T., 126
Burnside, Iain, 113
Burrows, Stuart, 114
Butterworth, George, 118–119

C

Caccini, Giulio, 114
Cadenzas, 51
Caldara, Antonio, 114, 116
Cambiata, 150
Cambiata Concept, 138
Canon(s), 66–67
Canon singing, 66–67
Carreras, José, 122
Cartilages, of larynx, 23, **24**, 28
Cash, Johnny, 112
Cats, 123
Chanting, 57–58, 64, 69
Chest register, 59
Chest voice
   registration, 68, 145
Choir
   alto in, 68–69
   baritone in, 69–70
   bass in, 69–70
   soprano in, 67–68
   tenor in, 69
"Choir, The," 190
Choir concert, 84
Choir schools, 58
Choral blend, 71

Choral breathing, 65
Choral ensembles
　description of, 64, 70
　gender diverse individuals in, 168
Choral rehearsals, 65
Choral singers
　as alto, 68–69
　as baritone, 69–70
　as bass, 69–70
　lifelong singing by, 72
　as soprano, 67–68
　as tenor, 69
Choral singing
　challenges of, 70–71
　history of, 63–64
　solo singing versus, 64–65, 72
　teamwork in, 19
　tuning and, 70
　two-part, 67
　women in, 151
Choristers
　breathing by, 15, 65
　responsibility of, 85
Cigarette smoking, 177
Cisgender, **159**
Clarke, Rebecca, 110
Class presentations
　assessment form for, 131–132
　final presentation, 129, 132
　midterm projects and presentation, 128, 131
Classical training, 105
Closed vowels, 49
Clough-Leighter, Henry, 118
Cognates, 53
Colapinto, John, xiv
Collaborative pianist, 130
Collins, Don L., 138
Collins, Judy, 153
"Come Again, Sweet Love," 110
Conable, Barbara, 99
Consonant(s)
　articulation of, 51–52
　in French language, 54
　fricative, 76
　in International Phonetic Alphabet, 51–52
　in Italian language, 54
　nasal, 76
　singing versus speaking of, 52
　single, 51
　voiceless, 78
Consonant clusters, 51
Constricted breathing, 14
Contraltos, 68
Converse, Frederick Shepherd, 118
Cooksey, John, 138
Cool-downs, 20, 78, 83, **83**, 98, 179–180
Cooper, Irving, 138
Copland, Aaron, 106
Corniculate cartilage, **24**
Corniculate tubercle, **25**
Coughing, 181
Count singing, 38, **39**, 70–71, 90
Countertenor, 110, 121–122, 155
Crescendo, 60
Cricoid cartilage, **24**, 27
Cricothyroid muscle
　anatomy of, **25–26**, 27
　in voice production, 34
Cuneiform tubercle, **25**

D

Damasio, Antonio, 8
Dayme, Meribeth Bunch, 18
De Falla, Manuel, 109
Debussy, Claude, 107
Decrescendo, 60
Deep breathing, 14
Deep River Collection, The, 126
Delius, Frederick, 116
Deller, Alfred, 110
Dental consonant, 52
Diction, 55
Dido and Aeneas, 121
DiDonato, Joyce, 114
Die Zauberflöte, 123
Digital music, 188
Diphthongs, 49–50
Donaudy, Stefano, 114, 127
Dowland, John, 101, 110
"Down by the Salley Gardens," 117–118
"Drink to Me Only With Thine Eyes," 112
Drinking water, 175–176
Dropped octave, 147

Duke, John, 119
Duke, Vernon, 119
Dysphoria, **159**, 167

E

Ear, nose, and throat physician, 183
"Early in the Morning," 120
e-cigarettes, 177
Edema, 183
Edwin, Robert, 105
Effects of Heel Height on Head Position, Long-Term Average Spectra, Perceptions of Female Singers, The, 11
Eighth notes, 40
"Elevator Music," xviii
Embouchure formation, 86
Emerson, Ralph Waldo, 101
English language
   American Appalachian example, 53
   British example, 53
   consonants in, 51–52
   diphthongs in, 49–50
   International Phonetic Alphabet in, 49–51
   "r" in, 54, 71
   sounds only heard in, 50
   triphthongs in, 50
   vowels in, 49–51
   "y" in, 50
Ensemble
   choral. *See* Choral ensembles
   definition of, 58
ENT physician. *See* Ear, nose, and throat physician
Environmental irritants, 177
Epiglottis, **24–25**
Erythema, 183
Essentials in Conducting, 137
Estrogen, 162
Etiquette, performance, 129–130
Even scale, 58–59
Evidence-based vocal pedagogy, 5
Exercise(s)
   cool-downs, 78, 83, **83**
   vocal, 134
   warm-ups, 76–78, **76–82**
Exercise physiology, 179

Exhalation, 14–15, 172
Expiration
   muscles of, 29
   passive, 15, 29
Expressive singing, 47

F

Face, relaxing of, 7
Fach, 3–4, 33, 60
Facies medialis, **27**
Fact sheet, for vocal repertoire, **89**
"Fair and True," 114
Fairy Queen, The, 122
False vocal folds, 27
Falsetto, 155–157
Fatigue, 68
Fauré, Gabriel, 107
Feldenkrais Method, 101
Fermata, 87
Final presentation, 129, 132
Fingerings, 86
Finzi, Gerald, 113, 116, 118
Fischer, György, 116
Fischer-Dieskau, Dietrich, 133
Flexibility, in singing, 115–116
Flora, 123
Florentine Camerata, 57, 106, 113–114
Flow glottography, 34
Flow phonation, 18–19, 34, 108
Folk songs, 105–106, 111–112
Formant
   definition of, 32
   singer's, 33
   speaker's, 33
Formant frequencies, 32
Forrester, Maureen, 111
Foster, Stephen, 120
14 Songs on American Poetry, 120
Franklin, Aretha, 112
Freer, Patrick, 138
French art songs, 107–108
French language, 54–55
French mélodie, 107–108
Frequency
   fundamental, 34
   of phonation, 163
Fricative consonants, 76

Friml, Rudolf, 123
Fundamental frequency, 34

G

Gackle, Lynne, 138
Gallwey, W. Timothy, 101
Gastroenterologist, 178
Gehrkens, Karl W., 137
Gender diverse individuals
  in choral ensembles, 168
  in choral settings, 161
  definitions associated with, **159**
  hormones in, 161–162
  language choices, 165–166
  music educators working with, 167–169
  as singers, 167
  terms associated with, **159**
  transfeminine individuals, 161–162, 166
  transitioning in, 161–162
  transmasculine individuals, 161–162
  traumatization in, 160
  trust building with, 160
  verbal communication in, 162–163
  voice in
    articulation, 165–166
    intonation, 165–166
    modification to, 163
    overview of, 162–163
    pitch, 163–165
    prosody, 165–166
    resonance, 165
  working with, 160–161
Gender dysphoria, **159**
Gender expression, **159**
Gender identity, **159**
Gender neutral attire, 168
Gentle onset, vocal repertoire for, 108–113
Germany
  folk songs of, 106
  language of, 54–55
  Lieder, 106–107
GI. *See* Gastroenterologist
Gibbons, Orlando, 110
Gilbert & Sullivan, 85, 123
Gilman, Marina, 11
Glides, 50, 76, 164
Glottal onset, 19

Glottal resistance, 182
Glottal stop, 19, 108
Glottic cycle, 32
Glottic resistance, 173
Glottis
  anatomy of, 25
  definition of, 19, 25
Gluck, Christoph Willibald von, 122
Goblet cells, 28
Golden, Ruth, 113
Gondoliers, The, 123
Gordon, Ricky Ian, 113
Graham, Susan, 120
Green, Barry, 99
Gregorian chants, 64, 69
Growth and development, 3
Gunn, Nathan, 120
Gurney, Ivor, 118–119

H

Hair, 123
Halperin, Tamar, 122
Hamilton, 123
Handel, George Frideric, 85, 106, 121
"Hands, Eyes, Heart," 113
Harmonic roadmap, 71
Harmonic vacuum, 69
Hart, Lorenz, 123
"Have You Seen but a White Lily Grow?," 110
Head voice attitude, 69
Head voice register, 69
Health
  physical, 101
  vocal, 171–172
Hillyer, Robert, 120
Hixon, Thomas J., 15
"Holding your own," in canon singing, 66
Hopkinson, Francis, 106
Hormones, 161–162
Horne, Marilyn, 120
Housman, A. E., 106, 119
Humidification, 176
Humidifiers, 176
Humming, 164–165
Hundley, Richard, 113
Hvorostovsky, Dmitri, 122

Hydration, 101, 175–176
Hyoid bone, **24**
Hypernasal voice, 174

I

Imitation of sounds, 54
In His Hands, 126
"In stiller Nacht," 111
Indian Queen, The, 122
Inferior cornu, of thyroid cartilage, **24**
Infraglottic vocal tract, 28
Inhalation. *See also* Breathing
   description of, 14–15, 172
   efficiency in, 16
   methods of, 16
Inner Game of Music, The, 99
Inner Game of Tennis, The, 101
Inspiration, 29
Instrumental music education, 63
Instruments, voice versus, 2
Intensity, of voice, 34, 152
International Phonetic Alphabet
   consonants in, 51–52
   in English, 49–51
   exercise sheets, 78, **79–82**
   imitation of sounds as principle of, 54
   learning of, 48
   purposes of, 48
   in song writing, 87
   symbols, 47–50, 54–55
   as tool, 52–53
   value of, 48–49
   vowels in, 49–51
Intonation, 165–166
Intrinsic muscles, of larynx, 23, 25, **25–26**
IPA. *See* International Phonetic Alphabet
Irritants, laryngeal, 176–178
"It Was a Lover and His Lass," 116
Italian language
   "musical" quality of, 48
   sounds in, 54–55
   vowels in, 47, 76
Italian songs and arias, 106

J

Jahnke, Christine K., 150
Jo, Sumi, 122
Johnson, Graham, 113
Jong Ho Park, 116
Jonson, Ben, 112
Journaling, 101

K

Katz, Marilyn, 120
Kemp, Helen, 2
Kern, Jerome, 123
Ki, Kathleen, 116
Kinesthetic, 11
King Arthur, 121–122
Kinnell, Galway, 190
Koehler, Hope, 111

L

La constanza in amor vince l'inganno, 116
Laban Movement Analysis, 101
Labiodental, 52
Lamina propria, 173
Larmore, Jennifer, 121
Laryngectomy, 23
Laryngologists, 163
Larynx
   anatomy of, 23–29, **24–27**
   cartilages of, 23, **24**, 28
   intrinsic muscles of, 23, 25, **25–26**
   irritants of, 176–178
   mucosa of, 28
   muscle tension on, 182
   pathology of, 182–183
   soft tissue of, 28
"Lass from the Low Countree, The," 111
Lateral cricoarytenoid muscle, **25–26**
Leck, Henry, 138
Legato singing, 58–59, 64–65, 113–115
Lesson plans
   for art songs, 111
   for folk songs, 111
   for legato singing, 113–114
   for lullabies, 109
   for lute songs, 109–110
   for messa di voce, 121
   for phrasing, 113–114
   for range, 119
   for registration, 119

resources for, 134
for text painting, 117
for vocal agility and flexibility, 115
for vocal color, 117
Let Us Garlands Bring, 118
Levine, James, 122
Libretto, 58, 85
Lied, 107
Lieder, 106–107
Liederzyklus, 107
Lifelong singing
by choral singers, 72
merit of, 44
Limited range exercises, for adolescent singers, 144
Lip trilling, 76, 79, 164
Liturgical singing, 58
Looking for Spinoza: Joy, Sorrow, and the Feeling Brain, 7–8
"Loveliest of Trees," 119–120
Love's Labour Lost, 116
Ludwig, Christa, 112
Lullabies, 108–109
Lungs
cancer of, 177
natural recoil of, 17
Lute, 106
Lute songs, 109–110
Lux, Thomas, 189
Lyrical poetry, 85

M

Mahler, Gustav, 107
Marin, Alonso, 110
Mark Hayes Vocal Solo Collection: 10 Spirituals for Solo Voice, 126
Martineau, Malcolm, 120
Matched pitch, 43
Matched vowels, 70
Maurice, Glenda, 113
McKenzie, Duncan, 138
Measure, 38
Meditation, 101
Melodic patterns, 42, **42**
Mélodie, 107–108
Melody, unison, **65–66**
Memorization, 98
Memorizing sensations, 19–20, 99

Men
as baritones, 156–158
as bass, 156–158
falsetto voices of, 155–157
frequency range of voices, 163–164
overview of, 154–155
pitch in, 154–155
pitch range in, 164
as tenors, 155
vocal folds of, 173
Mental coordination, 6
Mental fatigue, 68
Mental relaxation, 7–8
Mental toughness, 101
Mental wellness, 181–182
Merrill, Robert, 112
Messa di voce, **60**, 60–61, 77, 120–122
Messiah, 85, 121
Meter, 87
Meter signature, 39–40
Mezzo sopranos, 68, 124–125
Microphones, for voice amplification, 181
Middle register, 59
Midterm projects and presentation, 128, 131
Mignaco, Valeria, 110
Mikado, The, 123
Mindfulness training, 99, 101
Mixed register, 59
Mixed vowels, 54
Monody, 64
Morley, Thomas, 53, 116
Mouth breathing
description of, 15–16
disadvantages of, 15
nasal breathing and, 16
Munro, George, 114
Murphy, Kevin, 120
Muscle antagonism, 17, **18**
Muscle tension, 6
Music
interpreting of, 127–128
purchase of, 134–135
reading, 41
rhythm of. *See* Rhythm
strategies for learning, 43–44
structure of, 38
Music educators
gender diverse individuals and, 167–169
as voice care team members, 183

"Music for a While," 121–122
Musical map, 41
Musical preparation, 90
Musical skill training, 3
Musical theater, 123
Musicianship skills, 37–38
My Favorite Spirituals: 30 Songs for Voice and Piano, 126
"My Lovely Celia," 114

N

"Nana," 109
Nasal breathing, 15–16
Nasal cavity, 32
Nasal consonants, 76
Nasal voice, 165
Nasal vowels, 54
Nationalism, 106
Neck, relaxing of, 7
Nelson, Eric, 112
Nestor, James, 15
New Anthology of Art Songs by African American Composers, A, 126
Niles, John Jacob, 111
Nodules, 171, 183
Nonbinary, **159**
Nonpitched exercises, for adolescent singers, 142–143, **143**
Note learning, 3, 41–42

O

"O cessate di piagarmi," 122
"O del mio amato ben," 114
"O del mio dolce ardor," 122
"O Fair to See," 112–113
"O Mistress Mine," 118
"O sole mio," 105
"O Waly Waly," 111
Oblique arytenoid muscle, **25**
Octave displacement, 144
Oedipus, 122
Old American Songs, 106
"Ombra mai fu," 121
"On the breath," 19
Onset of sound, 19
Open vowels, 49
Opera, 57–58, 85, 116, 123
Operettas, 85, 123
Opus, 57–58
Oral cavity, as resonator, 32
Oratorio, 85
Orchestra concert, 84
Oropharyngeal cancer, 177
Otolaryngologist, 183
"Out of the Morning," 113
Oxford Diction of Pronunciation for Current English, 53

P

Palestrina, Giovanni Battista, 60
Paride ed Elena, 122
Parsons, Geoffrey, 114
Passaggio, 59
Passive expiration, 15, 29
Pavarotti, Luciano, 105, 114
Pears, Peter, 111
Perfect pitch, 43
Performance
  etiquette in, 129–130
  mental toughness and, 101
  mindful preparation for, 100
  physical factors and, 101
Performance anxiety, 99–100
Perischetti, Vincent, 113
Pharynx, as resonator, 32
Phillips, Kenneth, 138–139
Phonation
  in adolescent singers, 141–142
  anatomy and physiology of, 173–174
  breathy, 34
  flow, 34, 108
  frequency of, 163
  infraglottic musculature during, 30–31
  myoelastic-aerodynamic mechanism of, 32
  neurophysiology of, 28–29
  perceptual aspect of, 163
  pressed, 34
  straw, 76
  support mechanisms for, 28–29
  volitional, 29, **30**
Phonetic transcription, 53
Phonotrauma, 171, 180, 182
Phrasing, 113–115
Physical health, 101
Physical relaxation, 6–7

Physical well-being, 3
Pianist, collaborative, 130
Pirates of Penzance, 123
Pitch
   absolute, 43
   definition of, 32
   determinants of, 173–174
   female-speaking, 164
   gender differences in, 163–164
   in gender diverse individuals, 163–165
   male-speaking, 164
   matched, 43
   perfect, 43
   range of, 59
   relative, 43
Pitch accuracy, 42–43
Pitch awareness, 43
Pitch glides, 164
Pitch recognition, 43
Point of articulation, 52
Polyps, 171, 183
Pope Marcellus Mass, 60
Popp, Lucia, 112
Posterior cricoarytenoid muscle, **25–26**
Posture
   seated, 11, **12–13**
   singer's, 6, 11, 20, 75
   standing, 8–11, **9–10**
Power of the Voice, The, 5
Practice
   goal setting for, 98
   joy in, 99
   mindfulness in, 99
   strategies for, 90
   styles of, 98–99
Practice logs
   importance of, 90
   sample, **91–97**
Precentral gyrus, 29
Pressed phonation, 34
Price, Leontyne, 110
Professional organizations, 188–189
Program notes, 129
Prosody, 165–166
Pseudostratified ciliated columnar epithelial cells, 28
Pulse, 39–40, 70, 86
Punctuation, 86
Purcell, Henry, 106, 121

Q
Quilter, Roger, 110, 112, 116, 118

R
"r"
   diphthongs influenced by, 50
   in English language, 54, 71
   minimizing of, before consonants, 53
Range
   definition of, 59
   in older voices, 152
   vocal repertoire for, 118–120
"Raspberries," 76, 78
Reading music, 41
Recital, 84
Recitative, 58
Recurrent laryngeal nerves, 27
Reflux, 178
Registers, 59, 69
Registration
   chest voice, 68, 145
   definition of, 59
   falsetto, 155–157
   head voice, 69
   speaking voice, 2–4
   vocal repertoire for, 118–120
Relative pitch, 43
Relaxation
   mental, 7–8
   physical, 6–7
   in warm-up, 75
Renaissance Florence, 57
Repertoire. *See* Vocal repertoire
Resonance
   anatomy of, 174
   definition of, 18, 174
   flow phonation, 18–19
   in gender diverse individuals, 165
   memorizing sensations, 19–20
   onset of sound, 19
   sound modification by changes in, 174
   vocal sound production and, 61
   in warm-ups, 75–76
Resonators, 28, 32, 174
Respiration, 173–175
Respiratory Function in Speech and Song, 15

Respiratory system, 173–175
Reverse breathing, 16–17
Revolutionary War, 106
Rhyming vowels, 53
Rhythm
 construction of, 40
 description of, 3, 70
 musical structure from, 38
Rhythmic patterns, 40, **41**
Rhythmic syllables, 40
Rhythmic symbols, **39**
Robeson, Paul, 112
Rodgers & Hammerstein, 85
Rodgers, Richard, 123
Rollings, Amelia, 11
Rorem, Ned, 110, 120
Rosen, Charles, 1
Rossetti, Christina, 106, 112
Rossetti, Gabriel, 118
Rote learning, xvi, 3
Rounds, 67
Rumi, Jalaluddin, 55
Rutter, John, 116

S

Salons, 107
Sataloff, Robert T., 172
Scale patterns, 77, **77**
Scarlatti, Alessandro, 122, 127
Scatting, 50
Schober, Franz von, 133
Schola cantorum, 58
Scholl, Andreas, 121–122
Schubert, Franz, 107, 133, 158
Schubertiades, 107
Schumann, Robert, 107
Score
 basics of, **38–39**, 38–40
 composition of, 85
 horizontal lines on, 38, **38**
 marking of, 71–72, **72**
 preparation of, 84, 87
Score study, 84
Seated posture, 11, **12–13**
Self-hypnosis, 101
"Selve amiche," 116
Semi-occulted vocal tract exercises, 76, 78

Sensations, memorizing of, 19–20, 99
"Sento nel core," 127
Shakespeare, William, 106, 116, 118, 122
Shaw, Robert, 71, 85
Sight-reading, 41
"Silent Noon," 118
Silent reflux, 177
"Silver Swan, The," 110
Singers
 adolescent. *See* Adolescent singers
 choral. *See* Choral singers
 classical training of, 105
 gender diverse, 167
 memorizing sensations by, 19–20
 "performance ready" position of, 6
 sharing the stage by, 101–102
 transgender, 167
 voice perception by, 19
Singer's diction, 55
Singer's formant, 33
Singer's posture, 6, 11, 20, 75
Singing
 agility in, 115–116
 aging effects on, 152–153
 basics of
  breathing. *See* Breathing
  definition of, 5
  posture. *See* Posture
  relaxation, 7–8
  resonance, 18–20
 bel canto, 47, 58–61, 64, 105, 120
 breathing for, 14–15
 canon, 66–67
 choral. *See* Choral singing
 as conscious act, 8
 of consonants, 52
 count, 38, **39**, 70–71, 90
 Dayme's description of, 18
 expressive, 47
 flexibility in, 115–116
 history of, 1
 intrinsic value of, 187–188
 legato, 58–59, 64–65, 113–115
 liturgical, 58
 in nature, 1
 solo. *See* Solo singing
 in 21st century, 188–189
 unison, 64–66, 70

    of vowels, 52
    warm-ups for. *See* Warm-ups
    wordless, 1, 50–51
"Singing on the breath," 108
Singing voice. *See also* Voice
    health of, 3
    speaking voice versus, 2–4
Singing with Your Whole Self: A Singer's Guide to Feldenkrais Awareness through Movement, 11
Single consonants, 51
Sing-Song: A Nursery Rhyme Book, 112
Singspiel, 123
Sleep, 101
Slides, 76
SLP. *See* Speech-language pathologist
Smoke, 177
"Smoker's voice," 177
So You Want to Sing CCM (Commercial Contemporary Music): A Guide for Performers, 105, 123
Solo singing
    breathing for, 15
    choral singing versus, 64–65, 72
    description of, 187
    teamwork in, 19
    in Western world, 57–58
Song(s)
    art, 107–108, 111–113, 126–127
    composition of, 85
    context for, 87–88
    description of, 187
    folk, 105–106, 111–112
    learning to sing, 84–87
    lute, 109–110
    preparing of, 85–86
    researching of, 88
    text of. *See* Text
    word mastery in, 85–86
Song cycle, 107, 118
Sopranos
    in choir, 67–68
    history of, 63–64
    mezzo, 68
    repertoire for, 124
    vocal fold vibration in, 174–175
Sound(s)
    imitation of, 54

    onset of, 19
Source-filter theory, 174
SOVT exercises. *See* Semi-occulted vocal tract exercises
Speaker
    formant of, 33
    voice perception by, 19
Speaking
    of consonants, 52
    of vowels, 52
Speaking voice, singing voice versus, 2–4
Speech-language pathologist, 183
Spirituals, 126–127
Staccato, 87
Staff (musical), 38, **38**
Stage fright, 99–101
Staggered breath, 65
Standing posture, 8–11, **9–10**
Steam inhalers, 176
Strauss, Richard, 107
Straw phonation, 76
Stress, 181–182
Stutzmann, Nathalie, 122
Subglottic pressure, 31–32, 34
Superior cornu, of thyroid cartilage, **24**
Supraglottic vocal tract, 28
Surface hydration, 176
Sutherland, Joan, 116
Sweet, Bridget, 138–139
System, 38
Systemic hydration, 175

T

"T," 39
Tactile feedback, 29
Tayloe, David, 122
Taylor, Henry, xviii
Tempest, The, 122
Tenors
    in choir, 69
    history of, 63–64
    men as, 155
    repertoire for, 125
Terfel, Bryn, 109
Tessitura, 59–60
Text

Text (*continued*)
    International Phonetic Alphabet symbols for, 87
    interpreting of, 127–128
    punctuation of, 86
    word mastery of, 85–86
Text painting, 116–118, **117**
Thinking Outside the Box: Adolescent Voice Change in Music Education, 138
30 Spirituals for Voice and Piano, 126
This Is the Voice, xiv
Thomson, Virgil, 106
Throat clearing, 181
"Through-composed," 127
Thyroarytenoid muscle, 23, **25**, 34
Thyrohyoid membrane, **24**
Thyroid cartilage, **24**
Thyroid prominence, 25
Tidal breathing, 172
Timbre, 61, 155, 174
Time signature, 39, 87
Tone
    in older voices, 152
    production of, 42–43
Tone quality, 61
Tongue
    in mouth breathing, 16
    relaxing of, 7
Torelli, Giuseppe, 114
Torricelli, Evangelista, 14
Trachea, **24**
Transfeminine individuals, 161–162, 166
Transgender, **159**
Transmasculine individuals, 161–162
Transverse arytenoid muscle, **25**
Trial by Jury, 123
Trilling, 76, 78, 164
Triphthongs, 50
Triplet pattern, 40
Troeger, Tom, 1
"Tu lo sai," 114
Tuning, choral singing and, 70
Twelfth Night, 118
Two-part arrangement, 67, **68**
Two-part choral settings, 67

U

Unison melody examples
    as canon, **66**
    illustration of, **65**
    in two-part arrangement, **68**
Unison singing, 64–66, 70

V

Vaping, 177
Vargas, Ramón, 114
Verbal communication, in gender diverse individuals, 162–163
Verbal thought processes, 3
Vibrato, 61, 190
Vital capacity, 14–15
Vocal agility and flexibility, 115–116
Vocal aging, 152
Vocal care team, 183–184
Vocal color, 116–118, **117**
Vocal conditioning, 178–179
Vocal exercises, 134
Vocal fatigue, 68, 171
Vocal fold(s)
    anatomy of, 25, 28, 173
    benign pathology of, 182–183
    cool-downs for, 20
    damage to, 182
    false, 27
    friction in, 175
    glottis, 19
    irritant exposure to, 177
    lamina propria of, 173
    layers of, 28
    lubrication for, 175
    of men, 173
    oscillation of, 34
    paralysis of, 27
    pathology of, 182–183
    positioning of, 20
    size of, 164
    upper portion of, 32
    vibration of, **31**, 31–32, 108, 163–164, 173, 175. *See also* Pitch
    warm-ups for, 20
    of women, 173
Vocal fold body, 28
Vocal fold cover, 28, 32
Vocal fold transition, 28
Vocal fry, 19
Vocal habits, 108

Vocal health
    amplification for, 181
    cool-downs for, 179–180
    description of, 171–172, 174–175
    hydration, 175–176
    laryngeal irritant avoidance, 176–178
    tips for maintaining, 189
    vocal conditioning for, 178–179
    vocal pacing, 180–181
    voice rest, 180–181
    warm-ups for, 179–180. *See also* Warm-ups
Vocal hygiene, 171
Vocal injury, 2
Vocal jazz, 50
Vocal ligament, **24**, **27**
Vocal pacing, 180–181
Vocal pedagogues/pedagogy
    messa di voce use by, 60–61
    21st century, 188–189
Vocal quality, 61
Vocal recitation, 58
Vocal registration/registers, 59, 69
Vocal repertoire. *See also* Lesson plans
    for alto, 124–125
    for art songs, 112–113
    for bass, 125–126
    for breath coordination, 108–113
    cool-downs, 78–79, 83, **83**
    description of, 187
    fact sheet for, **89**
    for folk songs, 111–112
    for gentle onset, 108–113
    learning of, 84, 105
    for legato singing, 114–115
    for lullabies, 108–109
    for lute songs, 109–110
    for mezzo soprano, 124–125
    for musical theatre, 123
    for phrasing, 114–115
    practicing of, 98–99
    for range, 118–120
    for registration, 118–120
    resources for, 134
    song. *See* Song
    for soprano, 124
    for tenors, 125
    for text painting, 116–118, **117**
    for vocal agility and flexibility, 115–116
    for vocal color, 116–118, **117**
    vocal habits affected by, 108
    vocal problems in, 84
    vocal skills learned through, 108
    warm-ups, 75–78, **76–82**
Vocal skills, 108
Vocal tract
    infraglottic, 28
    length of, 32
    resonance frequencies of, 32
    shape of, 32–33
    supraglottic, 28
Vocal training
    in adolescents, 139
    classical, 47
    formal, benefits of, 178
    vocal conditioning through, 178
    vocal tract shape affected by, 32–33
Vocalis muscle, 23, **25–26**
Vocalization, 29
Voice. *See also* Singing voice
    acute illness effects on, 181
    adolescent, 138–141
    aging of, 152
    amplification of, 181
    anatomy of, 23–29, 172–174
    cool-downs for, 20, 78, 83, **83**
    in gender diverse individuals. *See* Gender
        diverse individuals, voice in
    health of, 171–172
    instruments versus, 2
    intensity of, 34, 152
    life events and experiences' effect on, 188
    listener of, 19
    measuring the, 60–61
    as musical instrument, 5
    physical well-being and, 3
    physiology of, 23–35, 29–34
    as "seat of the soul," 6
    self-identity and, 168
    "smoker's", 177
    speaking, 2–4
    subsystems of, 174
    volitional production of, 29, **30**
    warm-ups for. *See* Warm-ups
    in women, 150–153
Voice care team, 183–184
Voice disorders, 34, 182–183
Voice recital, 84
Voice rest, 180–181

Voice source signal, 32
Voice teacher, 178, 183–184
"Voice You Hear When You Read Silently, The," 189
Voiceless consonants, 78
Volitional phonation, 29, **30**
Vowel(s)
   closed, 49
   English, 49
   Italian, 47, 76
   matched, 70
   mixed, 54
   nasal, 54
   open, 49
   placement of, 85
   rhyming of, 53
   singing versus speaking of, 52
   spectrum of, **33**
   understanding of, 86–87
   word association with, 87
Vowel sounds, 86–87

W

Wagorn, Bryan, 120
Wanderings of Oisin and Other Poems, The, 117
Warlock, Peter, 114, 116
Warm-ups
   breathing in, 75–76
   description of, 20, 75, 98, 179
   exercises for, 76–78, **76–82**
   posture in, 75
   purpose of, 76
   relaxation in, 75
   resonance in, 75–76
"Weep You No More, Sad Fountains," 110
Wellness, 171–172
Western world, solo singing in, 57–58
Wharton, Edith, 107–108
"When Daisies Pied," 115–116
"Wiegenlied," 109
Williams, Ralph Vaughan, 106, 113, 118
Williams, Ursula Vaughan, 113
Wolf, Hugo, 107
Women
   choral singing by, 151
   frequency range of voices, 163–164
   nonmusical endeavors that affect, 151–152
   pitch range in, 164
   vocal aging in, 152
   vocal folds of, 173
   vocal limitations and strategies in, 152–153
   voice in, 150–153
Wordless singing, 1, 50–51
Working with Adolescent Voices, 138

Y

"y," 50
Yeats, W. B., 106, 117
Youmans, Vincent, 123

Z

Zeldin, Theodore, 107